Contemporary Korean cinema

To Wonha and Jinsup Song

Contemporary Korean cinema

Identity, culture and politics

HYANGJIN LEE

MANCHESTER UNIVERSITY PRESS Manchester and New York

The right of Hyangjin Lee to be identified as the author of this work has been asserted by her in accordance with the Copyright, Designs and Patents Act 1988.

Published by Manchester University Press
Oxford Road, Manchester M13 9NR, UK
and Room 400, 175 Fifth Avenue, New York, NY 10010, USA
http://www.manchesteruniversitypress.co.uk

Distributed exclusively in the USA by
Palgrave, 175 Fifth Avenue, New York, NY 10010, USA

Distributed exclusively in Canada by
UBC Press, University of British Columbia, 2029 West Mall, Vancouver, BC, Canada V6T 1Z2

British Library Cataloguing-in-Publication Data
A catalogue record for this book is available from the British Library

Library of Congress Cataloging-in-Publication Data applied for

ISBN 0 7190 6007 9 *hardback*
ISBN 0 7190 6008 7 *paperback*

First published 2000

08 07 06 05 04 03 02 01 00   10 9 8 7 6 5 4 3 2 1

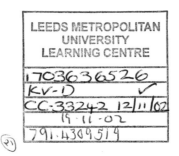

Typeset in Monotype Photina with Frutiger display
by Koinonia, Manchester
Printed in Great Britain
by Biddles Ltd, Guildford and King's Lynn

Contents

List of plates

Stills are reproduced courtesy of the Korean Motion Pictures Corporation, Chung Ji-Young, Chung Jonghwa, Han Sang Hoon, Lee Kwangmo and Pak Kwang Su.

Preface

The growing interest in Korean cinema by critics and scholars outside of the country has increased since the late 1980s. Despite these positive signs for Korean film studies, so far there has been no in-depth study written in this area. This book attempts to fill this vacuum, by providing a critical examination of the role of Korean film as a cultural text of contemporary Koreans in both North and South so that it discloses the conflicting self-identities of a people of a politically divided nation. This study started as my Ph.D. dissertation entitled 'Common Culture/Divided Nation: A Comparative Study of North and South Korean Film'. It has been developed to include further aspects of textual analysis and historical sources, and, as such, it presents a comprehensive survey of Korean cinema as an expression of self-perception of that society and its history.

I wish to acknowledge the following individuals who have provided me with invaluable suggestions and useful comments. I am indebted to Dr Richard Howells and Dr Graham Roberts of the University of Leeds, and Professor Fred Inglis of Sheffield University, Dr Hyangsoon Yi of the University of Georgia, George Turner, Dr Philip Charrier and Dr Rick Siddle of the University of Sheffield. I am very grateful for the support of the School of East Asian Studies at the University of Sheffield in granting me research leave to complete this project. Finally, I would like to express my gratitude to Manchester University Press for its support and recommendations.

Introduction

This book examines the ways in which Korean film reveals the ideological orientation of the society in which it is created and circulated. To understand the workings of ideology in contemporary Korea as a divided nation, this study takes a comparative approach to the films from both sides, considering gender, nationhood and class. A comparative analysis of the representation of ideology in the selected films clearly discloses, on one hand, the conflicting ideas of contemporary Koreans on their self-identity as a divided nation. On the other hand, these films show that Koreans are still strongly committed to their common cultural traditions despite their current partition into two states and the resultant political conflicts between them.

Film is a vital medium in both South and North Korean societies. As a mass entertainment, film portrays society. It is not only documentary but also feature films that provide the audience with images of the society in which they live. When a film presents socio-historical material in a concrete and realistic manner, the distinction between cinematic images and reality often becomes blurred, and the audience is disposed to perceive the fictional world on the screen as mirroring the actual conditions of the existing society.

Film is a cultural text produced in society. Among a variety of issues raised by film as a cultural text, those related with ideology are of critical importance. According to Graeme Turner, ideology is 'the most important conceptual category in cultural studies'.[1] To those film theorists and critics who are concerned with the relationship between social realities and cinematic representation, ideological forces behind the manifest message of a film text offer rich material for research. As Annette Kuhn points out, ideological analysis aims at a 'recovery and examination of the hidden work of ideology within film texts'.[2]

A filmic depiction of society cannot be fully understood in isolation from its dominant ideology. James Spellerberg emphasises that 'since its inception the cinema has rarely, if ever, been considered innocent of complicity in ideology'.[3] Film, similar to other cultural artefacts, tends to exhibit an underlying ideology that is embedded. Film can reflect and at the same time perpetuate the ruling ideology of society. Sergei Eisenstein's *Battleship Potemkin* (1925) well demonstrates how a dominant ideology figures in various aspects of the content and form of a film. By portraying society in a positive light, film can effectively disseminate a particular ideology supportive of the existing political system, projecting the given conditions of society as coherent with its historical needs and demands. Thus filmic images of society inevitably harbour a reality gap.

Society portrayed in film is essentially a construct. It is not the existing society but a creation reflecting salient aspects of a prevailing ideology. Through film, the audience can experience an imaginary social world which is reconstructed by a filmmaker from a particular point of view located in a particular historical moment. Hence, when the film is purposefully designed to approximate the actual conditions of society, its ideological effects dramatically increase because the audience tends to accept the mimetic correspondence between the image and its model as an authentic portrayal of social reality. As repeatedly stressed in film literature, the camera does not simply capture, record or report what happens in life, but it creates an imaginary world.[4] Even a work that appears faithfully to treat 'fact' has been filtered through the film-maker's interpretative eye, although it may be claimed to be an exact copy of reality and thus, has no intentional distortion or implicit bias. Despite its close resemblance to reality, film is fundamentally, the product of a complex mechanism fostered by various forces, political, economic, social and cultural; to say nothing of the film-makers' aesthetic perception. All these forces contribute to shaping a film in a certain ideological mould.

The present study analyses seventeen Korean films that treat socio-historical themes. History is a rich source of subject-matter. Film can accordingly reconstruct past events and situations in powerful verisimilitude. One of the historical materials widely available to film-makers is the folk tale. Traditional folk narratives are drawn on the collective, shared experiences of the community members in various realms of their lives. These narratives, therefore, contain time-endured, familiar motifs and themes for the audience. By utilising such motifs and themes, film can effectively transform a fictional space into a 'desirable world' with an instant emotional appeal to the audience. For this reason, film often becomes a wishful, imaginary projection of desires, which audiences cannot actually fulfil in their own lives. It is, therefore, not unusual that audiences respond to the cinematic depiction of their past in historical films as if it were an ideal version of their present society, which they find full of ills and hardship.[5]

The use of historical materials in film serves a double purpose. A cinematic reconstruction of past society puts history in a new perspective, and by doing so, it provides insights into the present state. While this study investigates these two interrelated aspects of the historical film, it is particularly interested in the latter effect: ideological messages that the film conveys about present society through its images of the past. By examining the ways in which previous experiences are reinvented on the screen, we can discern the subtle and complex operations of contemporary ideologies in everyday life. In historical films, specific sets of socio-political concerns of the present moment are often interwoven with seemingly timeless storylines.

A central methodological question raised in this study is this: How can we critically read the cinematic text to grasp its underlying messages about present society? An appropriate answer to this question would be one based on an approach that probes the link between the operations of ideology in the text and the historical and cultural contexts of the text. In this sense, film is a socio-cultural form of practising ideology. To analyse the ideological elements of each selected film, this study explores, first of all, in what way specific socio-historical material is reconstructed in the film. Second, it examines the latent meaning of the film text, given the tension between the specific ideological needs of the present society and the inherited cultural tradition that can be assumed to condition the audience's general attitude toward its society. These questions, however, do not aim at an 'objective' historical truth but rather an interpretation of the past created through a constructed ideology. This ideology tends to reflect contemporary societal norms and values.

To approach the most compelling ideological issues for the contemporary Korean people as a divided nation, this study investigates three groups of films from the North and the South. The first group deals with the cultural tradition from pre-modern Korea shared by both sides; the second set of films is concerned with the historical course of the national division and its aftermath; the third category commonly depicts the social realities of the divided nation. My analysis focuses on the character portrayal and main themes of the films. A comparative reading of South and North Korean films exhibits the patterns of similarities and dissimilarities in terms of their ideological orientations. Films dealing with the same subject-matter are particularly useful because different perceptions and expressions between the South and the North Korean film-makers are explicitly contrasted. The significance of ideological colouring is clearly discernible in such films. Moreover, it can be further related to the general discussion of the cinematic representation of society.

One of the recurring themes of Korean cinema is the burden of the ideological heterogeneity between the communist North and the capitalist South. Ironically, the complexity of this theme stems from the keen awareness Koreans have of their cultural homogeneity, which, rooted in their shared tradition from the past, has remained unchanged in essence despite the recent political partition. The co-existence of these contradictory strands characterises contemporary Koreans' self-perception, giving rise to two distinct traits in Korean films. On the one hand, the regimes in the South and in the North are both depicted as claiming historical legitimacy over the other.

On the other hand, Korean films from both sides subtly adopt the rhetoric of 'one nation', justifying the necessity to reunify the country. This rhetoric, in a way, reflects the genuine aspiration of the Korean people to restore their cultural homogeneity and solidarity, which, they believe, transcends the current ideological confrontation. The idea of 'one nation' is deeply valued by the public on both sides, as it appears to be grounded in their firm sense of ethnic homogeneity. The idea of ethnic unity is bolstered by the fact that the Korean people maintained one polity in the Korean peninsula for more than a millennium. Their political unity ceased as recently as 1945 with the Liberation from Japanese colonial rule. The long history of single nationhood explains the strong ethnic cohesiveness among Koreans even after the half century of division into capitalist and communist states. The idea of 'oneness' in contemporary Koreans' self-identity is epitomised in their frequent allusion of their country to an extended family. While the metaphor of familialism is not unique to Korean culture, its impact in political ideology is unusually powerful and deeply rooted.

Familialism is commonly used in the South and the North Korean films as a way of defining 'proper' or 'desirable' relations among individuals and between an individual and state. This kind of cultural norm derived from the common Confucian past confirms the lasting power of cultural heritage that resists the heterogeneous political ideologies that have been forcefully implemented in relatively recent times.

This study is informed by several theories of ideology, which provide basic terminology to describe not only unequal power relations in society but also key factors determining such relations, including gender, class and national identity. Prime consideration is given to those theories that are directly relevant to political film studies, such as Marxism and post-structuralism/postmodernism. These schools of thought all address the significance of film as an ideological apparatus. They approach film essentially as a constructed image of society that is sifted through its ruling ideology. Therefore, the insights they provide into the relations between ideology and the cinematic construction of social realities serve as indispensable conceptual resources in this book.

In film studies, scholarly interest in the subject of film and ideology has evolved into a distinct tradition of political criticism. Marxism was crucial in establishing the fundamental theoretical framework for political film studies. Arguing that social existence determines consciousness, Marx formulated the basic tenet that the base determines the content and form of the superstructure. This definition of the relationship between the base and the superstructure constitutes the foundation of the Marxist theory of culture and ideology. According to Marx, 'culture cannot be the primary force in history, but it can be an active agent in historical change or the servant of social stability'.[6] In *The German Ideology*, he claims that 'the ideas of the ruling class are in every epoch the ruling class: i.e. the class, which is the ruling material force of society, is at the same time its ruling intellectual force'.[7] Hence he views mass culture as one of the 'ideological forms of the superstructure' and the function of ideology as concealing the realities of class exploitation and oppression of bourgeois society.[8] In this view, ideology is 'false consciousness' or 'illusion', which is no more than an expression of the interests of the ruling class.[9]

The Marxist concept of 'ideology' is based on economic materialism, whose deterministic tendency has drawn much criticism recently from cultural studies. John Storey pointed out that the deterministic approach to ideology often results in a 'vulgar Marxist "reflection" theory of culture'.[10] For Marxist sociologists, ideology functions largely as an instrument to 'misrepresent "the real"' and to 'mask any political struggle', whereas for those in cultural studies ideology is 'the very site of struggle'.[11] Hence cultural theorists reject the Marxist notion of ideology, shifting the focus of their discussion from the economic basis of ideology to its cultural implications. John B. Thompson, for example, said that to study ideology means 'to study the ways in which the meaning (or signification) serves to sustain relations of domination'.[12]

Despite this criticism, Marxism – especially its notions of superstructure and ideology – continues to be the main source of inspiration for a number of critics interested in the socio-political aspects of film.[13] Among the various branches within the Marxist tradition, the Althusserian approach to ideology is most illuminating in analysing the cinematic representation of society. Louis Althusser's idea of ideology provides a useful and relevant conceptual ground for the present study.

Althusser defines ideology as 'the imaginary relationship of individuals to their real conditions of existence'.[14] This definition provides theoretical guidance for critics who explore the issues of why and how dominant ideology functions to legitimise the existing society. Althusser helps to situate film within the larger realm of the interplay between history and ideology. He has revised some of the key concepts in classical Marxism in such a way that they become more pertinent to the study of the ideological manipulation of film. Neo-Marxism has incorporated many of Althusser's ideas and has become a powerful basis for today's political film criticism.

An ideological critique of film relies specifically on Althusser's explanation of social formation and relative autonomy of the superstructures. The notion of the relative autonomy of the superstructures is an important element in Althusser's theory of ideology. His mention of the 'contradiction and overdetermination' between the base and the superstructure highlighted the reciprocal action of the superstructures on the base.[15] Informed by the works of Fredriech Engels and Antonio Gramsci, Althusser introduced this notion to revise the traditional model of economic–materialistic Marxism. By adding autonomy to the superstructures, Althusser took a major step from the original Marxist definition of the term 'superstructure'.[16] Althusser's theory enables film critics to address how ideology operates historically in its functional relation with the economic, political and cultural aspects of class society. His theory of ideology has indirectly helped to thrust political film studies into the post-structuralist/postmodern era.

In some respects, Althusser's revision of Marxist theory, and especially his notion of the 'relative autonomy' of the superstructure, echo the work of Gramsci, which opposes the economic determinism of Marxism. Gramsci devised the concept of hegemony which refers to the 'domination' and 'intellectual and moral leadership' that wins consent to unequal class relations.[17] Gramsci maintained that the relationship between dominant and subordinate groups depends not only on economic forces but also on cultural or ideological forces. He conceived the popular culture as a 'site of struggles between the forces of resistance of subordinate groups, and the forces of incorporation of dominant groups in society'.[18] By shifting the focus from economy to culture, Gramsci attacked, as Althusser did, the Marxists' dogmatic and mechanistic reduction of the 'superstructure' to materialistic factors.

Post-structuralism and postmodernism have recently offered another important conceptual basis for political film criticism. While Marxist film theorists concentrate on economic and class conflicts, post-structuralists and postmodernists tend to emphasise hegemonic coalitions formed on the basis of ideological and cultural interests. The Marxist groups criticise the latter for replacing the materialistic relation between the exploiting and the exploited with the non-materialistic relation between the dominating and the dominated. Marxist theorists also claim that the postmodern theory of domination and resistance stresses the uniqueness and individuality of the film, which is nothing but a redundant explanation.[19] These disagreements serve as indispensable theoretical resources in contemporary political film studies. Commonly centred around the notion of 'power', Marxism, post-structuralism and postmodernism provide film critics and film historians with differing yet equally useful paradigms with which to explore the ideological elements of the cinematic text.

In essence, post-structuralism and postmodernism have broadened the context for discussing the issues of the power relationship between the dominating and the dominated. A good example of the salient differences between post-structuralism and postmodernism, and Marxism, can be cited from the feminist analysis of the image of women in the mainstream films. Feminist filmmakers and critics show that the suppression of women in patriarchal society is reinforced through more than one channel. This multichannelled mechanism of suppression operates through economic exploitation, political exclusion and cultural discrimination of women.[20] The invisible orchestration of all these different practices of political power on women demonstrates that economic class is no more than one of the many categories of society's power structure. Contemporary political film critics take a similar stance to the feminist group on the issues of power. They attempt to differentiate various kinds of oppression represented in film. In the Marxist film studies, 'seeing films politically' means divulging the workings of a single factor, that is, the economic relation between the film and class society. In contrast, post-structuralists and postmodernists insist that films should be examined in the light of the interrelated networks of divergent elements, which range from politics, economy and culture to ideology.

For the last two decades, film theorists oriented towards post-structuralism or postmodernism have critically informed film studies. They have been directly affected by the ongoing debate on 'postmodern culture'. Many theorists have enriched this debate by proposing different perspectives regarding the central concerns of ideology. Among numerous works touching on this subject, Foucault's theses on the relation between power and knowledge have played a vital role in articulating the post-modern cultural discourse. His Nietzschean concept of genea-logy, which traces the power–knowledge relation, has drawn much attention from cultural studies and has created a con-siderable resonance among political film critics.[21]

Foucault's 'genealogical' study of power has introduced new concepts of 'domination' and 'resistance' to post-modern film studies.[22] The meanings of these concepts are succinctly sum-marised by his statement: 'as soon as there is a power relation, there is a possibility of resistance'.[23] The term 'resistance' in the cinematic context refers to refusing the 'domination' of the film's ideological effects. It is a denial of the repressive power that is located not only in economic and political sites but also in cultural and ideological sites. The concepts of domination and resistance, along with the idea of hegemonic coalitions, are enthusiastically received by the contemporary film critics who study the ideological and cultural struggle as inscribed in the film text. They apply Foucault's theory to all aspects of the film-producing and film-viewing activities.[24]

Foucault's argument on power–knowledge relations has had a broad impact. In his *Orientalism*, the prominent critic Edward W. Said, for example, remarks that Foucault's idea is useful in identifying a Western discourse on the Orient.[25] Foucault main-tains that the discourse of sexuality constitutes knowledge of sexuality and that the history of sexuality reveals the power–knowledge relations of sexuality. Modelled on this theory, Said describes 'Orientalism as a Western style for dominating, restruc-turing, and having authority over the Orient'.[26] In other words, 'the Orient' is a European 'invention' and 'the Orient has helped to define Europe (or the West) as its contrasting image, idea, personality and experience'.[27]

As illustrated by Said's application of Foucault's theory, the ideological interpretation operates most effectively with films which deal with socio-historical materials. In this sense, Foucault's ideas are pertinent to the present study. Above all, they help to justify why we need to look at the hidden meanings of the texts from multiple perspectives. Second, they suggest that the most meaningful way of comprehending the ideological aspect of a film is to analyse the functional relation of the contextual elements of the film. This strategy enables us to locate the ideological sites within the film text where power is exercised at particular historical moments.

Film can, of course, be studied solely for its internal aesthetic qualities. Yet, the present study does not embrace an exclusively aesthetic approach to film. So far as film functions as a cultural text in society, this study shares the interests of political film critics in relating the film text to its external contexts. A cultural text cannot be properly understood without looking at the power contestation among individuals or between individuals and their community, which is not always observable from the surface of their social interactions. In reading the latent ideological meanings of Korean films, this study treats the works as stories told by the Korean people about their daily lives, investigating their complex implications by situating them in specific temporal and spatial contexts.

For an interpretative procedure for the latent meanings of the film texts, the present study subscribes to hermeneutic and semiotics. Among the previous hermeneutic studies of cultural texts, Clifford Geertz's is of particular importance to this study. His essay, 'Deep play: notes on the Balinese cockfight' supplies diverse conceptual insights into and practical strategies for handling film as a cultural text. As Geertz puts it, the culture of a people is 'an ensemble of texts'.[28] Furthermore, the concept of culture is essentially a semiotic one, and the analysis of culture is not an experimental science in search of law but an interpretative one in search of meaning.[29] In adopting a hermeneutic perspective, the present study pays particular attention to its limitation of which Geertz rightly reminds us in his study of Balinese life: a hermeneutic approach is not to be regarded as '*the* master key' to the text.[30]

As a methodological apparatus, the hermeneutic approach has several advantages over the traditional methodologies drawn from natural sciences. First of all, a hermeneutic understanding of cultural texts is fuller and more dimensional than the 'scientific' explanations of social lives. The hermeneutic approach allows the researcher to focus on why, as well as how, people construct their lives in a particular fashion. Experiential meaning in social phenomena, especially relating to the question of why people act the way they do, cannot be fully examined from experimental methods that rely upon statistical measurements. Second, the hermeneutic approach exempts researchers from arguing on the quality of texts. The central concern of the hermeneutic approach is to find out how the subjects make a sense out of cultural texts, not to make a value judgement of the texts with the researcher's yardstick. Works of art are not an exception to their fundamental premise of hermeneutics. As Geertz says, 'works of art are elaborate mechanisms for defining social relationships, sustaining social rules, and strengthening social values'.[31] From the hermeneutic point of view, how and why people impart a significance to works of art in their local context should be the locus of investigation.

The hermeneutic approach has a dual task of reinterpreting the interpretation. This prime characteristic of the hermeneutic methodology is clearly expressed by Geertz: 'societies, like lives, contain their own interpretations. One has only to learn how to gain access to them'.[32] The reader of the text who gains an entry into the story constitutes an essential component in the mechanism of interpretation. After all, understanding meaning in cultural texts is a retelling of stories of the people from the researcher's point of view. Hans-Georg Gadamer conveys this idea succinctly: 'understanding belongs to the being that which is understood'.[33]

The hermeneutic paradigm of analysis helps to secure the reader's place in the whole process of interpretation of cultural texts. The importance of interpretation, as is argued by hermeneutics is noted by film theorists such as Dudley Andrew, who, in *Concepts in Film Theory*, remarks: 'cinematic figures openly require the work of interpretation to complete them. Interpretation is integral to the specific structure of discourse they constitute'.[34] Andrew's argument indicates that to complete films as cultural texts, there should always be the subject to interpret them. The complexities of the hermeneutic methodology involve these multi-layered perspectives of the subjects and the researchers. This once more reinforces the multi-faceted and multi-dimensional nature of the hermeneutic approach.

In exploring the deeper meaning of a cultural text, a hermeneutic perspective can be further strengthened by Barthes's methodological model. Compared with scientific film semiotics, which is capitalised on by the works of Christian Metz, Barthes's theory provides a more persuasive and applicable paradigm for researchers who are interested in the ideological aspects of film texts. Obviously, Barthes is dissatisfied with the semiotic framework, which is strictly based on linguistic rules. Unlike early theorists and practitioners of film semiotics, Barthes attempts to transcend the linguistic model of signification process by dividing the levels of signification into two: denotation and connotation. The former indicates the literal meaning of the text, and the latter expresses its cultural meaning. Denotation is the first level of signification, involving the obvious, straight meaning of a sign, whereas connotation relates to the second level of signification, referring to the associated meanings which may be conjured up by the object signified. Barthes stresses that layers of meanings lying beneath the surface of texts often deny or conflict with a simple description at the first level of signification. Barthes's point, which sheds interesting light on the present study, is that the interpretation of the second level requires a deeper knowledge of, or familiarity with, the culture in which the text is located. This is why Barthes's approach is considered useful in disinterring the latent ideology of cultural texts. His textual analysis illustrates how "'semic [semiotic] space is glued to hermeneutic space'".[35]

A hermeneutic paradigm enriched by Barthes's semiotic ideas helps us to understand the workings of ideology in Korean films. The texts analysed in this study all treat historical or socio-historical materials. Because of their historical nature, the films reflect more transparently than any other genres in Korean cinema, Koreans' perception of their own past at the present moment. In other words, the representation of history in Korean films contains various images that Koreans hold about themselves. An interpretative methodological procedure based on hermeneutics and semiotics is especially effective in explaining the similarities and dissimilarities between the South and the North Korean films in handling their past, in relation to the ideological orientations of the two states.

This book consists of four chapters. The first chapter examines the social and political milieu in which the Korean film industry developed from its beginning during the Japanese colonial period to its bifurcation into South and North Korean cinemas. Ever since film was introduced to Korea in 1903, the industry has been under strict governmental control. Hence a considerable part of this chapter is devoted to describing the political and economic interventions made first by the colonial authorities and then by the North and the South Korean governments. This chapter exposes how the seemingly opposite state ideologies of the two Korean regimes in fact, produced essentially similar film policies for the purpose of legitimising their political and economic status quo.

Chapters 2 to 4 present a critical analysis of the selected films, which were all made between 1960 and 1990. The selection of the films was based on the extent and depth of their treatment of gender, nationhood and class, three major factors in defining the cultural identities of the contemporary Korean people. Chapter 2 concentrates on the treatment of gender in five films, all of which are adaptations of a famous traditional love story, *Ch'unhyangjŏn* (The Tale of Ch'unhyang). The differing images of Ch'unhyang in the five films show the changing views of ideal womanhood in contemporary Korea. My discussion attempts to relate these images to the different ideologies of the North and the South. This comparison, however, reveals that these adaptations ultimately revert to the Confucian family values and sexual morality. These traditional values constitute a common cultural legacy, which influences the perception of gender relations in the North and the South Korean films, regardless of their differing political ideologies.

In addition to gender issues, Chapter 2 investigates the differences between the North and the South Korean films in their interpretations of the class distinction in traditional society. Despite their ideological disagreements, films from both sides commonly advocate traditional Confucian ethics as a fundamental guideline for an 'ideal' relationship between ruler and subjects. This tendency is not detected at the surface but at a deeper level of the text. The defence of the Confucian patriarchy implicitly justifies the present social hierarchy in both North and South.

Chapter 3 concerns the subject of nationhood by looking at how the North and the South Korean films portray the origin and consequences of the recent national division. All of the six films chosen for this chapter describe the rise and fall of the regimes in the North and the South in light of their contending ideologies. The North Korean films invariably attempt to justify the necessity of establishing a classless society, articulating anti-imperialism as the pivotal element of North Korean nationalism. The films also stress unceasing loyalty to Kim Il Sung and his son Kim Jong Il. Less rigid on the surface, yet equally coercive in its application to the film industry, is the anti-communist ideology adopted by the South Korean military regime throughout its thirty-year rule. The government has used anti-communism as a deliberate means to suppress the film-makers' freedom of expression.

Following the analysis of the six films, Chapter 3 briefly discusses the cultural elements that the North and the South films employ to delineate ideal Korean nationhood. The films analysed in this chapter emphasise the traditional family values as an appropriate moral foundation and cultural root with which contemporary Koreans of both North and South can overcome their ideological conflicts and establish an integrated nation in the future.

Chapter 4 probes the notion of class in contemporary Korea by examining the cinematic representations of individuals' heterogeneous class experiences in the 'classless' North or the capitalist South. The six films discussed in this chapter were all produced the 1980s, a watershed in the two societies. During this period, the full social consequences of the state-initiated drive for industrialisation projects, during the previous decades in both North and South Korea, became apparent. These films vividly portray the historical context in which socio-economic structures were formed on both sides. They also deal with the problematic of selfhood with which individuals have to cope in their everyday lives within the given structure. The North Korean films attempt to deny the existence of class-related conflicts between the state and the masses, under the unitary working-class system; whereas the South Korean films are more openly critical of the class relations controlled by the authoritarian rule of the military regimes. Ironically, though, despite their super-ficial differences, the six films commonly expose the extent to which contemporary Koreans rely on public recognition and respect as important barometers of their social standing, regard-less of the ideological bases of their class system. The films once again reinforce the indispensability of the cultural tradition and especially the Confucian precepts on interpersonal relations in understanding the operation of ideology in contemporary Korean society.

Finally, the Conclusion reiterates the major points that this study raises on the role of ideology in Korean cinema. It also suggests issues that merit further research in this and other related areas.

Spelling and style conventions used in this book

All the dialogues quoted from the films were translated into English by the author.

In romanising Korean names and words, I have generally followed the modified MacCune–Reischauer system, except in cases where a different method has long been established, such as *Juche*, Syngman Rhee, Park Chung Hee, and so forth. With regard to personal names, I adopted those whose English spel-lings are consistent. For those names whose English spellings are inconsistent, the modified MacCune–Reischauer system was applied throughout this book.

In East Asia, the family name comes before the given name. I have transcribed all Korean names, including characters', authors of Korean materials and directors in the East-Asian convention, except the authors who have given their English-spelled names in their works.

Concerning characters' names, I used their given names throughout my discussion, but in cases where the films use their surnames and titles, such as Miss, Mr, Comrade, Sir, Chairman, General (or other occupational titles), and so on, I used their surnames without titles.

Throughout this book, film titles are given in English to render things easier for the reader. The original Korean titles are listed in the Filmography on pp. 194–221. In translating the film titles into English, I adopted those widely circulated among film critics and scholars. However, when such English titles were unavailable, I attempted to render the translations as closely as possible to their meanings in the original language.

Notes

1 Graeme Turner, *British Cultural Studies: An Introduction*, 2nd edn (London, Routledge, 1996), p. 182.

2 Annette Kuhn, *Women's Pictures: Feminism and Cinema*, 2nd edn (London, Verso, 1994), p. 83.

3 James Spellerberg, 'Technology and ideology in the cinema', in Gerald Mast and Marshall Cohen (eds), *Film Theory and Criticism: Introductory Readings*, 3rd edn (New York, Oxford University Press, 1985), p. 761.

4 Jean-Louis Comolli and Jean Naraboni, 'Cinema/ideology/criticism', in Bill Nichols (ed.), *Movies and Methods Volume I: An Anthology* (Berkeley, University of California Press, 1976), pp. 22–30; and Marcelin Pleynet, 'Economical–ideological–formal', in Sylvia Harvey (ed.), *May 1968 and Film Culture* (London, British Film Institute, 1978), p. 59.

5 A good example is Sergei Eisenstein, *October* (Sovkino, 1928).

6 Karl Marx and Frederick Engels, *Selected Letters* (Peking, Foreign Language Press, 1977), p. 92, quoted in John Storey, *An Introductory Guide to Cultural Theory and Popular Culture* (Hertfordshire, Harvester Wheatsheaf, 1993), p. 99.

7 Karl Marx and Frederick Engels, *The German Ideology: Parts I & III*, ed. and trans. R. Pascal (New York, International Publishers, 1963), p. 39.

8 Karl Marx, 'Preface to *A Contribution to the Critique of Political Economy*', in David McLellan (ed.), *Karl Marx: Selected Writings* (Oxford, Oxford University Press, 1977), p. 390.

9 Marx and Engels, *The German Ideology: Parts I & III*; and Louise Althusser, *For Marx*, trans. Ben Brewster (London, Verso, 1996), pp. 140–1.

10 Storey, *An Introductory Guide*, p. 98.

11 Turner, *British Cultural Studies*, p. 182.

12 John B. Thompson, *Studies in the Theory of Ideology* (Cambridge, Polity, 1984), p. 4.

13 Gerald Mast and Marshall Cohen, 'Film: Psychology, society and ideology', in Mast and Cohen (eds), *Film Theory and Criticism*, p. 669.

14 Louis Althusser, 'Ideology and ideological state apparatuses', in *Lenin and Philosophy and Other Essays*, trans. Ben Brewster (London, Monthly Review Press, 1977), p. 153.

15 Althusser, *For Marx*, pp. 87–128.

16 Louis Althusser, 'The errors of classical economics', in Louis Althusser and Étienne Balibar, *Reading Capital*, trans. Ben Brewster (London, NLB, 1970), pp. 99–100.

17 Antonio Gramsci, *Selections from the Prison Notebooks*, eds and trans. Quintin Hoare and Geoffrey Nowell-Smith (London, Lawrence & Wishart, 1971), p. 57.

18 Storey, *An Introductory Guide*, p. 13.

19 J. Dudley Andrew, *Concepts in Film Theory* (Oxford, Oxford University Press, 1984), p. 115.

20 Claire Johnston, 'Women's cinema as counter-cinema', in Nichols (ed.), *Movies and Methods Volume I*, p. 211.

21 Michel Foucault, 'Critical theory/intellectual history', in Lawrence D. Kritzman (ed.), *Michel Foucault: Politics, Philosophy, Culture*, trans. Alan Sheridan *et al.* (London, Routledge, 1983), pp. 17–46.

22 Michel Foucault, *The History of Sexuality I: An Introduction*, trans. Robert Hurley (London, Penguin Books, 1979).

23 Michel Foucault, 'Power and sex', in Kritzman (ed.), *Michel Foucault: Politics*, p. 123.

24 Dana Polan, 'Powers of vision, visions of power', *Camera Obscura*, 18 (1988), 106–19; and J. P. Telotte, *Voices in the Dark: The Narrative Patterns of Film Noir* (Urbana, University of Illinois Press, 1989).

25 Edward W. Said, *Orientalism: Western Conceptions of the Orient* (London, Penguin Books, 1985), p. 22.

26 Said, *Orientalism*, p. 3.

27 Said, *Orientalism*, pp. 1–2.

28 Clifford Geertz, *The Interpretation of Culture: Selected Essays* (London, Fontana Press, 1993), p. 452.

29 Geertz, *The Interpretation of Culture*, p. 5.

30 Geertz, *The Interpretation of Culture*, p. 417 and p. 452; (my italics).

31 Clifford Geertz, *Local Knowledge: Further Essays in Interpretive Anthropology* (London, Fontana Press, 1993), p. 99.

32 Geertz, *The Interpretation of Culture*, p. 453.

33 Hans-Georg Gadamer, *Truth and Methods*, trans. William Glen-Doepel (London, Sheed & Ward, 1989), p. xxxi.

34 Andrew, *Concepts in Film*, p. 172.

35 Kaja Silverman, *The Subject of Semiotics* (Oxford, Oxford University Press, 1983), p. 257.

1

The creation of national identity: a history of Korean cinema

One of the most distinctive traits of Korean film is its strong political nature. Since its introduction in 1903, film in Korea has always been under governmental censorship. During the Japanese colonial period (1910–45), the government severely suppressed those films that would inspire anti-colonial sentiments among the Korean audience. On the other hand, the colonial government employed film as a powerful means to legitimise their rule in Korea up until their surrender to the Allies in 1945. The dissemination of propaganda through film continued throughout the USA–Soviet occupation period from 1945 to 1948. After the devastation of the civil war (1950–53), there was an inevitable ideological divide between the communist North and the capitalist South. As a result, governmental control over the film industry was further strengthened. For the last decades, both states enforced various policies on film for political purposes.

This chapter will examine the historical development of Korean film. Since the Korean film industry is inseparable from the political situation of the country, my survey of its development follows the general periodisation of the political history of modern Korea. From a broad perspective, the history of Korean film can be described in terms of governmental intervention and resistance to such interference. The emergence of Korean film during the colonial period testifies to the dynamics of these two oppositional forces. As the Korean Workers' Party adopted strict guidelines on every aspect of film-making and distribution, North Korean film has served exclusively as a propaganda instrument. The South Korean film industry was also subject to government censorship. However, the capitalist system in the South enabled film-makers to pursue freedom of expression amidst various political constraints from the government.

Korean film during the Japanese colonial period

Korea, in the late nineteenth century, was regarded as an object of colonisation by great powers such as Japan, the USA, Britain, France and Russia. These countries attempted not only to force Korea to open its doors to international trade, but they strove also to establish their political and social influence in the Korean peninsula.

The Korean government's seclusionism, and especially its suppression of the Catholic missions from the West, led Korea to wars with the USA and France. Japan soon became aware of the collapse of the isolationist policy of the Korean government and forced it to sign the Treaty of Peace and Amity in 1876. After the Sino-Japanese War from 1894 to 1895 and the Russo-Japanese War in 1904, Japan took the initiative by colonising Korea with diplomatic and economic support from the USA and Britain. In 1910, Japan's colonisation effort was concluded with an annexation of the Korean peninsula with unequal treaties.

To establish Korea as a base for food supplies and a military advance into China, Japan devised numerous programmes to change the economic structure of Korean society, including one to increase agricultural production, particularly rice, the main staple of the region. In addition, Japan put various cultural programmes into effect to demoralise Koreans as colonial subjects. Japan's cultural control over Koreans aimed to root out their sense of national identity as demonstrated by the prohibition of the Korean language in schools and the forced change of Korean family names into a standardised Japanese style.

Despite the colonial government's mounting military pressure on various sections of Korean society, Koreans continued to vigorously resist Japanese rule. The Tonghak Peasant War in 1894 and the disparate yet consistent attacks by the remnants of the Korean royal troops are examples of the Koreans' efforts to liberate their country from Japanese rule. Koreans' anti-colonial resistance culminated in the 1 March Independence Movement, a mass-scale popular liberation movement that occurred in 1919 and the provisional government of the Republic of Korea was founded in Shanghai in the same year.

The introduction of motion pictures to Korea

The seclusionism of the Chosŏn Dynasty collapsed in 1876 as the Korean government was forced to sign the Treaty of Peace and

Amity by Japan. Along with this change, Western goods and cultural products began to flow into Korean society. Motion pictures were introduced as part of the propaganda campaigns by foreign powers. Western films were an obvious case of cultural imperialism because they were used by the great powers as a means to win favour with Koreans for political and economic purposes. To most Koreans, film was an object of curiosity and rarity, rather than an artistic or scientific invention from the West.

It was through foreign companies, diplomatic corps and missionaries that motion pictures came into Korea for the first time during the late Chosŏn Dynasty.[1] These agencies showed films to Koreans as a way of introducing Western cultures and civilisation, and more importantly, as a sign of their prosperity. Foreign companies, such as the Hansŏng Electric Company, and the Yŏngmi Tobacco Company used films as part of their sales strategies. Western diplomats also showed films to high-ranking officials, government-patronised groups and pro-Japanese civil groups at hotels and social functions.

It was only in 1903 that foreign films were presented to the Korean public for the first time through an advertisement.[2] The film advertisement column in a newspaper *Hwangsŏng Shinmun*, dated 23 June 1903, illustrates a trick used by the foreign companies to increase sales by accepting admission fees in the form of proof of purchase of their companies' products.[3] The Hansŏng Electric Company, which was founded in 1898 with a joint stock of the Korean Royal Household and Americans, Henry Collbran and H. R. Bostwick, built the first electric railway in Seoul. This company used films to draw customers by charging them admission fees or selling them their streetcar tickets. Similarly, the Yŏngmi Tobacco Company allowed Korean audiences to pay the entrance fee with empty packets of the cigarettes made by their company. *Hwangsŏng Shinmun*, the contemporary newspaper, reported that audiences exceeded 1,000 per day.[4]

The appearance of Korean film[5]

With the influx of foreign films through both Japanese and Western agencies under the protection of the Japanese colonial government, Koreans could not develop their own film industry, which required substantial financial backing and strong economic and social infrastructure. In the late nineteenth century, the film industries of the dominant Western powers made efforts to conduct their business enterprises in their colonies, which they viewed as potentially profitable markets. This situation applied to Korea as well. Film as a business enterprise attracted enormous interests for foreigners in Korea. They could thus secure official, political backing from the Japanese colonial government. It was, therefore, not surprising that it was extremely difficult for Koreans to develop their own native film industry under such political, economic and social constraints.

This problem is clearly reflected in the complexity of determining the beginning of Korean film. Film historians are faced with several questions as to how to decide on what was the 'first' Korean film. Factors to consider include, among others, when the film was produced and when it was premièred; whether the general public was accessible to its première; whether it was shown to a special audience; who financed its making; and who directed it, a Korean or a Japanese. Moreover, such historians need to clarify their positions concerning those films where productions were completed, yet which were not distributed to the public because they had fallen foul of government censorship. As we shall see, these diverse factors account for the widely differing views on when Korean film actually began. The lively debate on this, and other related issues, still goes on among film scholars and critics.

Currently, the majority of film historians consider *The Righteous Revenge* to be the starting point for Korean film, made by a Korean director, Kim Tosan and released in 1919.[6] This film was a screen and stage play (i.e. kino drama), using motion pictures as an auxiliary part of the stage play. Shot by a Japanese cameraman, produced by Pak Sŭngp'il and premièred at the Tansŏngsa theatre, the film dealt with the story of Songsan's revenge against his wicked stepmother and her clique for their conspiracy to kill him and seize his inheritance. Promoting virtue and reproving vice, *The Righteous Revenge*, like other kino dramas of the time, depicted Korean life without any social and historical context, concerned only with personal problems, such as conflicts and intrigues over an inheritance, or accounts of amorous relationships.

The majority of film historians and scholars, however, consider *The Plighted Love under the Moon* (1923) as the first Korean feature film. *The Plighted Love under the Moon* is a full-scale feature film. It is not part of a stage drama like *The Righteous Revenge*. Its script was written, and subsequently directed by Yun Paengnam: it was the Japanese colonial government that produced the film with the aim of encouraging the salvation of Korea. Yŏngdŭk, the protagonist of the film, is addicted to sensual pleasures and squanders all of his family's financial resources. His *fiancée*, Chŏngsun, saves him from all his troubles by using her savings. The colonial government forced Koreans to see the film, which was, in fact, the beginning of a series of propaganda films made by the government to instil the spirit of obedience into the colonial rule.

Recently, Kim Chongwŏn and Cho Hŭimun proposed a different view on the origins of Korean film. They argue that Kim Tosan's *The National Borders*, which was screened 13 January 1923, should be considered the first feature film in Korean film history. Until Kim's and Cho's studies on early Korean films were published in 1993, *The National Borders* had been widely considered an unfinished work, and consequently, had been excluded by the majority of historians from their discussion on Korean film history.[7] This dominant view is challenged by Kim and Cho, who claim that the film was finished and even released to the public. For evidence, they point out the advertisement of its première in *Dong-A Ilbo* of 11 January 1923. This date indeed precedes the first viewing of *The Plighted Love under the Moon* on 9 April 1923. According to Kim and Cho, the existence of *The National Borders* became uncertain because the colonial government banned it immediately after the première night on the basis of its 'undesirable' political content.

The first sound film, *The Tale of Ch'unhyang*, was directed by a Korean, Yi Myŏngu, and produced by the Kyŏngsŏng Studios and financed by the Japanese in 1935. This film is based on a love story between a lower-class woman and an upper-class man who overcome discrimination and social stigma in the rigid caste Chosŏn society prevailing at that time. The appearance of the sound film in Korea resulted in establishing larger and more systematic production companies. But the majority of the Korean film production companies were too small to produce sound films. Moreover, the colonial government severely censored those films that were recorded in Korean. The weak financial basis of the Korean production companies, coupled with harsh censorship, led to the decline of the young Korean film industry at the very beginning of the sound-picture era.

The production, distribution and reception of Korean film during the Japanese colonial period

Western films were imported into the Korean market as cultural products. After realising the commercial values of films to the Korean audiences, Japanese and foreign traders monopolised the Korean film market under the political and economic protection of the Japanese colonial government. American traders, such as George R. Allen, H. G. Morris and G. Taylor, together with Japanese partners, could import films made by American companies such as Paramount, Universal, Warner Brothers, FBO, Fox, and the French companies, Méliès and Pathé. There were only two distribution companies established by Koreans, the Kishin Yanghaeng and Tongyang Film Stock Company, which imported films through the American, British and Russian companies, such as Paramount, British International Film Company and Sobkino.

Most of the imported films were shown at commercial theatres. Stimulated by the popularity of foreign films, business people built more and more theatres in Korea. In 1912 two new theatres were built, Kodŭng Yŏnyegwan and Hwangŭm Yŏnyegwan, and in 1913 Taejŏnggwan was opened exclusively for the Japanese who were living in Seoul. For the Korean audiences, Tansŏngsa, which was the first stage theatre opened in Korea 1907 was renovated in 1918 for cinema. Chosŏn Kŭkchang was another new theatre built in 1922 for Koreans. By 1935 approximately thirty-nine film theatres were established all over the country,[8] and the number of Korean moviegoers increased year by year from about 2,600,000 in 1927 to about 8,800,000 in 1935.[9] The 1935 data is estimated to have been one-third of the entire Korean population at the time.

Korean film-makers also attempted to establish their own production companies. For Korean film-makers, a commercial distribution of their films was the only source of funds to finance their productions. However, the funding was neither sufficient nor reliable. Their total lack of funding led them to depend on Japanese proprietors who were, in fact, the owners of the majority of the theatres run for Korean audiences and managed by Koreans. On rare occasions, when Korean film-makers could finance their own work, they usually had to give up the project at an early stage because they could not secure enough money to continue the filming. Even though their first film might become a box-office hit, it was often insufficient to finance any long-term film-making. Besides, Korean audiences had become more and more accustomed to the style of imported films. Such a Westernised taste among audiences added another problem for Korean film-makers. They were already suffering from a lack of financial backing and weak economic infrastructure, and were unable to compete with richer foreign importers.

Statistically, there were about sixty production companies operating in Korea during the Japanese colonial period, and they made more than 160 films in total. Two Japanese production companies and four Korean companies were established by 1926 when *Arirang* was made and became the biggest box-office success. From 1926 until 1935, when the first sound film was produced, about fifty film production companies were built for commercial profit. Most of these closed after producing one or two films; however, three companies, Chosŏn Kinema, Kŭmgang Kinema and Naun'gyu Production continued, producing five feature films. In this situation, Korean film-makers could not but depend upon Japanese investors whose share constituted approximately 40 per cent of the total capital owned by all the production companies in Korea at the time. Korean film-makers also had to rely on Japanese technology in the early stage of the silent-picture era from 1923 to 1926.

Foreign films, which were distributed during the colonial period, overwhelmingly outnumbered Korean films. For instance, of films released in 1925, 2,130 films were American and 124 films were European, whereas only 8 were Korean.[10] Imported foreign films were thus the overwhelming majority in the Korean film market. Two or three Korean production companies could make sound films from 1935, and the proportion of sound films in the total number of films released grew every year from 20 per cent in 1933 to 85 per cent in 1935.[11] In 1934 the Japanese colonial government began to put pressure on all the theatres to raise the ratio of Japanese films to 50 per cent of the entire number of the films they showed.[12] In spite of the increasing number of theatres and audiences, the actual conditions of Korean film production during the colonial period were thus inhospitable for developing a systematic film industry in Korea. Consequently, the Korean film industry was always dominated by the imported film distribution business conducted by foreign proprietors, and the Korean audiences were no more than consumers of the imported cultural goods.

Film policies during the Japanese colonial period

The film policy of the Japanese colonial government focused primarily on obliterating Korean culture and manipulating the colonial subjects ideologically. This attitude was a natural outcome of their overall colonial policy to integrate Chosŏn into Japan and impose the Japanese language on Koreans. The colonial government regarded film as an effective means to eradicate a sense of sovereignty and independence from the Korean people and to exact total submission to their rule. Using the popularity and effectiveness of film as a mass medium, the Japanese attempted to justify and reinforce the significance and the inevitability of their colonisation. For this purpose, the colonial authorities established the Motion Picture Section within the government in 1920, which produced its first film, *Cholera*, in the same year.[13] Beginning with this, the government made about 230 propaganda films for over twenty-five years until the Liberation in 1945.[14]

Film censorship was enforced even before the appearance of Korean film. In 1922, the government passed the Entertainment and Theatres Regulations to censor motion pictures and films. From 1924 all foreign films to be shown to the public were inspected by the government, and this censorship applied later to Korean films made by Koreans. The Motion Pictures and Films Censorship Regulations were further enacted in 1926 and revised in 1928. The censorship of films and scripts was enforced through each provincial police bureau. Both films and their audiences were under police surveillance at all the theatres. This system of theatre inspection was aimed at tightening control over Korean audiences and films. In 1934, the Motion Pictures and Films Censorship Regulations were changed to the Motion Pictures Surveillance Regulations to strengthen the censorship. When the first sound film, *The Tale of Ch'unhyang*, was made in 1935, the censorship became more strict towards the Korean films which were recorded in Korean. The government forced the Korean film-makers to produce pro-Japanese films and made it compulsory to show propaganda films to Korean audiences at public institutions.

In 1940 the Chosŏn Film Regulations were enacted. This law allowed the government to prosecute Korean production companies that refused to make pro-Japanese films. The film production and distribution system was also changed from a registration system to a license system. Organising the Chosŏn Film Distribution League in 1941, the colonial government banned film distribution itself, except for pro-Japanese Korean films and those films brought from Japan or its allies, Italy and Germany. A new company called the Chosŏn Film Production Ltd. Company was founded in 1942 under the supervision of the colonial government. However, the government revoked all the registrations of the Korean production companies, and thus deprived Korean film-makers of their freedom to undertake film production of their choice. The number and kind of films to be produced were decided by the government. The distribution of raw film stock was also restricted because it was regarded as military supplies. To intensify the Korean Language Prohibition Law enacted in 1938, the government completely prohibited the screening of films recorded in Korean in 1942: from this year, all Korean films produced by the Japanese were recorded and titled in Japanese, and all the Korean film-makers, including directors and casts, were also named in Japanese. The colonial film policy changed over the four decades. It became progressively more rigid, eventually forbidding Korean film-makers to engage in free enterprise and thus, forestalled an opportunity for them to develop a native form of film and their own independent film industry.

1　　　　Yi Kyŏngson's *Long Cherished Dream* (1926) is representative
of *Shinp'a* dramas produced in that period

Major directors and films

Despite the severe censorship and restrictions for film-making, the
Japanese colonial period produced more than 160 Korean films,
including eight kino dramas. Most of them belong to the *Shinp'a*
drama ('new school drama') whose melodramatic contents and
forms are based on love affairs, sex, murder or money matters.
These dramas appealed to the Korean audiences by providing
them with an escape from their grim social reality and their
unpleasant life as the colonised. The first *Shinp'a* drama is *Jade
Tears* (1925) directed by Yi Kuyŏng. Adapted from a popular
Japanese novel *My Crime*, the film depicts the tragedy of a
woman who gives birth to a boy from an extra-marital affair. In
terms of box-office hits, the most successful *Shinp'a* dramas were
Yi Kyŏngson's *Long Cherished Dream* (1926) adapted from
another popular Japanese novel *Gold Demon* written by Ozaki
Kōyō and Yi Kuyŏng's *Mutual Love* (1929), a tragic love story
between a beautiful *kisaeng* (courtesan or female entertainer) and
an artist.

　　Along with the *Shinp'a* dramas, historical films that dramatise
folk tales or classic novels were also very popular with audiences.
Yi Kyŏngson's *The Tale of Shimch'ŏng* (1925) and Pak Chŏnghyŏn's *The Tale of Changhwa and Hongnyŏn* (1924) are considered
the best pieces in this genre in both artistic and commercial
merits, together with *The Tale of Ch'unhyang* made in 1935. Pak's

The Tale of Changhwa and Hongnyŏn has special importance in Korean film history as the first truly 'Korean' work in all aspects of its making: the material, cast, film crew, directing and finance. The first Korean cinematographer Yi P'ilu made his début in feature film with this work.

Yi P'ilu is perhaps, the most important figure in the technological evolution of the early Korean cinema, heralding the era of sound film with *The Tale of Ch'unhyang*. Other notable figures in the early Korean film industry include Pak Sŭngp'il, the producer of *The Righteous Revenge* and the 1924 *Tale of Changhwa and Hongnyŏn*, and Yun Paengnam, the director of *The Plighted Love under the Moon* and *The Story of Unyŏng* (1925) and producer of the 1925 *The Tale of Simch'ŏng*, and Yi Kyŏngson, the director of *Long Cherished Dream*, and *The Tale of Shimch'ŏng* (1925).

Among these melodramatic Korean films, however, a few nationalistic resistance films appeared in 1926.[15] The success of *Arirang*, which was the first of a series of nationalistic resistance films, brought some prosperity to the Korean film industry. It aroused an interest among Korean audiences for Korean films and resulted in a rapidly growing number of film productions by Koreans in the ensuing years. As will be discussed later, the appearance of *Wandering* in 1928, the first of the so-called 'tendency films' which were made by the KAPF (Korean Art Proletarian Federation) film-makers, is often ascribed to the successful reception of *Arirang* by the public.[16] Tendency films articulated a socialist ideology, and the makers of these films were considered leaders of the Korean proletarian art movement during this period.

The colonial government, of course, did not ignore the growing interest in nationalistic films. In the 1930s, they enforced the censorship more strictly, banned the release of any nationalistic resistance films, and coerced Korean film-makers into producing pro-Japanese films only. Interestingly, Korean film-makers turned to literary films as a reaction to the government's control, viewing them as a way to escape from the forced production of pro-Japanese films on one side and to avoid conventional melodramas on the other. Subsequently, literary films became a new trend in the Korean film industry. Along with literary films, however, pro-Japanese military films were also produced in large number from this point. With the first military film, Sŏ Kwangje's *Troop Train* appearing in 1938, pro-Japanese films began to prevail in the Korean film industry until the Liberation.

Korean films during the Japanese colonial period can be divided into five categories according to their subject-matter and themes: melodramas; nationalistic resistance films; 'tendency films'; literary films; and pro-Japanese films. Among these five categories, nationalistic films and 'tendency films' deserve closer examination because they made a significant contribution to awakening a critical perspective in Korean directors on the political and social realities surrounding them and illustrated a cinematic approach to them. The following section will thus treat these two kinds of films in detail.

Nationalistic films and Na Un'gyu

Arirang was made by Na Un'gyu in 1926. The title derives from a famous Korean folk song of that name. The theme of this film is the resistance of the poor against the oppression of the rich. Depicting the problems of the feudalistic relationship between the supervisor of a tenant farm and a peasant in a rural community, the film treats for the first time in the history of Korean cinema, anti-imperialist sentiment against Japanese colonisation. The film's enthusiastic reception by audiences led to the production of numerous Korean films of a similar kind later. Na made another nationalistic film entitled *Searching for Love* in 1928. This film is often praised by film historians for its message concerning the need for national independence and awakening a keen political consciousness in the audience.[17] Many parts of this film were cut out by the Japanese colonial censors at that time, hence the original story cannot be restored in full.

Arirang and *Searching for Love* had a profound influence on Korean audiences as well as on the film-makers. Their indelible impact can be seen especially in that Korean film-makers who were provoked and inspired by Na's films tried their hand at a variety of nationalistic, anti-Japanese films in the following years. Yi Kyuhwan's *A Boat without a Boatman* released in 1932 is one of the most representative films modelled on Na's works, portraying the miseries of a Korean fisherman and his daughter who are mistreated by the landed class. Na's influence is also strongly felt in Yun Pongch'un's *A Big Tomb* (1931) which deals with anti-Japanese fighters tragically killed by the Japanese. Yun appeared in about thirty films, including five of Na's pieces. He also made four films of his own between 1927 and 1942 and then left the film circle, refusing to make films under the umbrella of the Chosŏn Film Productions Ltd. Company. For this reason, he has been regarded as an exemplary anti-Japanese, nationalist film-maker as well as actor by many South Korean film historians and critics.

Following his initial success, Na produced about twenty films, established Naun'gyu Productions in 1927, and even acted in his own and his colleagues' films until he died in 1937. Beginning with the early nationalistic films, Na's *œuvre* ranges from

2   Cast and staff of Na Un'gyu's *Searching for Love* (1928).
Na is second from left, first row

melodramas to pro-Japanese films. Although Na earned a high reputation as a 'nationalistic' director for his early works, he in fact tried his hand at a wide variety of subjects and forms. He was willing to make popular commercial films, guided by keen business instincts. The most controversial aspect of Na's career is the pro-Japanese films he made in the later years. He drew particularly serious criticism from Korean intellectuals for the propaganda films that are represented by *To Send a Husband to a Border Garrison* produced in 1931. This film features a Korean couple who are devoted to Japan's military cause.

Film scholars are divided in their assessment of Na's importance in the history of Korean film.[18] Despite this disagreement, Na's contribution to the development of the Korean film industry, especially his early works with anti-colonial themes, merits recognition. Although he was engaged in pro-Japanese activities towards the end of his career, it cannot be denied that the Korean film industry finally reached a take-off point with Na's *Arirang*. In this sense, his works marked a crucial turning point, a new phase in Korean film history. They showed Korean film-makers their strong potential to build a truly national film industry. This is why leading scholars such as Yu Hyŏnmok said that 'the silent picture era in Korean film history is Na's era'.[19]

'Tendency films' and KAPF

Arirang strongly appealed to Korean audiences, arousing in them an aspiration for national independence. The appearance of the

KAPF films can be understood in the context of such newly arisen nationalism in the film community. The acronym 'KAPF' stands for the Korean Artista Proletariat Federate in Esperanto.[20] Formed as a school among literary figures and artists in Korea in the early part of this century, the KAPF initiated a proletarian art movement. *Wandering*, made by an avant-garde poet and KAPF film-maker, Kim Yuyŏng, in 1928 was the first 'tendency film' in Korean film history. It depicts the life of Korean peasants exploited by the landed class. As is the case with Kim, the KAPF members made films under the slogan, 'art as arms for the class struggle', and their films formed another new trend in the Korean film industry. Considering film as a tool for political struggles, the KAPF film-makers tried to represent the social realities of the Korean proletariat on the screen. They produced five films between 1928 and 1931. The historical significance of these films can be seen in the argument proposed by a group of Korean film critics and historians that the contemporary anti-government, pro-labourer film movement in South Korea has its historical origins in the KAPF's 'tendency films'.[21]

Interestingly enough, however, most of the KAPF films were left unfinished mainly due to the directors' lack of experience in film-making and of funds combined with the government's censorship. Only four films were finished and distributed to the theatres, and their fifth film, *The Underground Village*, was produced in 1931, but banned before its release by the authorities. Those four released films turned out to be commercial failures, yet they sparked an unprecedented controversy in the literary and film communities concerning the social function of film. These debates, however, merely resulted only in inducing a harsher ideological control from the colonial government. In 1927, KAPF established a foreign film distribution agency, the Tong-yang Film Stock Company, which enabled them to finance their film-making to a limited extent in the face of continuing box-office failures. In 1928 they also reorganised their production system and founded a new company called the Seoul Kino with the aim of making more films along the lines of socialist realism. *The Imbecile Street* (1929) and *The Underground Village*, released through this production system, depict the wretched life of the poor who were living on the outskirts of Seoul. In 1931 those KAPF film-makers who were involved in producing *The Underground Village* were arrested by the police, and subsequently resistance films disappeared from Korean film history for a number of decades.

After their release from prison, most of the KAPF members' activities changed dramatically: some collaborated with the

Japanese authorities, some quit film-making altogether, or started making non-political, literary films.[22] It was the KAPF critic Sŏ Kwangje who made *Troop Train*, which was the first pro-Japanese military film. An Sŏkyŏng, who was a co-writer of *The Underground Village*, also made a military film entitled *The Volunteer Soldier* (1941). The group of directors who turned to literary films include Kim Yuyŏng, who made three out of the five KAPF resistance films before his imprisonment. Among the members who stopped making films were Kang Ho and Yun Kijŏng. Kang was the leader of KAPF and made *The Dark Road* (1928) and *The Underground Village*.

After the Liberation of 1945, some of the former KAPF film-makers – along with a number of poets, novelists and critics – went over to the North. Some, however, were abducted by the North Korean authorities or declared missing during the civil war. Among them, Im Hwa, who was the central figure of KAPF and leading theorist, was executed by the Korean Workers' Party in 1953, charged with 'pro-Japanese' activities, along with his 'anti-revolutionary' tendency. Most of those who moved to the North were denounced by the Korean Workers' Party on ideological ground and eventually 'purged', after devoting themselves to establishing a socialist-realist tradition in the early 1960s North Korean cinema. Under the so-called '1967 anti-sectarianism struggle', the party finally eliminated those who continued the KAPF line, such as Pak P'allyang, Pak Kŭmch'ŏl, Kim Toman and An Hamgwang, at the Central People's Committee in 1967, charging them as anti-party revisionists and as being anti-revolutionary.[23] Those who chose to remain in the South, such as An Sŏkyŏng and Sŏ Kwangje, met similar fates as other victims in the North. The struggle and defeat of KAPF film-makers clearly demonstrates the vulnerability of film to the politics of the colonial and post-colonial Korean society.

With all the political and economic limitations imposed upon them, the KAPF film-makers could not but ultimately relinquish their belief in accelerating the liberation of the Chosŏn proletariat class through 'tendency films'. As is seen in the different paths the KAPF members voluntarily or involuntarily took, their film movement as a whole is multifaceted. Given that the achievements of the individual members of this organisation have not yet been thoroughly studied in depth, the previous approach to their activities as an organised film movement appears to be somewhat simplistic. To a certain extent, the successive failure of all their works at the box office also suggests that their strong belief in the 'sacred' role of cinema as a political weapon for the socialist revolution and its ability to address audiences ended in vain. They failed to present film as a form of mass-cultural products or a medium to communicate with the masses.

After the dissolution of KAPF, the Korean film industry entered the era of sound film. Korean film began to use sound from 1935. Between 1935 and 1945, about sixty films were made, which tend to fall into two categories. One group of films were outright pro-Japanese. The other category of works simply avoided topical subjects, concentrating on stories that have nothing to do with the abject political realities. Although a new generation of directors emerged along with the introduction of sound film during this period, their works were totally devoid of social themes, let alone any nationalistic sentiment. Yi Kyuhwan, Ch'oe In'gyu and Pang Hanjun, who represented this generation, either actively co-operated with the colonial government or totally dismissed patriotic concerns. In this sense, the last ten years in Korean film history before the Liberation in 1945 can be characterised as a 'dark' period.

The development of North Korean film

The Liberation from Japan in 1945 meant another ordeal for the Korean people. After Japan surrendered, the Allies decided to divide the Korean peninsula against the wishes of the majority of Koreans. In August 1945, the Soviet and the USA forces occupied the North and the South, respectively, militarily dividing Korea. In July 1946, the North Korean Workers' Party was formed in the North under the chairmanship of Kim Tubong, an experienced communist from China with the vice-chairman Kim Il Sung backed by the Russians. Following this, the South Korean Workers' Party was also formed in November 1946 under the leadership of Pak Hŏnyŏng, who was the most influential figure in the indigenous Korean communist movement in the colonial period. After three years of Soviet occupation, the People's Democratic Republic of Korea was established in the North, and Kim Il Sung was appointed as head of the state by the North Korean Workers' Party. In June 1949, the North Korean Workers' Party formally absorbed the South Korean Workers' Party and renamed itself the Korean Workers' Party. Kim's rule lasted for nearly half a century until his death in 1994. Afterwards, his son Kim Jong Il succeeded to power and has been ruling North Korea ever since.

The political history of North Korea is perhaps the single most important force that has shaped North Korean film as we understand it today. In most capitalist societies, including South Korea, film is viewed chiefly as a form of entertainment. However, in North Korea, like other many socialist countries, it is conceived

Contemporary Korean cinema

primarily as an instrument for socialisation and effective political propaganda of the masses. The late Kim Il Sung repeatedly stressed the significance of film in the society as 'the most important and powerful mass educational means'.[24]

In North Korea, all artistic activities, including cinema, are based on the so-called *Juche* theory of art mandated by the Party. *Juche*, which means self-reliance, encourages 'a creative adaptation of Marxism–Leninism to the Korean situation' for revolutionary purposes.[25] The definition of the term was explained by Kim Il Sung in 'On eliminating dogmatism and formalism and establishing *Juche* in ideological work', a speech he gave on 28 December 1955.[26] According to the 1972 North Korean Socialist Constitution, the Party defines art as a vehicle to inculcate communism in people and as an ideological weapon to teach them how to raise working-class consciousness and achieve a communist revolution in Korea. The *Juche* theory of art was adopted as the official principle in North Korea. This theory serves to implant Kim Il Sung's '*Yuil* [monolithic] thought' in every sector of North Korean society.

North Korean film policies and the *Juche* theory of cinematic art

As pointed out above, North Korean film policy is based on the Party's definition of art and the *Juche* ideas. According to this policy, art is no more than a revolutionary instrument for national, class and each individual's liberation. By indoctrinating people with communist ideology, art functions as the pabulum of revolutionary thought. As such, art should express the spiritual energy of a self-sufficient human being and the struggle of the masses who pursue independence from feudalistic bondage.[27]

It is mainly through Kim Jong Il, the son and the successor of Kim Il Sung, that the *Juche* theory of art has been applied to filmmaking in North Korea. Kim Jong Il has supervised every aspect of the film industry since he was appointed as the director of film art in 1968, which belongs to the Propaganda and Agitation Bureau within the Party. Under his direct supervision, the North Korean film industry launched a full-scale development plan in the late 1960s and the 1970s. Through his active involvement in cinema and other arts, Kim Jong Il finally received the Party's recognition of his leadership in inspiring the masses with its official guidelines. He also gained his father's confidence as a successor by making a series of films promoting loyalty toward his father. In 1974, he was named the sole successor of his father by the Party during the Party's Central People's Committee meeting.

Kim Jong Il's extraordinary interest in film is fully demonstrated by his successful abduction of the leading South Korean

3   Kim Jong Il on location during shooting c
An Chunggŭn Shoots Itō Hirobumi (1979

film director and his actress wife, Shin Sangok and Ch'oe Ŭnhŭi
in 1978. This popular director–actress couple were regarded as
the leaders of the 'Golden Era' in the South Korean film history.
Shin made sixty-four films before his abduction, and Ch'oe
played title roles in many of his films. Their abduction tells us not
only about Kim's personal and somewhat excessive enthusiasm
for film but also about the great importance of film as a propaganda tool in North Korea.[28] According to the testimony given
by Shin and Ch'oe after they had escaped from North Korea in
1986, Kim Jong Il's personal film collection is in excess of
15,000 in number. They also revealed that a screening room
was available wherever Kim visited, and that he watched films
'nearly every night'.[29]

    Kim Jong Il published a book in 1973, *Yŏnghwa Yesulron*
(*The Theory of Cinematic Art*).[30] Outlining the official North
Korean theory of art, this book is regarded as the bible of film
art by North Korean film-makers. In this book, Kim expounds
the theory that an actor should perform in such a way that he/
she faithfully portrays the experiences and emotions of the
working-class people, and that directors should work in a
collective directing system. Kim also asserts in this book that
the *Juche* ideology is what distinguishes North Korean film art

from that of the West, which seeks only to 'flatter' the audiences. He argues furthermore that when a film expresses the *Juche* ideology successfully, the film becomes a 'complete' piece of art. Thus he urges all North Korean film-makers to translate the *Juche* ideas into their cinematic art. More specifically, film should picture North Koreans as a people unfailingly loyal to the Party and willing to work for the construction of a classless society with a firm class-consciousness. To make a 'complete' work of art for 'people', everyone involved in film-making must have first-hand experiences that the 'people' actually have in order to be able to describe their emotions, demands and aspirations realistically on the screen.

Another main strand which constitutes North Korean film theory is that of nationalism. Kim's book stresses that North Korean films should capture not only the mentality of the working-class people but also their 'nationalistic sentiment'. In other words, North Korean films are expected to undertake the historic task of inculcating the audiences in their duties and responsibilities for unifying Korea and building an ultimately classless society. A film can function only when it appeals to the audiences by conveying the urgency of these tasks. When a film fulfils such expectations, it achieves a 'nationalistic form' and thus the status of art as delineated by the Party. Besides, only those films that have attained the status of 'nationalistic form' can satisfy the popular taste of North Koreans.

On the basis of this theory, the Party provides film-makers with a specific set of principles that govern each stage of film-making in North Korea. These principles of film-making consist of the 'seed theory', 'modelling' and the 'speed campaign'. The 'seed theory' means that every film should treat 'proper' material and themes that feature the revolutionary thoughts of Kim Il Sung and the Party line like 'seeds' to be planted in the audience's mind. The principle of 'modelling' is concerned with how to portray the struggles of the working class to achieve class and national liberation. It requires film-makers to present an idealised picture of North Korean society and its people. The 'speed campaign' is to meet the demands of the Party to make films of high ideological and artistic quality rapidly and to strict schedules.[31] This principle rejects a 'passive' attitude in film-making. Film as an ideological weapon should be produced as quickly as possible to accelerate the revolutionary process. These film-making principles are imposed upon all 'film workers'. The majority of the North Korean films which are made according to these principles are called 'collective works'.

The socio-political characteristics of North Korean film

It is not surprising that mainstream North Korean films strictly adhere to the national policy of the Korean Workers' Party. The Party formulated an official criterion for describing the history of art. The periodisation of North Korean film history, therefore, also conforms to the official criterion of periodisation of any other form of art in North Korea. The Party names each period with a particular term deriving from their interpretation of Korean history. In the following section, I will examine the socio-political nature of the North Korean film history, which is categorised according to the criteria set by the Party.

Along with this categorisation of the history, I examine the recent developments in North Korean cinema since 1967 in three stages. According to the Party's official periodisation, there is no further periodical division from 1967. However, as is discussed earlier in this chapter, during the last thirty years or so, a series of significant changes and developments have continued in the North Korean cinema. Such changes are mostly linked to the rise of Kim Jong Il as the power-successor and his monopolised supervision on the film industry during the last three decades. Also, the stability of the socio-political structure under the rapidly changing international environments, especially, the fall of communism in Eastern Europe and the former Soviet Union, and the death of Kim Il Sung exerted a significant influence in the recent trends of North Korean cinema.

The period of 'peaceful construction': August 1945 to June 1950

After the Liberation in 1945, North Korea attempted to eradicate the remnants of feudalism and Japanese imperialism, punishing pro-Japanese intellectuals and the landed class. To achieve its purpose, the Party encouraged North Korean film workers to make films for the cause of constructing an 'anti-imperialistic, anti-feudalistic and democratic' national culture. The films should represent the loyalty of the North Koreans, particularly the working-class people, such as factory workers and peasants, to their country and the Party.

The Party declared the end of Japanese colonial rule as the starting point of North Korean film history. While South Korean film historians tend to include the Japanese colonial period in Korean film history, North Korean historians exclude it, officially labelling the colonial era as the period of the Party's anti-Japanese revolutionary activities and nationalistic struggles. After the Division of Film Production was established within the Party in 1946, it produced the first North Korean silent film, *Our Construction*. It is a documentary film commemorating the anniversary of the 1 March Independence Movement in 1919. The first North Korean feature film, *My Hometown*, was made in 1949. It is a story of a revolutionary who participates in the anti-Japanese partisan activities and underground resistance to landowners. This film was the first of a series of films that were awarded the title of the People's Prize Winner. Commissioned by the Party, this award has been given to films and film-makers that are perceived as fulfilling the role of an 'excellent textbook' for the Party. *The Blast Furnace* (1950), another feature film that came out during this period, treats the efforts of the working class to lay the foundation of the socialist economy in North Korean society after the Liberation. All in all, fifteen documentary films and two feature films were produced during this period, all of which were designed to propagate the historical legitimacy of the Korean Workers' Party and the leadership of Kim Il Sung. In other words, films that belong to this period are all attempts to renounce the South Korean government and its president, Syngman Rhee and justify instead that North Korea succeeded the legitimate line of Korean history.

The period of 'the great national liberation': June 1950 to July 1953

This period corresponds to the period of the Korean War. Because of the war, most films that came out during this period are either documentaries or newsreels. The Film Production Division of the Korean People's Army made about seventy documentary films and five feature films during the war period. The titles of these feature films clearly illustrate the themes of heroism of the masses and optimism for victory in what they termed as the 'Fatherland Liberation War': *The Frontier Guards* (1950); *The People's Armed Corps Fighting in Defence of the Village* (1952); *Go to the Front Line, Once Again* (1952); *The Combat Unit of Fighter Plane* (1953); and *Scouts* (1953). These films interpret the Korean War as a national liberation struggle against American imperialists who schemed to colonise Korea again. They also interpret the war as a class struggle against the puppet regime of the United States, referring to the South Korean government which, they claim, protected pro-Japanese intellectuals and the landed class after the Liberation.

The period of 'struggle for post-war reconstruction and establishment of the socialist foundation': July 1953 to 1958

After the signing of the Truce in 1953, the Party began to concentrate on reconstructing the war-torn economy and turning North Korea into a tightly woven socialist society. Films and film-makers were again used by the Party for this purpose, following its official guideline faithfully. They emphasised the post-war restoration efforts and the importance of the *Juche* ideology in the process of restoration. In a 1955 address, Kim Il Sung told all writers and artists in North Korea that they should serve the cause of rebuilding the post-war economy.[32] He stressed that the *Juche* ideology would be the only way to root out 'doctrinism' and 'formalism' from their mental activities. The North Korean preoccupation with post-war reconstruction is well testified by the two films, *The Newly Married Couple* (1955) and *The Beautiful Song* (1955), both of which glorify the industriousness of North Koreans in the rapid reconstruction of the post-war economy. During the years 1953 to 1958, more than twenty films were made for the purpose of 'enlightenment' of the people's socio-political consciousness.

The period of 'struggle for an all-out construction of socialism': 1959 to 1966

North Korean film-making of this period strongly reflects Kim Il Sung's slogan, 'Creating literature and art which serve for the period of *Ch'ŏllima*'.[33] The '*Ch'ŏllima* Movement' was an intense campaign to exhort the people to devote all their energies to rebuilding the economy fast. Kim insisted in his 1964 address 'Concerning the creation of revolutionary literary art', that the aim of literature and art was to provide people with direct instructions on, as well as indirect experiences of, the revolutionary struggles so that workers could develop a revolutionary perspective on the world.[34]

During this period, scores of films were produced every year. Among them, *The Demarcation Village* (1961) and *The Spinner* (1963) received the People's Prize Winner for their 'excellent' handling of the themes which were promoted by the Party. The first of the two portrays a woman who heroically endures the hostilities of her neighbours after her husband joins the South Korean army, and resists the efforts of South Korean agents to recruit her as a spy. The second film epitomises the spirit of this period through a protagonist who suffered during the Japanese colonial rule but then became an exemplary worker, full of the *Ch'ŏllima* spirit. She works happily in a factory that is owned by North Korean workers themselves. All the films of this period, including these two, aimed to create positive images of labour which were essential in constructing a 'socialist paradise' and enhancing the sense of loyalty to Kim Il Sung.

The period of 'struggle to advance the victory of socialism': 1967 to the present

The fifth period of North Korean film history can be examined from the viewpoint of Kim Il Sung's address at the Korean Workers' Party Executive Congress, which was held in October

4 The assassination of the first Japanese residential colonial governor Itō on his visit to China in 1909. From Ŏm Kilsŏn's *An Chunggŭn Shoots Itō Hirobumi* (1979), awarded People's Prize Winner in North Korea in 1979

1966: 'The present state of affairs and the task of our Party'. This speech is focused on promoting the '*Yuil* thought' of the Party by consolidating ideological education and action.[35] Kim also issued a statement entitled 'About producing a revolutionary film' in which he repeats the importance of '*Yuil* thought' and explains the role of film-makers in constructing a socialist society. In addition to these statements by Kim, this period deserves particular attention for Kim Jong Il's publication of *The Theory of Cinematic Art* in 1973. Through this book, which can be considered a manifesto on North Korean cinematic art, Kim Jong Il, an enthusiast of film, began to exercise a profound influence on North Korean film-making.

The number of films produced during this period steadily increased; the average number of films made per year reached nearly thirty. In this period, which brings us to the present, eight films have been awarded the People's Prize Winner: *Five Guerrilla Brothers I–III* (1968–69); *The Sea of Blood* (1969); *The Flourishing Village* (1970); *The Fate of a Self-defence Corps Man* (1970); *A Worker's Family I & II* (1971); *The Flower Girl* (1972); *An Chunggŭn Shoots Itō Hirobumi* (1979); and *The Brigade Commander's Former Superior* (1983). Most of the films made in this period focus on Kim Il Sung's leadership. In the films depicting the struggle against Japanese colonial rule, he is portrayed as the only person who can liberate Korea from Japanese domination. The films, which are set during the Korean War, treat his leadership as the only real force that could end the war with the North's victory over the South. A numbers of films depict the life of North Koreans after the Liberation, but the dominant and typical theme of these films is still the people's admiration and glorification of Kim Il Sung and his ideology. However, a close analysis of the films that have been produced since 1967 reveals the Party's strong motivation to cease their internal power struggle and reinforce the political basis of Kim Jong Il as the only successor to their late leader, Kim Il Sung.[36]

The cult of Kim Il Sung cultivated by Kim Jong Il clearly divides the North Korean film history into two: before and after Kim Jong Il's control over the film industry. At first, the most significant change in the late 1960s and 1970s was to advocate the 'Suryŏng hyŏngsang munhak' ('Great Leader's literature') and 'anti-Japanese revolutionary literature' as the absolute premise of the North Korean film. The elimination of the KAPF film-makers through the '1967 anti-sectarianism struggle' was the starting point of his denouncement of the 'socialist realistic tradition', one of two theoretical bases of the North Korean art and literature.[37] He criticised that, whereas the 'socialist realistic tradition' led by the KAPF had stressed the detailed depiction of the everyday life of the ordinary working class, it did not present the decisive role of the 'Suryŏng' in the class revolution nor promote his leadership to the masses. Furthermore, echoing his father's 1966 speech, he insisted that the expurgation of the KAPF must be 'to eradicate the feudal Confucian thoughts, capitalistic ideas, flunkeyism, dogmatism ... and strengthen the Yuil thought of the Party'.[38] In other words, since 1967 the theoretical base of North Korean film moved from that of the KAPF and anti-Japanese revolutionary literature to the latter only.[39] Also, the 'Great Leader's literature' substituted the 'socialist realism' as the major tenet of North Korean cinema.

One of the notable changes of the 1980s North Korean cinema is marked with the appearance of 'hidden hero' films. In contrast to the anti-Japanese revolutionary films ensuing the conventional 'Great Leader's literature', many of 'the hidden hero' films deal with the various ordinary workers' hidden efforts, difficulties or despair in the present society. The People's Prize-awarded film, *The Brigade Commander's Former Superior* (1983), as well as *Bellflower* (1987), are probably most representative among the 'hidden hero' films produced during this period.

Interestingly, the appearance of the 'hidden hero' films tends to coincide with the Party's gradual recognition of the growing discontent among its people. This is especially evident with regard to the economic gap between the city and countryside, conflict between generations or restlessness among the groups located in the different strata of the present 'classless' society.[40] Also, it seems to suggest the needs of the Party to reinforce the ideal working-class consciousness as a major theme, together with the loyalty towards the Party and Kim Il Sung within the mode of the 'Great Leader's literature'. Therefore, regarding the representation of social reality of working class, the difference between the films made in this period and the films made by KAPF film-makers is the emphasis on the close ties between Kim and the masses, likened to the relationship between a father and his children.

Another new feature of the 1980s North Korean film is the production of a series of films that reduce the ideological content in response to popular demands for mass-entertainment films. The stories that are isolated from the ordinary people's interests, repeating the same stereotyped moralistic lesson on the history without any specific entertaining elements, were finding less favour with audiences, especially the post-war generations. The re-emergence of historical films and their popularity after the 1950s, such as *The Tale of Ch'unhyang* (1980; 1985), *The Tale of Ondal* (1986) and *The Tale of Imkkŏkchŏng I–V* (1988–89) can be understood in this context.

The characteristics of North Korean film in the 1990s are probably summarised with the re-examination of the issues of working class, and nationalism.[41] Along with the loyalty towards the Party, these two themes have been proclaimed as the most important tenets in the North Korean film by the Party from inception, but since the late 1960s the priority tended to be given to the loyalty of the Party and Kim Il Sung. The reassurance on the significance of nationalistic notion and working-class consciousness in the North Korean cinema reflects the general response of society to the changing climate of international politics in the post-Cold War era. This also highlighted the direct concerns of the Party regarding the anticipated social unrest among the masses after the death of Kim Il Sung in 1994. The restoration of the KAPF tradition, or re-evaluation of Na Un'gyu's works in Korean film history, also indicate the various efforts of the Party to strengthen the nationalistic sentiments of the masses. It also reflects their working-class consciousness to protect the socio-political system against the increasing foreign influences or popular discontent.

The fifty episodes of *The Nation and Destiny* (1992–99), which officially represents the 1990s North Korean cinema, succinctly express these concerns of the Party.[42] Kim, defending this, stated that 'the seed of *The Nation and Destiny* is that the destiny of Nation is that of individuals' and 'the essence of the destiny of nation is a question about the autonomy of nation'.[43] For example, the treatment of the extremely extravagant lifestyles of the rich upper classes is contrasted with the abject poverty and grim conditions of the masses in the South or other capitalist countries. The intention is to convince the audience of their 'happy life in the socialist paradise protected by its national autonomy'. Also, the various episodes feature a wide spectrum of people, such as South Korean spies or defectors, KAPF writers, Japanese Koreans, the so-called 'comfort women' who were forced to serve for the Japanese soldiers during the Second World War, exiled pro-North Koreans, and the present-day North Korean working class. The message of these films is that, despite their differences, the characters are forgiven for any crimes and betrayals and welcomed back to their 'true nation'. All of the characters stress the desire to return to or devote themselves to their 'fatherland', reiterating the superiority of 'our style socialism'.

Despite the Party's efforts in contriving film plots, the testimonies of the North Korean defectors and refugees reveal that the audience are inclined to be fascinated with the affluent and lavish lifestyles of the capitalist societies reconstructed on the screen. Ironically, they tend to show an intense curiosity – if not fascination – towards the outside world. This 'undesirable' response of the audience betraying the calculated political purposes of the films, evinces the limitation of the role of cinema as a propaganda and socialisation of the masses in the society and warns of the failure of the Party's film policy.

North Korean film production, distribution and reception

Film-making in North Korea is a national enterprise. From the stage of conception to that of the final distribution, every aspect of film-making is under the total control of the state. All the films are produced under the direct supervision of the General Bureau of Cinema in the Department of Culture and Art of the Party. In the 1980s and the early 1990s, more than 130 films were made annually, including thirty or so feature films, sixty documentaries, thirty science and about ten children's films. In the last two decades, on average, thirty feature films have been produced by three studios, among which the Korean Film Studios is the largest. Built in 1947 and further expanded in 1970, this Korean Film Studios occupies 800,000 square meters. It contains ten film-producing sub-groups within its organisation, such as the

Paektusan Creative Workshop, the Poch'ŏnbo Creative Workshop and the Taehŭngdan Creative Workshop. Each workshop produces two to three films per year. Another film production unit is called the Korean 2·8 Film Studios, which has lately changed its name to the Korean 4·25 Film Studios.[44] It belongs to the Korean People's Army, and produces five to seven feature films, with most of them relating to the war. The Korean 2·8 Film Studios (or the Korean 4·25 Film Studios) has three sub-groups: the Wŏlmido Creative Workshop, the Taedŏksan Creative Workshop and the Wŏlbisan Creative Workshop. Shin Films was established in 1978 for Shin and Ch'oe, the couple abducted from South Korea. Under Kim Jong Il's special patronage, Shin and Ch'oe made about seven feature films and were involved in thirteen other projects until they fled from North Korea in 1986.

The Korean Workers' Party takes the training and re-educating of film workers very seriously. They refer to these people as the 'creating members of the country' or 'creating workers'. The Party founded the P'yŏngyang Drama and Film University in 1953 and reorganised it as the P'yŏngyang Film University in 1972, and have held several film workshops and contests of film literature. It is interesting to note that until the late 1970s, except for some films produced under the name of Kim Il Sung, the majority of the North Korean films do not contain the names of the individual workers who were involved in the film-making process. Each work is considered a collective production of the 'creating workers'.

A rather unique element in the way in which films are distributed in North Korea is that their citizens must see all the films produced there under the supervision of the Party, not just feature films but also documentary, science and even children's films. According to the *Korean Film Yearbook*, the number of films made in 1986 was 129, and this figure includes thirty-one feature films. The number of screenings in 1986 was about 1,900,000, and the size of the audiences was about 236,440,000.[45] A typical North Korean viewer tends to see more than nine films a year. This figure is quite surprising considering that the size of the North Korean population is approximately 25,000,000. Most films are shown in the name of 'the work of film supply' at workshops, co-operative associations and factories. In 1986, only 5 per cent of the entire films were shown at public theatres that belong to the Party, and 7 per cent of the audiences viewed films there. The data from this yearbook suggest that every North Korean must see all the films distributed there and attend film-screening workshops whether they want to or not. In other words, film viewing is a compulsory activity for every North Korean citizen as her or his most important political education.

Major genres of North Korean film

Films on the revolutionary tradition of class struggle

The two most popular themes of North Korean films, which often appear in combination, are the class struggle against exploitation by the landed class during the feudal era and the anti-Japanese resistance for national independence. The films of these themes include *The Sea of Blood* (1969), *The Fate of a Self-defence Corps Man* (1970), *The Flower Girl* (1972) and *An Chunggŭn Shoots Itō Hirobumi* (1979). These feature films were screened between the late 1960s and 1970s as the classic examples of the North Korean cinematic art. Kim Il Sung praised them, saying they supplied an 'exhaustive' answer to the issue of man's '*Chajusŏng*' (autonomy), which is raised with the advent of a new historical era in which the masses have emerged as the masters of history, and thus can determine their own destiny.[46] These films, therefore, were not only made People's Prize Winners but were also recommended by the Party to the people as works of great significance that should not be missed. The Party's comments on these films were that they elevated the North Korean cinematic art to a new dimension of ideological substance and artistic eminence by rendering the '*Yuil*' (thought) of the Party.

Some of the North Korean feature films that contain the theme of class struggle are specifically on Kim Il Sung's leadership in the anti-Japanese struggle. Starting from *My Hometown* (1949), the first feature film made in North Korea, to such films as *The Story of a Detachment Commander I & II* (1965), *The River Flows* (1967), *Five Guerrilla Brothers I–III* (1968–69), *Star of Korea I–X* (1980–87), *Beautiful Valley* (1989) and *The Sun of the Nation I–IV* (1987–90), typically depict Kim Il Sung's underground resistance activities, organising the 'Down with the Imperialism Union' and the 'Anti-Japanese People's Guerrilla Army' in 1932. Used to educate people in the communist revolutionary spirit, these films attempt to confirm the validity of Kim's ideology. In these films it is also claimed that the anti-Japanese struggle should be understood fundamentally as a class struggle, and that Kim was the central figure in such a struggle and the champion of revolutionary thought.

A series of films produced in the late 1980s, as a variant of the 'Great Leader's literature', heroically dramatise the anti-Japanese, revolutionary struggles of Kim Il Sung's family: *The Green Pine Tree I & II* (1985) and *Dawn I & II* (1987) about his father Kim Hyŏngjik; *Wait for Me* (1987), *Leaving the Headquarters* (1987) and *Royal Fighter* (1987) about Kim Chŏgsuk, who is Kim Il Sung's first wife and Kim Jong Il's mother; and

Contemporary Korean cinema

Revolutionary Fighter (1987) and *Eternity I & II* (1987) about Kim Il Sung's younger brother Kim Ch'ŏlju. All these works are directly related to the Kim Jong Il's anxiety about the legitimacy of his power-succession, using the old Confucian, patriarchal ideas on the 'proper' family line and his 'sacred revolutionary blood' as the only successor of his father. As discussed above, although one of distinctive traits of the 1980s North Korean film can be said to be the popularity of the 'hidden hero' films and historical films, the films adherence to the principle of the 'Great Leader's literature has also been continuously emphasised up to the present.

The consistent pattern of vindicating Kim Il Sung's anti-Japanese activities continues in historical films. The primary purpose of North Korean historical films lies in advocating the construction of a classless society as the only and ultimate dream of the Korean people. Essential to this purpose is a need to justify Kim's indispensability in realising such a dream. Films, such as *The Tale of Shimch'ŏng* (1957), *The Tale of Ch'unhyang* (1959, 1980 and 1985), *The Tale of Honggildong* (1980) and *The Tale of Imkkŏkchŏng I–V* (1988–89), all call for a class consciousness among the working class and demonstrate how they can confront the landed classes. These films usually end with a message that the earlier collective struggle against the exploitation of the landed classes during the pre-Kim period could not but fail without Kim, as proved by the actual historical experiences.

Films on the Korean War and unification[47]

North Korean War films have been produced mostly by the Korean 2·8 Film Studios of the North Korean army. Their war films are filled with heroic actions of North Korean patriots during the war. The Film Production Division of the Korean People's Army, the predecessor of the Korean 2·8 Film Studios, produced five films during the three-year-long war period, all of which were intended to be morale boosters for people engaged in military action.

Even after the Truce in 1953, films utilising material from the Korean War continued to be made, but this time as a powerful way of arming North Korean citizens with anti-American sentiment. Their ultimate purpose was to prepare North Koreans for the 'imminent' national liberation war. Among the films which belong to this category are: *Ch'oe Hakshin's Family* (1966), *Unknown Heroes I–IIX* (1979–81) and *Wŏlmi Island* (1982) are selected by the Party as the best and 'representative' war films, which raised the standard for artistic expression of the North Koreans' fighting spirit and patriotism. A key element commonly found in all of these films is strong jingoism, which the Party uses for indoctrination.

The jingoistic tendency is also found in the films that treat issues related to national unification. The most prominent examples of films on unification are *The Path to Awakening* (1965), *Yŏngsu and Yŏngok in the Socialist Homeland* (1969), *The Fate of Kŭmhŭi and Ŭnhŭi* (1974), *Nunsŏk of Spring Days* (1985) and *Red Maple Leaves I–III* (1990) and *The Nation and Destiny I–VX* (1992–99). These films inculcate hostility in the audience towards the USA and its 'puppet regime' in South Korea. Touching on the volatile issues of the current division between the North and the South, these films stress that unification is an urgent historical task, and that the occupation of South Korea by the USA imperialists is the very cause of the prolonged split of the nation. They perceive the South–North division as an unprecedented national tragedy in Korean history. Latent under this strong political undercurrent in films, however, is an equally strong motive, a kind of ulterior motive of the Party, to divert the people's attention from the widespread dissatisfaction with their failing economy, rigid political system and, more importantly, the power struggle recently taking place within the Party itself.

Films on the development of a socialist economy

The last group of North Korean films treats themes connected to the North Korean economy. The Party shows the public films that convey North Korean workers' sense of happiness and achievement in putting the Party's economic plans into effect. The films emphasise the current occurrence of 'miracles' and innovations in their economy and the further need of them in the future. *The Fourteenth Winter* (1980), *Three Girls on the Sŏlhan Ridge* (1984), *Bellflower* (1987) and *Chŏng Ryulsŏng, the Musician* (1992) share protagonists who conduct exemplary activities towards building a strong socialist economy, and who thus present themselves as a source of inspiration for other workers. As model citizens, leading characters of these films account for why and how their devotion to the Party's economic plan goes hand in hand with political revolution. Other films with economic-related themes, such as *The Spinner* (1963), *The Flourishing Village* (1970), *When We Pick Apples* (1970), *Get over the Trials* (1983), *The Young Heart* (1990) are focused more narrowly on the process of revolutionisation and making the people working class. Regardless of the specific details of each film, these films commonly point out the importance of being obedient to the Party's guidelines and the beauty of single-minded devotion to constructing a socialist paradise in North Korea.

The development of South Korean film

When Japanese rule ended and the American army occupied the South in 1945, the South Korean film industry was mainly engaged in importing and distributing American films. Some Korean film-makers also attempted to make Hollywood-style films. The audiences were heavily exposed to imported American films and even gangster films from Hong Kong, which were mostly a superficial imitation of the Hollywood films. Consequently, Korean moviegoers quickly became accustomed to the Hollywood style. The Americanisation of the viewers' taste accounts for the major developments in the South Korean film industry during the years that cover the Korean War and American military administration.

South Korean film has always been ideologically controlled by its government. Even until the early 1990s, directors were easily arrested or banned from making or releasing their films because of an alleged violation of national security. Moreover, the conservative nature of Korean culture, which is rooted in a Confucian tradition, has imposed considerable constraints on film-making on moral and ethical grounds. The Korean Motion Picture Act enacted in 1962, for instance, clearly forbids films that may offend the moral standards of the public (i.e. government). Naturally, the range of materials and forms available to South Korean film-makers is therefore quite limited.

Since the late 1980s, however, the Korean film industry has entered a new phase. Against the fast expansion of the foreign film distribution network, especially after the lifting of the government's sanction of the operation of UIP (United International Pictures) in the Korean market in 1987, Korean film-makers have made desperate efforts to overcome the chronic stagnation of the industry. They have tried to upgrade the artistic and technical qualities of their films to counter the audience's fading interests in the domestic cinema as well as to attract foreign audiences. A group of young directors have sought to establish more effective and specialised film production and distribution system to compete with the vigorous attacks of foreign (American) companies on the domestic market. Due to these efforts, the South Korean cinema has slowly recovered its confidence in the competition with foreign films since the mid–1990s.

Also, as part of their endeavour to revitalise the industry, Korean film-makers have also searched for a solution to the problem of ideological restraint which has been one of the major obstacles to a healthy growth of South Korean film art. Some radical film-makers have refused to produce films under the

5　　　　South Korean film directors' desperate efforts to check UI
direct distribution in the domestic market: on the right is Pak Ch'ŏls
reading a statement condemning UIP (office of the Association c
Film Directors, 1988

existing production system, leading a film movement which, steeped in nationalism, targets an open treatment of 'urgent' issues like unification of the country and labour-related issues. They insist that a pressing task of Korean film-makers is to present the actual political and economic conditions of the present-day Korea on the screen.

The socio-political characteristics of South Korean film

South Korean film history can be roughly divided into three periods, according to the economic and political interventions of the government and to the prosperity and recession of the film industry itself. Each period shows that the film industry reacted sensitively to political changes in society. The governmental interventions were most manifest in the film policies that restricted the freedom of expression at various levels of film-making.

The fixation of the national division and South Korean film, 1945–59

The Liberation of the country in 1945 by the Allied armies brought about political chaos and the tragedy of a national division. In South Korea, conflicts among various political factions created all kinds of hindrances to establishing a powerful government through a democratic process. The political disruptions were also accompanied by socio-economic disorder. The film community could not remain immune from these problems.

During the years immediately following independence, South Korean film-makers tended to divide themselves into two groups, including those used to making pro-Japanese military films or who had been actively involved in other pro-Japanese activities in previous years. One group was composed of those who supported the anti-communist American military government and Syngman Rhee, who became the first Korean president after the occupation period, and those who tended to refuse to take sides, defending 'humanism' or 'pure art'. The other group consisted of those who leaned toward the communist North and opposed Rhee's government as well as the American occupation forces, and those who were not sympathisers of the North but strongly advocated radical reforms for the newly liberated Korea. The former, pro-South group was formed around the Chosŏn Film Scenario-writer Association and Korean Film Director Club in 1946 and later formed Korean Film Association in 1948. The central figures of this group were An Sŏkyŏng, Ch'oe In'gyu, Pak Kich'ae, An Chonghwa and Yun Pongch'un. Whereas, the latter, the progressive, left-wing directors organised the Chosŏn Film Confederation in 1946, unifying the Chosŏn Film Construction Centre and Chosŏn Proletariat Film Confederation, both of which were organised in 1945. Their leaders were the former KAPF film-makers, Ch'u Min, Kang Ho, Sŏ Kwangje and Kim Chŏnghyŏk, among others. Because the two groups were incompatible in their political views, confrontation was unavoidable. Their mutual antagonism continued into the post-colonial period, illustrating the degree to which Korean film has been subject to the political climate and ideological pressure. The hostility between the two groups continued, surfacing frequently in the form of public disputes, until some of the leading left-wing film-makers finally decided to defect to North Korea. Under such unstable conditions, both external and internal, up to twenty feature films were made before the Korean War broke out.

In 1946 the American military government abolished the 1939 Chosŏn Film Regulations and established another similar censorship. During the three-year occupation period, about fifteen films were produced, half of them silent films. The overwhelming majority of the films distributed to commercial theatres were American, imported through the Central Motion Picture Exchange, an American corporation jointly established in 1946 by the eight film distributors, the Department of the Army and the State Department.

Despite the dominance of imported American films in the

market, the Korean film industry slowly but steadily attempted to create its future direction until the outbreak of the Korean War in 1950. Perhaps the most memorable event during this period is the introduction of colour film to the Korean audience in 1949: Hong Sŏnggi's *The Women's Diary*. As the first colour film in the history of Korean cinema, the significance of Hong's work lay in its attempt at technical experiment rather than in its artistic merits. The audience's response to this film was also not so enthusiastic as to create a boom for colour films in the film industry. It was only in the 1960s that colour film finally gained popularity among Korean audiences.

The first commercially successful film made in this period was the patriotic *Hurrah! for Freedom* (1946). Directed by Ch'oe In'gyu, this film inspired a number of simplistic imitations by other film-makers in the following years. Ch'oe's – and the group of films that he inspired – celebrate the newly gained independence. Explicitly nationalistic and anti-Japanese in tone, the films treat the subject of independence and the political changes exclusively in terms of the simple emotional responses of ordinary Koreans. They never raise such questions as: Why was the Liberation not realised by Koreans themselves but by the great powers' external intervention?; Why was Korea occupied by foreign countries again?; Why should Koreans be engaged in an ideological war with each other?

In 1949 Ch'oe In'gyu made his next film *Seasonal Fish Market* in which the main character, who is a fisherman, dreams of the good life of the mainland. After he has indulged in this lifestyle, he eventually returns disillusioned to life as a traditional fisherman. Before he made *Hurrah! for Freedom* and *Seasonal Fish Market*, the director, Ch'oe In'gyu had produced pro-Japanese military films during the colonial period, such as *Sons of the Sun* (1944) and *Love and Pledge* (1945). It is somewhat ironic from a historical perspective, then, that he has been often cited as one of the eminent nationalistic directors by film-makers and critics alike.[48]

Although the Korean War destroyed virtually all the obsolete equipment and facilities for film-making in South Korea, the film industry began to restore its base in the mid–1950s. Syngman Rhee, the first Korean president, exempted tax from Korean films from 1953 as an incentive to revitalise the industry. This rather unusual gesture immediately resulted in a number of positive signs of restructuring old systems in the industry. In 1955 Yi Kyuhwan's film *The Tale of Ch'unhyang* marked a rare box-office hit. The number of films produced increased every year. From the end of the 1950s, about 100 feature films were made yearly, and more than 200 feature films were released. The majority of these feature films fall into one of four categories in terms of subject-matter and theme: historical drama, melodrama, comedy and anti-communist drama.

Government interventions and anti-communist policies towards South Korean film, 1960–79

The 19 April Student Uprising in 1960 brought freedom of expression to South Korean film-makers and along with it, a shift of authority for film censorship from the government to civil organisations. But this freedom was short-lived due to the 16 May military *coup d'état* in 1961. The military leaders who succeeded in the *coup* created the Third Republic of Korea. This government, heavily anti-communist in orientation, aggressively pushed the export-centred economic development plan, which resulted in widening the gulf between the rich and the poor, and between the urban and the rural.

Between the 1960s and the 1970s, each film production in South Korea was determined by the censorship authorities on the basis of whether a film deals with the present social structure positively or not. The military regime set up a standard with which it could censor or ban any cinematic representation of the political and economic conflicts in Korean society, especially the poverty of the working class. With its staunch anti-communist policy, the government also took extreme ideological sanctions against political material that could be potentially favourable to North Korea.

It was during this time that the first Korean Motion Picture Act was established in 1962. These new legal regulations on the film industry deprived South Korean film of one of its important functions of art, that is, its social criticism. As a way of expanding its control over the industry, the government also established Grand Bell Awards in 1961, a form of film recognition system. In 1965, the government limited the number of foreign films imported to no more than one third of Korean films produced each year and introduced the Screen Quota System of sixty to ninety days a year for domestic films at theatres.

Governmental intervention in the development of the film industry was clearly evident when the government introduced the Quality Film Reward System in 1965. Similar to the last period of Japanese colonial rule, the measure led to the revival of good-quality, artistic literary films in a relatively short period. Kim Suyong's *The Sea Village* (1965) initiated the boom of literary films during this period, regarded the most successful and representative literary films produced in this period. Also, as a sub-genre of the literary films, a large number of anti-communist films were produced in this period, starting with Kim Kidŏk's

South and North (1965), Yu Hyŏnmok's *Martyr* (1965) and Pak Sangho's *The Demilitarised Zone* (1965).

However, the literary films produced in this period were mostly aimed at the allocation of the foreign film import quota. In other words, they were not the outcome of artistic pursuits of individual directors nor did they pander to popular demand. Furthermore, despite the strong backing of the government and the artistic achievements of the films, the majority of the literary films failed at the box office. In fact, the commercial success of the films was not the primary concern of the film producers because their main financial sources are the import of foreign films as reward for producing literary films. Therefore, it is not surprising that the literary films immediately disappeared when the government discarded the reward system in 1973.

During the period, melodrama re-emerged as the dominant genre, typically portraying upper-class life, love affairs or the lives of bar hostesses. Prominent here was a group of films, which dealt with the relationship between a rich man and a poor barmaid. Borrowing the meaning of 'barmaid' from the English loanword 'hostess' in Korean, films of this kind were conveniently labelled 'hostess films'. By focusing on personal problems only, these films enabled Korean film-makers to avoid topics related to their immediate social environment and political circumstances to some degree. In other words, it was a form of cinematic escapism.

In accordance with the military government's film policy, a set of propaganda films was also produced, and this genre quickly became another major feature of the Korean films during this period. The most successful military film was *Red Scarf* (1964). Directed by Shin Sangok, *Red Scarf* is a story about the fighters of the Korean Air Force. Since then propaganda films reinforcing the anti-communist ideology were subsidised by the government. A quasi-travelogue type of film *Sights of the Eight Provinces* (1967), directed by Pae Sŏkin, is representative of another sub-genre of propaganda films from this period, portraying economic prosperity under the leadership of President Park Chung Hee and his economic development plan.

In the prevailing mood of propaganda films, some films still caught the attention of the film authorities with their 'undesirable' views on the social reality or their interpretation of history. When the government signed the 1965 Korea–Japan Basic Treaty for the normalisation of relationship with Japan against the popular anti-Japanese sentiments, there was nationwide support for the student demonstrations. In response, the government imposed martial law in order to repress the widespread riots. The government further tightened its control on the film industry. Many films were ordered to resubmit to the Censorship Board and many film-makers were arrested, or taken into custody and charged with violating public morals or threatening national security.

The confiscation of Yi Manhŭi's *Seven Women Prisoners* (1965) by the police authorities and the trial of the director on the charge of being pro-communist exemplify the military regime's hard-line approach. Yi Manhŭi is regarded as one of the most important directors in the 1960s and 1970s film history by many film critics and scholars, often referred to as offering a critical view on the Korean War and its aftermath. Including *Seven Women Prisoners*, his war films, such as *The Marine Who Never Returned* (1963) or *The Legend of Ssarigol* (1967) depict the inhumane nature of the civil war and the devastation brought on the people. However, his war films also can be regarded as typical war films in that they emphasise anti-communism without any explicit interpretation of the origins of the war nor national division. Neither does he express any pro-communist sentiments in his films. In this sense, the war films produced at that time require to be re-examined from a more critical point of view. The criteria should be based on how individual films or directors investigate or explore issues related to recent history and social reality; rather than how far they fulfilled the ideological demands of the government.

With the third revision of the Korean Motion Picture Act in 1973, the South Korean film industry gradually began to decline from the mid–1970s. The revised law was the outcome of the 'Yushin' (renovation), the ruling ideology of the military government of the Third Republic. This was quite similar to the Chosŏn Motion Picture Act enforced during the Japanese occupation. It facilitated governmental intervention, banning any filmic criticism of the military dictatorship or the monopoly of the Korean industry by a few conglomerates. The new Act replaced the registration system of film production and distribution with a licence system. A double censorship also began to be enforced: this meant all films had to be reported to the censor before production and submitted again for a second censorship before being released to the public. Furthermore, the revised act prevented the industry from importing expensive foreign films by imposing a heavy tax on film-makers and theatre owners. Only a few relatively large companies could survive such regulations, but only by importing films of low price and quality. The general decline of the industry is clearly reflected in the overall production of the films during this period; the number of feature films made between 1969 and 1977 decreased from 229 to 101. The total number of feature films made in the 1970s was 1,392, and yearly production decreased constantly throughout this decade. The size of the audiences also shrank from approximately 170,000,000 in the 1960s to 44,443,000 in 1981.[49]

The democratisation movement and South Korean film, 1980 to the present

The assassination of Park Chung Hee in October 1979 was a decisive event in the history of the country. He was assassinated by his own fellow military academy graduate and KCIA (Korean Central Intelligence Agency) director, Kim Chekyu at the president's private drinking party. This incident suddenly triggered an unexpected end of Park's military dictatorship due to an internal power struggle. However, behind this façade, there is a more significant development, the growing scepticism of his regime's ruthless repression of the civil society even within his power base. Indeed, despite mounting repressive measures of the government to the labour strikes and student demonstrations, there was strong public demand for democratisation, fair economic distribution policies, the abolition of the anti-labour policies and freedom of expression. Therefore, the political chaos which met the shocking news of his assassination was soon overwhelmed by the fever for democratisation which was endemic throughout society.

Nevertheless, this democratic mood of the entire society, which surfaced in the momentary period that is called 'Spring of Seoul', was suppressed by military hard liners led by General Chun Doo Hwan in May 1980. He led another military coup in December 1979, immediately after Park's death and imposed full martial law, arresting many leading dissents and labour activities, including Kim Dae Jung, the veteran opposition leader and current South Korean president. Following his arrest, the large-scale demonstrations of university students and citizens on 18 May in violation of the martial law decree occurred in Kwangju, the capital of the province where Kim comes from. This event saw the beginning of the Kwangju uprising, which claimed almost 200 lives (according to the official governmental account) with a considerable number of citizens declared missing. Chun pushed the masses' will towards the democratisation of the country and reversed the direction of South Korean history. Despite the rapid economic development and other achievements during Chun's and his successor and former General Roh Tae Woo's regimes, the government could not gain legitimacy from the Korean people. Moreover, the deep scars and memory of the Kwangju massacre are still too painful for many

6   Yi Kwangmo's *Spring in My Hometown* (1998). The film depicts
the Korean War through the eyes of children caught up in the conflict

Koreans, regardless of the Kim Dae Jung government's pardon of
Chun's life sentence for the crime related to the December 1979
coup and the May 1980 Kwangju massacre in 1998.

In this milieu, the latest phase of South Korean film history,
from 1980 to the present, is characterised by two developments:
the international recognition of Korean films and the emergence
of socially conscious young film-makers. Since the late 1980s, a
series of South Korean films has begun to draw attention from
international critics. Three of Im Kwŏnt'aek films won the Best
Actress Awards in international film festivals: *Surrogate Mother*
(1986) at the 47th Venice Film Festival in 1987; *Come, Come,
Come Upward* (1989) at the 16th Moscow International Film
Festival in 1989; *Adada* (1987) at the 12th Montreal World Film
Festival in 1988. Pae Yonggyun's *Why Has Bodhi Dharma Left for
the East?* (1989), and Chŏng Chiyŏng's *White Badge* (1992)
received the Grand Prix at the 42nd Locarno Film Festival in
1989 and at the 5th Tokyo International Film Festival in 1992,
respectively. Chang Sŏnu's *Passage to Buddha* (1994) won the
Creative Film Award (Alfred Wauer) at the 44th Berlin International Film Festival in 1994, and Pak Ch'ŏlsu was recognised
at the 20th Montreal World Film Festival in 1996 for his artistic
achievement with *Farewell My Darling* (1996). Yi Ch'angdong's
Green Fish (1998) and Yi Kwangmo's *Spring in My Hometown*
(1998) received the Grand Prix at the Vancouver Film Festival in
1998 and at the 52nd Locarno Film Festival in 1999, respectively. These directors and their works have been considered to

be 'South Korea's new wave' or 'South Korea's new cinema' by film critics and scholars outside of the country.

A more important development in this period than the international reputation earned by these Korean films is the slackening of political pressure on the film industry. With the social upheaval resulting from the Kwangju Uprising in 1980, Korean film-makers began to see the possibility of utilising socio-political material and directly communicating their views to the audience. With this change, a group of radical young directors, who were centred around university communities, challenged the existing film producing system. These directors took a 'revolutionary' stance against the external ideological suppression, making anti-government films outside the established industry. The most radical among them established an organisation called Changsan'gonmae and initiated the National Film Movement. They defied the conventions of the mainstream Korean films, refusing not only to make commercial films but also to distribute their works in the existing film market. Their favourite subject-matter included the struggle of the working class and the contradictions of the political and economic structures of contemporary Korean society. Because of their tendency to address labour-related issues, their films have coined the term 'labour film'. *Oh, the Land of Dreams*, which was made in 1988, treats the legitimacy of the Kwangju Uprising in 1980, and the responsibilities of the United States to the massacre of the innocent citizens by the brutal and ruthless military actions. *The Night before the Strike* (1990) depicts labourers' lives in Korea, their awareness of the economic inequity in society and their determination to solve problems of social injustice. This film has drawn audiences of 150,000, most of whom, according to the report by the National Film Research Institute, were labourers, students and intellectuals.[50] Many of the members of the Changsan'gonmae, including its leader Yi Yŏngbae, were charged with violating the Motion Picture Act and were wanted by the police. A leading critic Kim Sunam found their nationalistic orientation 'too radical' and pointed out that they approached film as a 'means for a proletariat revolution', echoing the *Juche* theory of cinema of North Korea.[51]

In opposition to Kim, many young critics, including Yi Hyoin, Yi Yonggwan and Yi Chŏngha consider this new film movement to be the 'most significant' event in recent Korean film history. Despite the different assessments of these directors, critics generally agree that they have provided the existing film community with a momentum for self-examination. Another important contribution made to Korean film is the directors' effort to elevate the status of film beyond that of commercial entertainment. They helped to highlight the function of film as social commentary. It is largely owing to their serious attitude to film that scholarly discussions of cinema began in Korea. A number of young directors, such as Chang Sŏnu, Pak Kwangsu, Pak Chongwŏn, Hong Kisŏn, Kim Hongjun and Yi Chŏngguk, who led the new 'realistic' South Korean cinema since the late 1980s, were directly or indirectly related to this resistance film movement before they started making films within the film industry.

South Korean film production, distribution and reception

The South Korean film industry recorded approximately 40 per cent market share at the box office in 1999, an astonishing feat given the aggressiveness of the direct distribution of Hollywood films since 1988. Despite the remarkable success, the industry presently experiences a decrease in overall production and an increase of imported films. The 1990s were marked by a continuous decline in the number of theatres as well as in film production. In 1993, about 64 feature films were produced, and about 700 theatres were in operation for about 48,231,000 moviegoers. In 1997, about 47,523,000 moviegoers saw 50 feature films at 497 theatres. Compared with 1970 when 229 feature films were produced and 690 theatres served more than 166,350,000 moviegoers, the current situation is evidence of how the Korean film industry has weakened during the last two decades.[52] In 1970, the typical moviegoer saw 5.3 films; this figure decreased annually to 1.1 in 1993 and 1.0 in 1997.

The following example illustrates the industry's depressed state: 73 feature films were released in 1986, but 31 of them failed at the box office at their first run in the Seoul area. In the same year, however, the ratio between Korean and foreign films shown at commercial theatres was 1:2. As testified to by this ratio, most film companies tried frantically to import foreign films to compensate for their loss with Korean films. The fifth Korean Motion Picture Act, which was revised in 1985, gave a little freedom to the industry for independent film-making, but this limited freedom was soon taken away in 1987 when the government revived the old censorship. In 1985 foreign films attracted about 67 per cent of the entire audiences and made up about 75 per cent of the films shown at public theatres. Furthermore, the abolishment of the quota link system between the production of domestic films and the import of foreign films in 1987 drew the attentions of many film investors mainly engaged in film imports. The proportion of foreign films within the Korean film market annually increased up to 1997. This was brought by the nation's worst economic crisis in decades. The opening up of the Korean market to foreign film distribution companies in 1987 worsened the already shrinking Korean film industry. The box-office record of 1993 illustrates that about 7,689,000 moviegoers saw Korean films whereas about 40,541,000 moviegoers attended foreign films. The foreign films attracted more than 84 per cent of the entire audiences, and their profit made up about 85 per cent of the entire box-office income of that year.

The problems of the recent Korean film industry have been compounded by the popularity of TV and home videos as well as the arrival of new mass-media, such as cable TV and satellite TV. Since the late 1960s, the film industry had already begun to lose audiences, especially those of 'home drama' and melodrama, to TV, where audiences had their own 'home theatre'. Therefore, instead of aiming at the 40-year old age group, it tried to attract the young, post-war generation, producing many youth and teenage films. With the initiation of colour broadcasting in 1980, the wide distribution of these two media, TV and home videos coupled with the audience's inclination toward foreign films, has even led some film-makers to try their hand at pornographic video for adult audiences. Foreign distribution companies such as UIP have also recently broken into the Korean video market. Furthermore, the rapid rate of the distribution of cable and satellite TV in the late 1990s demanded a much more complex and aggressive marketing strategy for the film industry. Therefore, the problem appears to be how to co-operate with the other visual industries in order to maximise their profits as the main suppliers of the programmes.

The direct distribution of American films, which started from 1988, caused uproar not only among Korean film-makers but also the public, who interpreted it as American cultural imperialism. Moreover, after the success of the direct distribution, the distribution companies demanded the abolition of the Screen Quota System to the Korean government, accusing it of unfair trade practice.[53] The tension between the foreign distributors and the Korean film community regarding this system has become more intense since the late 1990s. In this deteriorating situation, the abovementioned National Film Movement of the 1980s by the young film-makers created a new impetus, which helped the Korean film industry to recover. This film movement was a welcome sign of the general democratisation of Korean society, as well as of the film industry.

Major genres of South Korean film

It is difficult to classify South Korean films neatly into certain categories because, despite the political and socio-economic constraints on the film industry, South Korean films are still far more diverse than North Korean films in terms of the range of materials and forms they can experiment with. One way of classifying them is to group films that share certain similarities in subject-matter, theme and characterisation. Approached from the viewpoint of such similarities, the majority of Korean films seem to cluster around two major genres: melodrama and social commentary. These two genres have been the most conspicuous trends in the history of the South Korean cinema, and each comprises a few variations. The characteristics of the two genres and other related sub-groups of them will be discussed below, which will be followed by a brief sketch of the most up-to-date development in Korean feature films since the mid-1980s.

Melodramas

Throughout the history of South Korean film, melodrama has been the most abundant in terms of the sheer number of productions, and the most popular genre regardless of the changing circumstances of the film industry. Such films usually deal with women's private lives, focusing specifically on their love affairs. The earliest successful film of this kind is Han Yŏngmo's *Free Wife* (1956), which challenges the rigid moral code of Korean society by treating an extra-marital affair of the neglected wife of a college professor. Chŏng Soyŏng's *Hate But Once More* (1968) is probably the most representative work of this genre, often referred to as an archetype of the South Korean melodrama. Breaking the biggest box-office record at that time, Shin Sangok's *Sŏng Chunhyang* (1961), it led to the mass production of similar type of films dealing with a tragic love story between a successful middle-class married man (predominantly a businessman) and an innocent single woman. *Hate But Once More* type of melodramas deal not only with the issues of ex-marital relationship but also of illegitimate child from the point of view of the suffered. However, it can-not be said such sympathetic approaches of the films reject the prevailing ideas on the male-centred social values or family relationship.

Modelled upon these films, a great number of melodramatic romance films have been made since then, frequently based on serial novels in newspapers. This genre was particularly popular in the 1970s and 1980s. Yi Changho's *Home of Stars* (1974), Kim Hosŏn's *The Best Days of Yŏngja* (1975) and *Winter Woman* (1977) are some of the representative works that belong to this genre. By exposing the evils of the patriarchal culture, these films attracted a record number of viewers. Although this type of film proved to be quite appealing to the Korean audiences, directors could not find qualified screenplay writers. Hence they frequently borrowed stories from the novels serialised in the daily newspapers. Due to the lack of good screenplay writers within the industry, some film-makers also adapted works of *belles-lettres* on similar themes. Some of the best films from literary sources are Shin Sangok's *My Mother and the Lodger* (1961) and Yu Hyŏnmok's *Later Autumn* (1966).

An offshoot of melodrama of the South Korean film is a group of pornographic films that highlight graphic sex rather than the sufferings of women in a sexually suppressed society. The best-known examples of this are Lee Yŏngshil's *No More Sexual Life* (1982), Chŏng Inyŏp's *Madam Aema* (1982) and Yi Changho's *Between Knee and Knee* (1984) and *Ŏudong* (1985), and Yu Chinsŏn's *Prostitution* (1988). The alleviation of censorship on sexual expression on the screen in 1985 has resulted in the mass production of pornographic films, yet it has drawn considerable criticism of the industry from conservative audiences.

Another sub-genre of melodrama is historical romance. Such films are typically set in pre-modern Korean society. A close reading of a series of historical romances, however, reveals that there is virtually no difference between this category and contemporary melodrama, except for that of temporal settings. They both tend to focus on women's love affairs in their plot, treating the plights of 'wayward' women from a sympathetic perspective. *The Tale of Ch'unhyang* is a classical novel that neatly fits the requirements of the genre of historical romance. Thus, the story of Ch'unhyang has been adapted frequently by Korean film-makers.[54] Among the directors who have attempted to portray this famous story of forbidden love on the screen are Yi Kyuhwan (1955), Shin Sangok (1961), Pak T'aewŏn (1976), Han Sanghun (1987) and Im Kwŏnt'aek (2000). Other material for historical romance that has proved popular involves the death of a woman due to her romance with a man of a different class in caste-conscious Chosŏn society. Typical examples are Yi Tuyong's *The Death Cottage* (1980) and *Mulleya Mulleya* (1983), Pae Ch'angho's *Hwangjini* (1986) and Im Kwŏnt'aek's *Surrogate Mother* (1986).

In the 1990s, a new type of melodrama appeared, such as Yi Myŏngse's *My Love, My Bride* (1991) and Kim Ŭisŏk's *Marriage Story* (1993) and Yi Kwanghun's *Dr Bong* (1995). These films treat various issues relating to marriage, gender roles and relationships between men and women, with a light comic touch. In the late 1990s, Kang Chegyu's *Gingko Tree Bed* (1996), and Chang Yunhyŏn's *The Contact* (1997) and Chŏng Chiu's *Happy Ending* (1999) attracted the audience. Although they use the familiar motifs of romance and betrayal, their diverse cinematic experiments generated a considerable commercial success. These films reflect the changing attitudes of the young generation on these issues, raising questions about the traditional patriarchal values. Their continuous success at the box office has helped to revitalise the Korean film industry.

Finally, there is a series of films which resists being easily classified as melodrama. They are Pak Ch'ŏlsu's *301, 302* (1995) and Hong Sangsu's *The Day When a Pig Fell in the Well* (1996) and Chang Sŏnu's *To You from Me* (1994) and *Lies* (1999). These films are concerned with hidden violence in individual's private lives caused by sexual abuse, moral hypocrisy and sexual repression in a materialistic society.

Films of social commentary

This category includes a variety of films that approach individuals essentially as victims of political and historical incidents beyond their control, and of the unequal economic structure of the modern Korean society. In the early 1960s, films that take up social issues as their main concern started to appear. They attempted to represent problems of modern-day Korean society and culture realistically. *A Stray Bullet* (1961) directed by Yu Hyŏnmok well captures the tragic consequences of the Korean War in terms of the complete destruction of the protagonist's family. Ch'ŏlho, a poor yet hard-working man loses everything in the end despite his desperate efforts to survive the aftermath of the war: his wife in childbirth, his sister to a prostitute ring catering to the needs of foreign soldiers; his brother to jail for a petty burglary; and finally his mother to insanity.

A close relationship between the political situation and the production of social commentary films is clearly noted during the transitional period between the 19 April Student Uprising in 1960 to the 16 May military *coup d'état* in 1961. During this period, film censorship was handed over to a Film Ethics Committee, a civil organisation, and a series of films was made on social problems: Kang Taejin's *Old Pak* (1960) and *Horseman* (1961), Kim Kiyŏng's *The Housemaid* (1960), Chŏn Ch'anggŭn's *Ah, Paekbŏm Kim Ku* (1960), Yi Kangch'ŏn's *The Wayfarer* (1961) and Yi Manhŭi's *Kaleidoscope* (1961). As in *A Stray Bullet*, these films address dark social realities. Skilfully exposing the social disorder and economic unrest, they revitalised a native form of social commentary film in South Korean film history.

The directors of the 1980s who viewed film as a medium for social criticism touched on a variety of subjects in their works. Some of them focus on the social problems caused by the national division: Im Kwŏnt'aek's *The Banner Bearer without a Flag* (1979), *Tchakk'o* (1980), *Gilsottŭm* (1985) and *The T'aebaek*

7 One of the most representative social commentaries on the emerging problems of the urban poor, Yi Changho's *A Declaration of Fools* (1983)

Mountains (1993); Pae Ch'angho's *Warm It Was That Winter* (1984); Yi Changho's *A Wayfarer Never Rests on the Road* (1987); Chŏng Chiyŏng's *Southern Guerrilla Forces* (1990); Chang Kilsu's *Silver Stallion* (1991); Pak Kwangsu's *Berlin Report* (1991) and *To The Starry Island* (1993); and Yi Kwangmo's *Spring in My Hometown* (1998).

The growing gap between the rich and the poor, class issues and political corruption supplied provocative subjects for such films as: Yi Changho's *Nice Windy Day* (1980), *Children of Darkness* (1981), *A Declaration of Fools* (1983) and *Widow's Dance* (1983); Kim Suyong's *Maidens Who Went to the City* (1981); Pak Kwangsu's *Ch'ilsuwa and Mansu* (1988) and *Black Republic* (1990); and Pak Chongwŏn's *Kuro Arirang* (1989). The interest in topical subjects, which began in the 1980s, intensified in the following decade. The films of 1990s used some of the most controversial historical subject-matter. For instance, Pak Kwangsu's *A Single Spark* (1996) treats the labour movements of the 1970s, and Yi Chŏngguk's *Song of Rebirth* (1990), Chang Sŏnu's *A Petal* (1996) and Yi Ch'angdong's *Peppermint Candy* (2000) portray the Kwangju Uprising in 1980.

A group of films made in the 1980s and 1990s were concerned with the materialism and moral decay that pervaded contemporary Korean society. The representative works include Kim Hosŏn's *Three Times Shortly, Three Times Long* (1981), Pak

Ch'ŏlsu's *Mother* (1985), Chang Sŏnu and Sŏnu Wan's *Seoul Jesus* (1986) and Pak Chongwŏn's *Our Twisted Hero* (1992). The appearance of a number of films that specifically explore Buddhist teachings or monks' lives can be understood in light of the search for a moral vision of society. The most widely known of the Buddhist films are: Im Kwŏnt'aek's *Mandala* (1981); Pae Yonggyun's *Why Has Bodhi Dharma Left for the East?* (1989); and Chang Sŏnu's *Passage to Buddha* (1994). These films investigate the psychological and emotional insecurities that plague Koreans living in the hectic modern world. Toward the mid–1990s, a fresh look at the traditional arts and customs created a vogue in the film community, as is illustrated by Im Kwŏnt'aek's *Sŏp'yŏnje* (1993) and *Festival* (1996) and Pak Ch'ŏlsu's *Farewell My Darling* (1996). The attention these films drew from the public, and critics alike, can be read as a widespread interest among contemporary Koreans in re-examining their past.

The South Korean cinema also has its own genre of action or detective films. They tend to touch on the country's social and political problems, without any immediate resort to ideological or moralistic tones: Im Kwŏnt'aek's *Son of a General* (1990); Kang Usŏk's *Two Cops* (1994); Yi Ch'angdong's *Green Fish* (1997); Kang Chekyu's *Shwiri* (1999); and Yi Myŏngse's *Nowhere to Hide* (1999). They usually contain heroic stories based on colonial experiences, the national division, social chaos and political corruption. However, they are generally light-handed in their approaches to these serious topics. They continually broke box-office records, and such commercial appeal helped to convey the social themes to a broad range of audience in an enjoyable manner.

A noteworthy feature of the recent developments in South Korean film is the emergence of the young, ambitious and iconoclastic film-makers who slowly yet surely have generated a new energy in the existing film community. Their fresh perspectives on the future of South Korean film are already felt through their sharp criticism against government control over the industry. By avoiding the old traditional stories depicting love affairs or entertainment-oriented themes in conventional manners, they provide a fresh look into the fundamental preoccupations of average Koreans, such as the labour conditions, democratisation movements, political corruption and various kinds of contradictions latent in their everyday life. They also reinterpret the socio-political realities of contemporary Korea and its colonial/post-colonial history, specifically such volatile issues as the current national division and unification. Yet, their films address these issues without any explicit ideological slant. Furthermore, there are different interpretations and approaches. Some of the young directors vigorously resist the stereotyped representation of the pretentious, repressive social norms, or ideological impulse itself. They seek to express the confusing status of individuals and their moralistic chaos in the pursuit of the individualistic lifestyles against the psychological burden from the society and history. Led by Chang Kilsu, Chang Sŏnu, Chang Yunhyŏn, Chŏng Chiyŏng, Hong Sangsu, Kang Chekyu, Pak Ch'ŏlsu, Pak Chongwŏn, Pak Kwangsu, Yi Ch'angdong, Yi Kwangmo, Yi Myŏngse and Yŏ Kyungdong, this group of young directors offers a promising future for the industry. The final abolition in 1997 of the long-standing censorship helps them to explore their artistic visions with an unprecedented degree of freedom.

Notes

1 Different views exist concerning the precise year when film was shown to Korean audiences for the first time in history. Cho Hŭimun suggests that the first motion picture was introduced in 1899 by the American traveller, Elias Burton Homes. However, Aya Ichikawa, the Japanese film producer and author of *The History of Korean Film*, proposes 1897. Ichikawa claims that British Aster House showed films to the public in 1899, which had been produced by a French company, Pathé. Yu Hyŏnmok, a director and film historian, adopts Ichikawa's view in his widely circulated book, *Korean Film History*. Yi Chunggŏ maintains, however, that film was introduced to Korea in 1898 by two Americans, Henry Collbran and H. R. Bostwick. See Cho Hŭimun, 'Han'guk yŏnghwa kitchŏm-e kwanhan yŏn'gu' (A study of the beginning of Korean film), in Kim Chŏngok (ed.), *Han'guk Yŏnghwa-ŭi Saeroun Palgyŏn* (A New Discovery of Korean Film) (Seoul, Korean Film Academy, 1993), p. 8; Yu Hyŏnmok, *Han'guk Yŏnghwa Paldalsa* (Korean Film History) (Seoul, Hanjin, 1980), p. 42; and Yi Chunggŏ, 'Han'guk yŏnghwasa yŏn'gu' (A study of Korean film history) in Yi Chunggŏ *et al.*, *Han'guk Yŏnghwa-ŭi Ihae: Arirang-esŏbut'ŏ Ŭnma-nŭn Tolaoji Annŭnda-kkaji* (Understanding Korean Film: From *Arirang* to *Silver Stallion*) (Seoul, Yeni, 1992), p. 22.

2 It is difficult to pinpoint precisely when film was introduced to Korea because it was available only to small, limited audiences at the beginning. However, film historians generally agree on 1903 as the year in which a motion picture was shown to the public for the first time in Korea. See Cho, 'A study of the beginning', p. 9; Yu, *Korean Film*, p. 43; Yi Chunggŏ, 'A study of Korean film history', p. 21; Yi Hyoin, *Han'guk Yŏnghwa Yŏksa Kangŭi 1* (Lecture on Korean Film History 1) (Seoul, Iron-gwa Shilch'ŏn, 1992), p. 19; and Yi Chunggŏ, 'Han'guk yŏnghwasa' (Korean film history), in Korean Association of Professors of Film Studies (ed.), *Yŏnghwa-ran Muŏshin'ga* (What Is Film?) (Seoul, Chishik Sanŏpsa, 1986), p 185.

3 *Hwangsŏng Shinmun* (23 June 1903), quoted in Cho, 'A study of the beginning', p. 9.

4 *Hwangsŏng Shinmun* (10 July 1903), quoted in Cho, 'A study of the beginning', p. 10.

5　The term 'Korean film' is defined broadly in this study as a film by a Korean film-maker which deals with subjects related to Korea or Koreans' lives. Yet the usage of the term in this chapter, especially the part on Korean film during the colonial period, needs further explanation. Since the colonial authorities suppressed the use of the Korean language, and film-making at the time was financed mostly by Japanese proprietors, the term 'Korean film' in this chapter is used more liberally, indicating any film which treats Korea or Koreans' lives, made either by a Korean or a Japanese director and recorded either in Korean or Japanese.

6　In South Korea, 27 October has been celebrated as the 'Day of Cinema' since 1966. The government designated this special day to commemorate the birth of Korean film, following the première performance/screening of *The Righteous Revenge* at Tansŏngsa on 27 October 1919. Some scholars do not regard this work as a film because of its mixed genre, therefore, they consider *The Plighted Love under the Moon*, which was made in 1923, to mark the beginning of Korean film. The majority of film historians disapprove of this view because *The Plighted Love* was made by the Japanese colonial government whereas *The Righteous Revenge* was produced by the Koreans. The debate between these two groups and the government's ultimate decision on *The Righteous Revenge* illustrate the nationalistic attitudes prevailing among the Korean film community. See Cho Hŭimun, '"Han'guk yŏnghwa"-ŭi kaenyŏmjŏk chŏnghŭi-wa kijŏm-e kwanhan yŏn'gu' (A study of the major concepts in Korean film and its beginning), *Yŏnghwa Yŏn'gu* (Film Study), 11 (1995), p. 11.

Recently, Kim Chongwŏn has proposed another view that the first Korean motion picture is *The Past Sin*, which, produced in 1917, preceded *The Righteous Revenge* by two years. See Kim Chongwŏn, 'Ch'och'anggi-ŭi Han'guk yŏnghwasa kisul-ŭi munjejŏm-gwa saeroun kijŏm-ŭi yŏn'gu' (The problems of describing the early Korean film history and a redefinition of the beginning of Korean film), *Korean Film Critiques*, 5 (1993), pp. 12–15.

7　This view is partly based on personal recollections by film historians and critics on the sudden death of the producer and director Kim Tosan in a car accident. For instance, Yu claims that he heard about Kim's death from the crew who had participated in the making of *The National Borders*. See Kim Chongwŏn, 'The problems of describing', pp. 11–27; Cho, 'A study of the beginning', pp. 18–29; and Yu, *The Korean Film*, pp. 69–71.

8　Yi Chunggŏ, 'Ilje shidae-ŭi uri yŏnghwa' (Our film in the Japanese colonial period), in Yi Chunggŏ *et al.*, *Understanding Korean Film*, p. 144.

9　Yi Chunggŏ, 'A study of Korean film history', p. 60.

10　Yi Hyoin, *Lecture*, p. 49.

11　Yi Chunggŏ 'A study of Korean film history', p. 61.

12　Yi Hyoin, *Lecture*, p. 224.

13　Kim Sunam, 'Yun Paengnam-ŭi yŏnghwa insaeng yŏn'gu' (A study of Yun Paeknam's film and life), in *Han'guk Yŏnghwa Chakka Yŏn'gu* (A Study of Korean Film Directors) (Seoul, Yeni, 1995), p. 40.

14　Ch'oe Yŏngch'ŏl, 'Ilje shingminch'iha-ŭi yŏnghwa chŏngch'aek' (Film policies under the Japanese colonial rule) in Yi Chunggŏ *et al.*, *Understanding Korean Film*, p. 238.

15　The appearance of 'nationalistic resistance' films during this period is perceived as the most significant achievement in the entire Korean film history by most of the South Korean film historians. This is a rather odd phenomenon, given the intense censorship at the time.

Presently, no scholarly explanation is available on the question as to how these nationalistic films could pass the censorship.

16 Kim Taeho, Yi Hyoin and Pyŏn Chaeran, for instance, argue that the 'tendency films' are the origin of the Korean films that treat socio-political issues. See Pyŏn Chaeran, '1930 nyŏndae chŏnhu KAPF yŏnghwa hwaldong yŏn'gu' (A study of the KAPF film movement in the late 1920s and the early 1930s), in National Film Research Institute (ed.), *Minjok Yŏnghwa 2* (National Film 2) (Seoul, Ch'in'gu, 1990), p. 219.

17 Yu, *The Korean Film*, p. 129.

18 For the negative view of Na's so-called 'nationalistic' films, see Kim Sunam, 'Na Un'gyu-ŭi minjok yŏnghwa chaego' (Reconsideration of the nationalistic film of Na Un'gyu), in *A Study*, pp. 83–4.

19 Yu, *Korean Film*, p. 96.

20 It seems that Esperanto was popular among Korean intellectuals during this period.

21 Yi Hyoin, *Lecture*, pp. 88–91; and Pyŏn, '1930 nyŏndae chŏnhu', p. 220.

22 It was not only the 'tendency film' directors who began collaborating with the same film authorities who had earlier imprisoned them. During the latter half of the colonial period, a significant number of the popular Korean intellectuals and national leaders who had devoted themselves to the cause of Korean nationalism or socialist movement began to work for the Japanese colonial authorities up until the Liberation. Regarding the 'betrayal' of the KAPF film directors and critics, contemporary film historians point out their weak ideological stance as socialists as well as the fact that they were in difficult circumstances; they were often forced into becoming collaborators 'for the sake of Korea'.

23 Kim Il Sung, 'Hyŏngmyŏng chuje chakp'um-esŏŭi myŏt kaji sasang mihakchŏk munje' ('Some ideological and aesthetic problems in revolutionary works') (10 January 1967), in *Kim Il Sung Chŏjak Sŏnjip 21* (P'yŏngyang, Korean Workers' Party Publishing House, 1983), pp. 13–28; and Yi Uyŏng, *Kim Jong Il Munye Chŏngch'aek-ŭi Chisok-kwa Pyŏnhwa* (The Continuity and Changes of Kim Jong Il's Literature and Art Policy) (Seoul, the Research Institute for National Unification, 1997), p. 14. For further details, see North Korean film history section in this chapter, on pp. 36–8.

24 Kim Il Sung, 'Yŏngha-nŭn hososŏng-i nopaya hamyŏ hyŏnshil-boda apsŏ nagaya handa' ('Film should strongly appeal to the masses and advance them more than reality') (17 January 1958), in *Kim Il Sung Chŏjak Sŏnjip 12* (P'yŏngyang: Korean Workers' Party Publishing House, 1981), p. 9.

25 Kim Jong Il, 'Marx–Leninjuŭi-wa *Juche* sasang-ŭi kich'i-rŭl nop'i tŭlgo nagaja' ('Let us move forward with Marxism–Leninism and *Juche* idea'), in *Kim Jong Il Chŏjaksŏn* (Selected Works of Kim Jong Il) (Seoul, Kyŏngnam University Far-East Research Institute, 1991), p. 166.

26 Kim Il Sung, 'On eliminating dogmatism and formalism and establishing *Juche* in ideological work: Speech to Party propaganda and agitation workers', in *Kim Il Sung Works 9: July 1954 to December 1955* (Pyongyang, Foreign Languages Publishing House, 1982), pp. 395–417.

27 Literature Research Institute of Social Science Board, *Juche Sasang-e Kich'ohan Munye Iron* (Juche *Oriented Ideas on Literature and Art*) (P'yŏngyang, Social Science Publishing House, 1975), p. 12.

28 This couple were allegedly detained in North Korea for eight years. While they stayed there, they were actively involved in the North Korean film industry. They were also occasionally sent abroad by Kim Jong Il, as representatives of the North Korean film community. Much of Kim's rather unusual interest in film was known to the outside world through the testimonies by this couple after their successful escape from North Korea in 1986.

29 For further information on this incident, see Ch'oe Ŭnhŭi and Shin Sangok, *Kim Jong Il Wangguk 1 & 2* (The Kingdom of Kim Jong Il 1 & 2) (Seoul, Dong-A Ilbo, 1988).

30 Kim Jong Il, *Yŏnghwa Yesulron* (The Theory of Cinematic Art) (P'yŏngyang, Korean Workers' Party Publishing House, 1973).

31 The series of *Unknown Heroes I–IIX* had been known to be produced according to this theory: each film was made in forty-five days under the direction of Kim Jong Il during the years 1979 to 1981.

32 Kim Il Sung, *Kim Il Sung Chŏjak Sŏnjip 3* (Selected Works of Kim Il Sung 3) (P'yŏngyang, Korean Workers' Party Publishing House, 1975), p. 159.

33 Kim Il Sung, *Kim Il Sung Chŏjak Sŏnjip 2* (Selected Works of Kim Il Sung 2) (P'yŏngyang, Korean Workers' Party Publishing House, 1968), pp. 572–3.

34 Kim Il Sung, 'Hyŏngmyŏngjŏk munhak yesul-ŭl ch'angjakhalde daehayŏ' ('Concerning the creation of revolutionary literary art') (7 November 1964), in *Kim Il Sung Chŏjak Sŏnjip 18* (P'yŏngyang, Korean Workers' Party Publishing House, 1982), pp. 436–8.

35 Kim Il Sung, *Kim Il Sung Chŏjak Sŏnjip 6* (Selected Works of Kim Il Sung 6) (P'yŏngyang, Korean Workers' Party Publishing House, 1974), p. 276.

36 I will discuss this issue in detail in Chapter 3.

37 Kim Jong Il, 'Saeroun hyŏngmyŏng munhak-ŭl kŏnsŏlhalde daehayŏ' ('Concerning the creation of the new revolutionary literary art') (7 February 1966), in *Kim Jong Il Chŏjak Sŏnjip 1* (Pyŏngyang, Korean Workers' Party Publishing House, 1992), pp. 113–14.

38 Kim Jong Il, 'Pandang panghyŏngmyŏng punjadŭl-ŭi sasang yŏdok-ŭl ppurippaego tang-ŭi *Yuil* sasang ch'egye-rŭl seulde daehayŏ' ('Concerning the eradication of the poisonous thoughts of the anti-party, anti-revolutionary elements and the establishment of *Yuil* thought') (25 June 1967), in *Kim Jong Il Chŏjak Sŏnjip 1* (P'yŏngyang, Korean Workers' Party Publishing House, 1992), pp. 230–1.

39 Kim Chaeyong, *Pukhan Munhak-ŭi Ihae* (Understanding North Korean Literature) (Seoul, Munhak-kwa Chisŏngsa, 1994), pp. 217–19.

40 I will discuss this issue in detail in Chapter 4.

41 According to the official notion of the Party, nationalism means 'the ideas that the nation of Chosŏn is the greatest'.

42 Yi Sŏngdŏk, 'Rodong kyegŭp-ŭi saenghwal ch'ŏlhak-ŭl kuhyŏnhan segyejŏkin kŏljak (1)' ('The world's great work materialising the philosophy of life of the working class'), *Chosŏn Yŏnghwa* (Chosŏn Film), 267 (September 1995), p. 40.

43 Kim Jong Il, 'Tabujak yesul yŏnghwa *Minjok-kwa Unmyŏng*-ŭi ch'angjak sŏnggwa-e t'odaehayŏ munhak yesul kŏnsŏl-esŏ saeroun chŏnhwan-ŭl ilŭkija' ('Let's reach a new turning point in the construction of literature and art, based on the creative result of the multi-volume art film *The Nation and Destiny*') (23 May 1992) in

Chosŏn Chungang Nyŏn'gam 1993 (Chosŏn Year Book 1993) (P'yŏng-yang, Chosŏn Changang Tongshinsa, 1993), p. 50.

44 2·8 was used to stand for the foundation day of the Korean People's Army, but the North Korean government changed the foundation day from 8 February to 25 April in 1978.

45 Chosŏn Yŏnghwa Yŏn'gam 1987 (Korean Film Yearbook 1987), eds Ch'oe Chunghwi and Li Hoyun (P'yŏngyang, Munye Publishing House, 1987).

46 Korean Film Export and Import Corporation, Korean Film Art (Pyongyang, Korean Film Export and Import Corporation, 1985) [no page number is available].

47 Until the national division brought about by the Allies at the end of the Second World War, Koreans had maintained a nation-state for over thirteen centuries.

48 As exemplified by Ch'oe's case, evaluating film-makers in terms of the presence or absence of nationalistic elements in their work can be quite dangerous and misleading. The problem becomes far more serious when directors are labelled 'nationalistic' merely on the basis of a few films they made, especially when they have an undeniable record of co-operation with the colonial authorities by making pro-Japanese films. A more thorough and objective assessment of the film-makers of this period, therefore, should be based on the broad historical context in which they conducted their film-making and on a variety of factors which determined the nature of the environment for their cinematic enterprise.

49 Han'guk Yŏnghwa Yŏn'gam (Korean Film Yearbook), ed. Korean Motion Picture Promotion Corp. (Seoul, Tongmyŏng, 1989), pp. 99–112.

50 National Film Research Institute, 'P'aop Chŏnya-ŭi sŏnggong-gwa kŭ kyŏlshil' ('The fruits of The Night before the Strike and the evaluation'), in National Film Research Institute (ed.), National Film 2, p. 174.

51 Kim Sunam, 'A study of Yun', pp. 85–6.

52 Korean Film Yearbook, pp. 99–112.

53 Under the regulation of the current Motion Picture Act, a theatre should show domestic films at least 146 days a year.

54 Chapter 2 of this book is devoted to an analysis of five of these adaptations.

Gender and cinematic adaptation of the folk tale, *Ch'unhyangjŏn*[1] 2

This chapter discusses the cultural identity of contemporary Koreans by analysing five films based on a popular traditional folk tale, *Ch'unhyangjŏn*.[2] Three of the five films were made in South Korea: Shin Sangok's *Sŏng Ch'unhyang* (1961), Pak T'ae-wŏn's *The Tale of Sŏng Ch'unhyang* (1976) and Han Sanghun's *Sŏng Ch'unhyang* (1987). The other two films are from North Korea: Yu Wŏnjun and Yun Ryonggyu's *The Tale of Ch'unhyang* (1980) and Shin Sangok's musical, *Love, Love, My Love* (1985). Although using the same story, these films interpret the morals of the well-known narrative differently, and their differences are most lucidly discernible in their treatments of the issues related to gender and class.

The film adaptations of *Ch'unhyangjŏn* divulge the disparate interests of contemporary Koreans living in the divided nation, and their differences can be, as I intend to show in this chapter, attributed to their conflicting cultural identity. Norman Denzin elucidates several parameters that affect the moulding of one's selfhood: gender, ethnicity, race, religion, class and national identity.[3] Among them, gender, class and national identity are directly pertinent to defining the cultural identity of contemporary Koreans. *Ch'unhyangjŏn* features gender and class as the central subjects. The treatment of the two interrelated subjects in the film texts is tied specifically to the oppositional ideologies of the capitalist South and the communist North. Therefore, the varied portraits of Ch'unhyang can provide us with useful clues to the self-perceptions held by Koreans in the post-war era.

The significance of gender and class issues in *Ch'unhyangjŏn* can be glimpsed through the three variants of the film title.

Ch'unhyangjŏn literally means 'the tale of Ch'unhyang'. This title appears to tell nothing beyond the name of the protagonist, but the unequivocal femininity of its literal meaning – 'fragrance of spring' – implies that the protagonist is female.

The title *Sŏng Ch'unhyang* draws attention to the heroine's class background. 'Sŏng' is the family name of her *yangban* (the ruling class in the Chosŏn Dynasty) father. Born of a *yangban* and a *kisaeng* (courtesan or female entertainer), Ch'unhyang is legally assigned to her mother's class. Classified as such, she is forbidden to use her father's family name. Then there is the three South Korean directors' use of 'Sŏng' in their titles. The reason could be that the titles, by alluding to her partially noble blood, help the heroine to fit the picture of an ideal woman of the Chosŏn society.[4] The use of Ch'unhyang's family name suggests that her father is a prosperous aristocrat who can afford a *kisaeng* (concubine). The contrasts between her father's aristocratic background and her mother's humble status also point to the class conflict underlying the film.

The title of Shin's North Korean film, *Love, Love, My Love* situates the viewer firmly in a male-centred position. It conveys the ontological meaning of the story: Ch'unhyang's life does not exist without a man's presence in it. In other words, her story can be meaningful only when it is told through the controlling male consciousness. Thus the title foregrounds her lover–husband's point of view and also, implies Ch'unhyang's inferior position as an object of male desire.

My investigation proceeds in three phases. First, it defines the source material on Ch'unhyang briefly and reviews its significance in the Korean cinema. The second phase describes the dominant images of Ch'unhyang in each film. Ch'unhyang's character traits embody female virtues defined from the traditional patriarchal perspective, and, as such, they bring our attention to the ideal Confucian womanhood cultivated during the Chosŏn Dynasty. All five films portray their heroine's image on the basis of traditional sexual morality. The emphasis in Ch'unhyang's characterisation, however, shifts from one text to another, therefore, each film suggests a different idea of women's position and roles in society.

A full description of the representations of Ch'unhyang's character helps to prepare for the third part of this chapter, which explores how South and North Korean films tailor differently the common legacy of Confucian sexual morality and class distinction. This phase focuses specifically on the emerging patterns of similarities and dissimilarities between the South and the North in their interpretation of gender and class within the ideological contexts of the respective societies that produced the works. This section aims to show, on the one hand, the continuous influence of the traditional Confucian ethics upon the contemporary Korean cultural identity, regardless of their present ideological variance. On the other hand, the section demonstrates the inevitable fusion between the old value system with the pressing ideological demands of the divided nation. My analysis attempts to expose the cultural logic of the current society through an ideological critique of the structural contradictions and the moral systems in the traditional society. The complexity of the film as a cultural text helps us to grasp the complicated relationship between the state's attempt to enforce its ruling ideology and its cultural traditions.

Film can create an imaginary world in which sublime fantasy structure betrays various social constraints in the viewer's mundane day-to-day life. Since fantasies about the past cannot be created without the intrusion of the present, film about traditional Korean society can serve as an effective window through which we can contemplate the unfulfilled desires of modern Koreans. Set in a remote place and time, a historical film provides its viewers with a comfortable psychological distance to project their present situation onto the reconstructed past world. Through the imaginative participation in the fictional world, they try to grapple with their immediate concerns and find a meaning in their given circumstances. This explains why historical films are believed to offer a key to the self-perception of contemporary Koreans. As will be shown below, a nostalgic approach to filial duty, family honour and traditional marriage in the films tells us about the society's need for these values as a frame of reference to shape its present experiences into a meaningful form.

The origins of *Ch'unhyangjŏn*

Before a detailed analysis of the films begins, it would be useful to survey the folkloric origin of *Ch'unhyangjŏn* and its historical development. This will help clarify the significance of issues related to gender and class in the selected film texts. The story originated from *Ch'unhyang Kut*, a shamanistic ritual performed in the Namwŏn area in the south-western part of the Korean peninsula.[5] The purpose of the ritual is to appease the soul of a young girl named Ch'unhyang, who died of deep grief, which stemmed from her plain appearance. Local legend has it that she was so ugly that no one wanted to marry her or was ever attracted to her. Due to her homely looks, she died a virgin, without having had her sexual desire fulfilled.[6] Following her death, the area suffered from years of famine caused by a long drought, and the newly appointed magistrates of the region met with mysterious deaths, one after another. The local people believed that the calamities were due to Ch'unhyang's lingering woes about this world, so they decided to seek a way to vent her spite. Consequently, the *Salp'uri Kut*, a shamanistic ritual, was staged to exorcise her spirit, and along with it, a story was devised about her. In the story, Ch'unhyang appears as a beautiful girl. She marries a handsome man from the *yangban* class, and they live happily together. This oral tradition established the prototype of *Ch'unhyangjŏn*.[7]

The above invented story of Ch'unhyang made its way into *p'ansori*, a traditional performing art of storytelling and singing, which flourished in Korea in the eighteenth and nineteenth centuries. *Yŏllyŏ Ch'unhyang Sujŏlga* (The Tale of a Faithful Wife, Ch'unhyang) is the first existing text of *p'ansori*. As a *p'ansori* work, the folk tale gained a more elaborate narrative structure with the motifs of romantic encounter, secret marriage, forced separation, the heroine's trial, her lover's return and their happy reunion. New features were added to the characters and plot: Ch'unhyang became the daughter of a retired *kisaeng* and a *yangban* man.[8] One spring day, she meets Yi Mongnyong, the magistrate's son, and they fall in love at first sight. Mongnyong calls at her house at night, and upon his visit they marry secretly. But he soon has to move to Seoul with his father. After his departure, a new magistrate comes to the village and forces Ch'unhyang to serve him. Because she rejects his authority, she is imprisoned. Her trial is eventually ended when Mongnyong passes a state exam, returns to his hometown as a secret royal inspector and rescues her from a death sentence.

Korean fascination with *Ch'unhyangjŏn* comes partly from the way it touches on the traditional class system and its political implications. The story is set in the mid-eighteenth century when national sovereignty was in peril. Successive invasions by the Japanese (1592–98) and the Manchurians (1627–36) devastated the national economy and disintegrated the social structure of old Korea. One of the consequences of such tribulation was the emergence of nationalism between the late seventeenth and the early eighteenth centuries. It was led by the *Shilhak* (Practical Learning) scholars who advocated political, economic and social reforms as a way to regenerate the country. They renounced the China-centred worldview in their search for Korean identity and raised a critical voice against the incompetence of the ruling class, the widespread corruption among the local magistrates and the systematic exploitation of peasants by the landowners.

In *Ch'unhyangjŏn*, this socio-political background is mirrored in the commoners' dread of their exploiters and their scepticism about the oppressive class system.[9] The story also intimates the aspiration of the populace to live in a stabilised and, ideally, classless society. Ironically, this aspiration is expressed through their wish for the king to exercise absolute power to eradicate all the class-related social evils. What the people wish is to eliminate their exploiters, not to deny the legitimacy of the existing social order altogether. Such paradoxical longing characterises the historical period in which the story of Ch'unhyang is situated.

The *p'ansori* text, *Ch'unhyangjŏn*, is a story of romance and marriage between an upper-class man and a lower-class woman, which was forbidden by law during the Chosŏn Dynasty. Therefore, the text was subject to severe government censorship. The official persecution was particularly due to its 'suggestive' description of love scenes and direct criticism of the hypocrisy of the ruling class. Despite the censorship, however, the narrative has been handed down from generation to generation in both verbal and written forms. It was further embellished by people who found an outlet for their unfulfilled desires and hidden anxieties in the fictional world of the story. This explains to a great extent why Ch'unhyang's inter-class marriage is viewed as reflecting a popular desire to level the class distinction in traditional Korean society.

Through its source material and all the subsequent variants, *Ch'unhyangjŏn* is deeply rooted in the folk imagination of the lower-class people. From its rudimentary form, the story revolves around the themes of sexuality, marriage and social class, which are all tightly enmeshed. Ch'unhyang functions as the major signifier of erotic desire in the collective imagination in a repressed society, which prohibits public discussion or display of sexual matters.

Later versions of *Ch'unhyangjŏn*, including the five contemporary films, tailor specific aspects of the narrative according to the aesthetic standards and pragmatic needs of their times.[10] The original *p'ansori* text, however, highlights Ch'unhyang's loyalty to her husband Mongnyong, his filial respect for his father, and the subordination of the commoners to the ruler. These ethical principles, which Confucianism prescribes as the governing rules of 'proper' human relationships, entail a fundamental paradox. A scrutiny of the main characters' relations in the narrative indeed exposes underlying ideological contradictions in the established morals on sexuality and the institution of marriage. It is these problematic aspects of the story that this chapter will address.

The significance of *Ch'unhyangjŏn* in Korean film history

Ch'unhyangjŏn is a text apt for an ideological interpretation. This argument is born out by its history of cinematic adaptation. The tale has occupied an important place in Korean film industry from the beginning. The second silent and the first sound films in the history of Korean cinema were based on it. The story was first adapted in 1923 immediately after *The Plighted Love under the Moon* (1923), Korea's first silent film that the Japanese colonial government produced for propaganda purposes. Although the second in chronological order, it is *The Tale of Ch'unhyang* that actually ushered the Korean film industry into the silent film era. It was also the first commercial film made in Korea, and, as such, it made a tremendous contribution to forming the perception of film as a popular entertainment among the general public.

Ironically, the first Ch'unhyang film was directed by a Japanese film-maker who discerned the commercial potential of the entertaining elements of the narrative. Stimulated by the commercial success of the film, and especially by the fact that it was made by a Japanese director, Korean film-makers became increasingly self-conscious, claiming that a 'pure' Korean film should be made by Koreans for the Korean audience with indigenous material.[11] This idea bore the fruit in the production for another *The Tale of Ch'unhyang* in 1935, the first Korean sound film by Yi Myŏngu. The appearance of Yi's film, however, provoked severe censorship from the colonial government. In 1938, the government banned the use of the Korean language and Korean names in all sectors of Korean life, and the film industry was no exception to this policy. Incredible as it may seem, the Korean language had actually disappeared from Korean cinema by 1942. Despite the increasingly aggravating conditions, the 1935 *The Tale of Ch'unhyang* was received with great enthusiasm by the public. The surprising commercial success of the film demonstrated the Koreans' intense desire to have their own story to be told on the screen. As colonial subjects, the audience could identify themselves with Ch'unhyang and other lower-class characters who have to endure injustice, oppression and humiliation by those abusing their power. The past world unfolded in *The Tale of Ch'unhyang* reminded them of their lost images and their longing for a peaceful life free from foreign interference and exploitation.

Ch'unhyang continued to appear in Korean film even after the Liberation in 1945. In South Korea, Yi Kyuhwan adapted the story into a film in 1955: *The Tale of Ch'unhyang*. Following Kim Hyang's 1957 *The Great Tale of Ch'unhyang* and An Chonghwa's

8 The first Korean sound film, Yi Myŏngu's *The Tale of Ch'unhyang* (1935)

1958 *The Tale of Ch'unhyang*, Shin Sangok and Hong Sŏnggi also made *Sŏng Ch'unhyang* and *The Tale of Ch'unhyang*, respectively in 1961. Seven years later, another film, *Ch'unhyang* was directed by Kim Suyong. In 1971, Yi Sŏnggu made *The Tale of Ch'unhyang* as the first Korean 70 mm film in Korean film history. Among these, Shin's 1961 *Sŏng Ch'unhyang* holds a special place. When released, it marked an unprecedented box-office hit. Not only did it reach the widest audience in Korean film industry, but it also generated a sensation because of the rivalry between Shin and Hong, the two eminent directors, and their casting of the two leading actresses of the times as Ch'unhyang in their films. Shin's film also helped to generate a boom for colour cinema in the Korean film industry, which was first introduced in 1949 but had not been very popular until then.[12]

Furthermore, Shin's *Sŏng Ch'unhyang* set a trend for melodrama and historical romance in South Korean cinema. Shin's Ch'unhyang adumbrated an innocent, self-sacrificing lower-class woman as a typical heroine of these genres. Modelled on Shin's work, all kinds of melodramatic pieces came out whose plots revolved around forbidden love between a married man and a single woman, typically a prostitute.

In the 1970s and 1980s, two films were made on the basis of *Ch'unhyangjŏn*: Pak's *The Tale of Sŏng Ch'unhyang* (1976) and Han's *Sŏng Ch'unhyang* (1987). Im Kwŏnt'aek's *The Tale of*

Ch'unhyang (2000) was presented at the 53rd Cannes Film Festival. This was the first time that a quality Korean film could compete with other international films at this festival. Since the 1970s, however, the popularity of historical romance has sharply declined. The appearance of the three adaptations of *Ch'unhyangjŏn* during the last two decades regardless of this circumstance, illustrates the sustained interest of contemporary Koreans in the story. Directed by the younger generation of directors, Pak and Han's films take different approaches to the traditional Confucian morality of the story from previous adaptations.

In North Korea, three films were produced in 1959, 1980 and 1985, based on *Ch'unhyangjŏn*. Under the thorough control of the Korean Workers' Party, North Korean cinema in general stresses the revolutionary struggles of the working-class people toward a classless society. For this theme, the party does not consider the traditional society to be a proper setting for a film: it prefers the relatively modern settings, such as the Japanese colonial period, the Korean War years or the contemporary socialist society. Literature on North Korean film history lists a small number of films dealing with traditional society. Hence, it is somewhat astounding that, out of an estimated fifteen historical films ever made in North Korea, three drew on *Ch'unhyangjŏn*: Yun Ryonggyu's *The Tale of Ch'unhyang* (1959), Yu and Yun's *The Tale of Ch'unhyang* (1980) and Shin's *Love, Love, My Love* (1985).

Of the above three works, Yu and Yun's and Shin's are selected for this study. Concerning the former, it should be mentioned that its screenplay was written by Paek Injun who is known as the most significant figure in the North Korean culture and art because of his political espousal of the party's aesthetic guidelines. Shin made *Love, Love, My Love* on the basis of the Ch'unhyang story after he was abducted to the North in 1978. Yun's *The Tale of Ch'unhyang*, the oldest among the three, is not included in this study as it is inaccessible to critics as well as lay viewers outside North Korea.[13]

The popularity of the Ch'unhyang story among film-makers is obvious in both South and North Korea. Specific aspects of the folk tale that have inspired numerous film adaptations are examined in the following section.

The images of Ch'unhyang in South Korean films

The obedient and self-sacrificing wife in Shin's *Sŏng Ch'unhyang*

The Confucian ethics that regulated everyday Korean life in Chosŏn society defined a woman's meaningful existence exclusively in terms of her relationships with men as daughter, wife and mother (of a son, ideally).[14] This is the order of identities bestowed upon her by the society as she progresses in her life. A woman's desires can be fulfilled only when her father, husband or son acknowledges and realises them for her. Among the three stages of a woman's identity change, Shin's *Sŏng Ch'unhyang* singles out a modest, chaste, obedient and self-sacrificing wife as an ideal female figure.

In Shin's film the favourable feminine qualities are signalled through Ch'unhyang's shyness. The opening scene shows Mongnyong sitting on the back of a mule, staring at Ch'unhyang in a crowded market. Conscious of his attention, the embarrassed heroine cannot hold up her head. She tries only to avert his intense gaze.

The overbearing male gaze is reinforced by the high-angled camera position toward Ch'unhyang. The camera sets up the audience to identify their viewing position with Mongnyong's. The camera position remains the same even after Mongnyong disappears from the screen. In fact, the conscious lowering of Ch'unhyang's position before a male character continues when the new magistrate replaces Mongnyong. Aligned with the male gaze, the camera dwarfs Ch'unhyang's status, visually evoking her powerlessness and inferiority, which are equated with her femininity.[15]

The shifting movement of the camera angle and the heroine's shy reaction are also found in the nuptial night sequence. Mongnyong is sitting in the room, enjoying the sight of his beautiful bride. Yet Ch'unhyang with her eyes cast down, does not dare to look at him face to face. The audience is again invited to share Mongnyong's voyeuristic pleasure of looking down at her from an elevated position. Embarrassed, she is symbolically immobilised by his gaze, unable to escape from it. The purposefully sustained shots force the audience to read her shyness as a pronounced token of her well-educated manners, according to the Confucian semiotic signs.

Contrasted with the bashful bride, the 15-year-old bridegroom skilfully leads her in their nuptial-bed ritual. The film's message of male domination becomes clear when we compare the scenes with their counterparts in Pak's *The Tale of Sŏng Ch'unhyang*. In the latter, Mongnyong acts timidly, hesitating to approach his

9   The shy bride Ch'unhyang being wooed by her bridegroom
Mongnyong on the first night: Shin Sangok's *Sŏng Ch'unhyang* (1961)

bride. He even flinches when he takes off the bride's clothes – as is required by custom – and sees her half-naked body.

The thematic significance of Ch'unhyang's shyness can be explained in terms of the Confucian notion of 'romantic' which is often assumed to reflect aspects of femininity. According to the male–female sexual dynamics in traditional Korean society, the coyness of a girl was perceived as romantic allurement. Blushing or timidity was also believed to reveal her romantic nature.

However, Ch'unhyang's simple, spontaneous emotion such as shyness is loaded with layers of complex meanings. In the Confucian Chosŏn society, a romantic relationship can develop only through male initiative. A woman, especially a 'good' one is expected to react to it in a demure fashion. This is interpreted as a sign of modesty, which is in turn read as an indicator of her passivity in dealing with the various problems that she will face in life. Passivity is viewed as stemming from the woman's total acceptance of her inferior position to men, especially to her future husband. Shin's film communicates this point poignantly through Ch'unhyang's metaphorical statement to Pangja, Mongnyong's messenger, as a response in fact, to Mongnyong's proposal: 'A butterfly follows a flower, but a flower cannot follow a butterfly'.

In Shin's treatment of Ch'unhyang's relationship with Mongnyong, her social class does not weigh as much as her feminine virtues. The film evades any in-depth discussion of the obvious status gap between the two lovers. Mongnyong tersely remarks: 'If she is a daughter of a *kisaeng*, she is also a *kisaeng*. Is there a problem if a *yangban* calls a *kisaeng*?'. To the perceptive audience, Pangja's answer to his master's rhetorical question subtly touches on the tension from their class difference: 'Of course she is a *kisaeng*, but she is also a daughter of Sŏng who lives in Seoul!'. The insinuation of Ch'unhyang's upper-class side enables the film to prepare her for the role of a *yangban*'s wife. The reference to her alleged *yangban* father is thus necessitated by the internal logic of the narrative, which is centred on her role as an ideal wife.

Ch'unhyang in Shin's film is a model wife in that she fulfils acceptable cultural norms of feminine behaviour: obedient, faithful and self-sacrificing. She thus fits perfectly the ideal wifehood as demanded by her society. For instance, when Mongnyong, now secretly married, is distracted from his studies by thoughts of Ch'unhyang, she is far from being flattered: instead, she tries hard to make him concentrate on books. Such selflessness qualifies her for the status of a 'good' wife. It is only through this kind of paradoxical self-renunciation, that her moral attainment can be elevated to the level of the *yangban* class, and thus bring her happiness in due course. When Mongnyong is reluctant to move to Seoul alone as ordered by his father, who does not accept their marriage, Ch'unhyang urges him to not only leave her but also not regret their separation. She even insists that he should forget about her. Her noble mind and action in this scene are a perfect example of the notion of the respectable wife. Among the five directors discussed in this chapter, Shin is the most persistent in highlighting Ch'unhyang's image as a virtuous wife. His emphasis on Ch'unhyang's renunciation of herself for her husband's welfare reaches its climax when she resists the new magistrate's coercion to serve him: 'I already have an owner. I belong to him. Don't force me to serve you!'. This protest literally spells out Ch'unhyang's perception of her identity as an object in her husband's possession. Her dramatic description of her marital status in terms of ownership stands in marked contrast to the usual line: 'I am already married, and I have a husband'.

Ch'unhyang's image as the paragon of female virtues, however, is not totally convincing. From a Confucian perspective, she is not morally immaculate. She violates her society's injunction on pre-marital sex. By secretly marrying, she in fact challenges the institution of marriage, which requires initial parental consent for its validation.

Preoccupied with creating Ch'unhyang's image as a refined wife. who is commensurate with her husband's *yangban* status, Shin introduces supernatural elements into the film text. They are used to forestall a possible question: if she is so virtuous, how can she engage in a sexual relationship with Mongnyong without obtaining his father's approval of their marriage? Considering that Mongnyong's father is the only one who has the power to legitimise their marriage, her rash sexual act can be easily perceived as a moral flaw in her character. It can undermine all the ideal *yangban* attributes she demonstrates. To prevent this potential problem, Shin resorts to the indigenous folk beliefs, such as fortune-telling and dream sequences that transcend the logic of naturalism and has a strong grip on Korean spiritual life. Ch'unhyang's involvement with Mongnyong is presented as predestined by forces beyond her control. As the film begins, Ch'unhyang approaches a blind fortune-teller in the market, who rather conveniently predicts her unavoidable encounter with Mongnyong in the immediate future. Of course, the prediction is at once realised on the screen. Similarly, on the night when Mongnyong calls at Ch'unhyang's house, her mother Wŏlmae tells her daughter about a strange dream she has just awoken from: 'I saw a blue dragon entering your room thick with smoke and then flying away in the air, holding you in his mouth ... It strangely woke me up ... If you were a boy, it would mean that you will pass the state exam ...'. A similar kind of fortune-telling blended with a mysterious dream returns in the prison scene where Ch'unhyang is shown awaiting her death. The unearthly elements serve as an effective means to justify their unusual marriage: their meeting and marriage are the result of the play of inexplicable forces, and humans must obey the fate befalling them. These superstitious motifs are not non-existent in other films, but Shin utilises them most heavily.[16] Shin's efforts in portraying Ch'unhyang's character are solely directed towards cinematically realising the concept of virtuous *yangban* wifehood.

The youthful teenager in Pak's *The Tale of Sŏng Ch'unhyang*

Pak's *The Tale of Sŏng Ch'unhyang* presents a somewhat different image of Ch'unhyang from other South Korean films that depict her as chaste or sensual. Pak's Ch'unhyang is closer to a carefree, puerile adolescent girl than an emotionally and mentally mature adult woman. The dominating theme of Pak's adaptation is that one of youthful, true love can overcome the prejudices of the older generation, much in the vein of Romeo and Juliet's romance in the West. Pak removes the typical moralistic overtone from the story. Contrasted with Ch'unhyang's traditional tale, making every effort to act upon the societal norms of the respectable womanhood, Pak's protagonist remains an innocent teenager who meets a boy of a similar age and then falls in love with him. This Ch'unhyang does not agonise over Mongnyong's proposal as other Ch'unhyang figures tend to.

To some extent, Pak's film can be read as a response to the rising feminist voice in Korean society of the 1970s. It also reflects the rapid commercialisation of teenage subculture during this decade. Ch'unhyang's innocence, characteristic of her age, contains an element of subversion to the conventional ideas of female sexuality and marriage. A good example of her challenge to the traditional codes of conduct is found in the scene where the young Ch'unhyang freely goes out and talks to Mongnyong, a stranger. Her action is an outright violation of the moral dictum that girls of marriageable age should not go out during the daytime or speak to men. Pak's Ch'unhyang does not appear to mind such convention. She is undaunted by Mongnyong's sudden appearance in her place at night. Unlike other mature Ch'unhyang figures, she does not overly refuse his advances.

Ch'unhyang's childlike lack of inhibition in speech also conveys Pak's subtle indictment of the established ideas of womanhood. Ch'unhyang in the original tale and other film adaptations tends to observe carefully Confucian views on women's silence as one of their prime virtues. In Confucian ethics, verboseness is regarded as one of the seven grounds for a man to ask for a divorce from his wife.[17] Hence, Ch'unhyang is usually depicted as quiet, and Wŏlmae plays the role of an intermediary in her communication with Mongnyong. In some films, she is silent even after she has spent the night with Mongnyong. She breaks her silence only when she painfully realises his impending departure. Contrary to the idealised image of a quiet woman, Pak's Ch'unhyang acts like any buoyant teenager who does not hesitate to express herself freely to Mongnyong, a boy whom she has just met for the first time in her life. She is not suddenly struck dumb by his proposal. Her action overturns the preconception of the audience about Ch'unhyang as a demure, reserved adult woman.

Ch'unhyang is liberal not only in her attitude toward language but also in physical activity. She appears to disregard the virtue of moderation in physical activity emphasised by Confucian codes of conduct. She plays on the swing until she gets totally exhausted. The idea of moderation in movement was strongly impressed upon women in Chosŏn society. They were taught to avoid excessive physical activity because it was read as a sign of aggressive personality. Contrary to this teaching, Pak's Ch'unhyang tends to exert herself in sports and games. This is another

10   Wŏlmae tries to protect her naïve daughter
Ch'unhyang from the *yangban* boy Mongnyong:
Pak T'aewŏn's *The Tale of Sŏng Ch'unhyang* (1976)

character trait that sets Pak's Ch'unhyang apart from other
directors'.

Ch'unhyang's overall image in Pak's film imparts a note of
individualism. It is clearly demonstrated by the initiative she
takes in her own marriage. She is not the familiar type of docile
daughter seen in other films. When Mongnyong pays a nocturnal
visit to her house, she leads him into her own room without her
mother's knowledge. Nor is Wŏlmae an authoritarian parent.
Instead of manipulating her daughter to marry a *yangban* boy, as
she often does in other adaptations, Pak's Wŏlmae is more concerned about protecting her naïve daughter from Mongnyong's
approach. She insists on him visiting Ch'unhyang in a proper
manner if he 'really intends to marry' her; that is, more openly,
in daylight, without fearing others' eyes. In other films, Wŏlmae
is entrusted with the matters of Ch'unhyang's marriage. Wŏlmae's
secondary role in Pak's film helps to highlight the heroine as a

relatively independent individual. Through the rather unconventional characterisation of Ch'unhyang, Pak stresses the theme that a romantic relationship is primarily a matter of love and determination of those involved, and also, that marriage is an institution for the couple rather than one for their families.

Pak's film, however, does not portray Ch'unhyang with a purely positive image. She is both carefree and childlike. She is sometimes even inconsiderate, if not outright selfish. Her innocent vulnerability is most vividly displayed when she quickly hides herself behind her mother, scared by Mongnyong's appearance at her house. She instinctively feels for her mother's breasts, as a nervous child might do. Practical matters do not interest her, such as collecting spring vegetables in the field as girls of her age usually do to help the family. Her action sometimes appear to be driven by a fun-loving, somewhat immature, juvenile temperament. For instance, she simply disappears to the pond to feed fish without telling her maid, Hyangdan, who is in the meantime desperately looking for her missing mistress. Pak's Ch'unhyang emits the dual image of a free-spirited adolescent who is yet to be bridled by the patriarchal codes of conduct and a vulnerable child who needs strong parental protection.

The sexually attractive entertainer in Han's *Sŏng Ch'unhyang*

Han Sanghun's *Sŏng Ch'unhyang* stresses Ch'unhyang's image as a sexually appealing entertainer rather than as an obedient wife. The film's focus on Ch'unhyang's erotic aspect is clearly indicated when Pangja tells Ch'unhyang in the woods: 'It's you. You send your smell from under the skirt to prick his nostrils'. As is illustrated by this crude, insulting remark, the film is far less concerned with Ch'unhyang's chastity and self-restraint than with sensuality, which is demanded of her as a *kisaeng*.

One of the major signifiers of Ch'unhyang as the object of male sexual desire is the *kayagŭm*, a traditional string instrument. During the opening credit scenes, Ch'unhyang is seen in the background playing the *kayagŭm*. The instrument is traditionally played by a woman at men's drinking parties. Therefore, a *kisaeng* and the *kayagŭm* are closely associated through evocative eroticism. When Mongnyong jumps over the walls of Ch'unhyang's house, she is again seen playing the *kayagŭm*. Also when he promises to marry her, Wŏlmae brings in wine and summons her daughter to entertain him with music. In this 'first night' scene Ch'unhyang's *kayagŭm* performance is seamlessly followed by her undressing.

The *kayagŭm* is later identified with Ch'unhyang's body when Mongnyong revisits her room on his return from Seoul, by despairing at her imprisonment. The camera shows him entering

11   The night before their separation, Ch'unhyang plays the *kayagŭm*
for Mongnyong in her room: Han Sanghun's *Sŏng Ch'unhyang* (1987)

Ch'unhyang's empty room only to find her *kayagŭm*. Abandoned
and broken, the instrument symbolises Ch'unhyang's wretched
condition. In great dejection, Mongnyong caresses the *kayagŭm*
as if it were Ch'unhyang herself. The instrument is used in other
films, but none of them make such an explicit linkage between
the *kayagŭm* and Ch'unhyang's body as in Han's work. In Shin's
film, the instrument is only briefly shown. In Pak's, Ch'unhyang
never plays it. In the two North Korean films, Ch'unhyang plays
the *kayagŭm*, but the scenes focus on her musical ability.
Mongnyong is immersed in her music, showing deep respect for
her talent. Nor do these scenes include any wine drinking.

Unlike Shin's heroine, who forsakes earthly pleasures, Han's
heroine actively seeks them out. After the nuptial night scene,
the bride and groom go on a picnic enjoying their secret union.
This is quite different from Shin's rendition of the same sequence,
in which Ch'unhyang sews clothes beside Mongnyong who
studies for the state exam. In Pak's film, the night scene is
followed by their separation. In the North Korean film by Yu and
Yun, Ch'unhyang works on the morning after their first night
together.

Han also throws light on Ch'unhyang's self-assertiveness as a
social entertainer. She does not passively wait for his attention to
be drawn to her. Conscious of her sexual appeal to him, she takes
the initiative, leading him to promise marriage to her. When
married, Ch'unhyang does not adhere to the conventional norms

of the *yangban* wifehood as eagerly as Shin's heroine.

The effective use of space in Han's film strengthens the film's priority on Ch'unhyang's profile as an attractive entertainer. When Mongnyong visits her house, Wŏlmae first finds him in the garden. She then leads him to Ch'unhyang's room right away. In other films, Mongnyong is led to the entrance hall of the house, not further into Ch'unhyang's chamber. In Chosŏn society, an inner room is reserved for women only as their private space. Traditionally, men were not allowed to enter the inner quarters of a *yangban*'s house. They were designated as private and personal precisely because they were forbidden to male visitors. The rule of the space division in a house was strictly observed even between husband and wife. They were not supposed to share rooms but stayed in separate quarters in a residence.[18] In light of the spatial segregation rule of Confucian sexual ethics, Wŏlmae makes a highly unusual move in leading a man – virtually a stranger – to the inner room and serving wine. Without doubt, it is not an acceptable behaviour in this society. Wŏlmae's action suggests Ch'unhyang's low upbringing in the household of a *kisaeng*.

Ch'unhyang's images in the three South Korean films may appear to diverge from each other. But a close look at her imagery patterns reveals that they constitute different facets of an ideal female constructed in a male fantasy: a virtuous and yet sexually attractive woman with childlike vulnerability. This composite Ch'unhyang figure is wife, lover, sister and many others at the same time, who appeals to the male's erotic desire as well as his ego as provider and protector. This figure can turn contradictory attributes into complementary and compatible ones and embrace them all. The character Ch'unhyang is thus, remarkably adaptable to the male-centred gender dynamics. In this sense, the three films do no place it in the larger context of gender issues. In fact, they all tend to appropriate feminist concerns for their immediate commercial profits. Moreover, they avoid the subject of social class all together.

While the South Korean films tend to be concerned chiefly with sexuality and marriage, the North Korean adaptations centre Ch'unhyang's images on her class background. The two North Korean films interpret Ch'unhyang as the representative working-class woman whose foremost merit is her self-discipline and courage to challenge the 'contradictions' of the traditional class society.

The images of Ch'unhyang in North Korean films

The model worker in Yu and Yun's *The Tale of Ch'unhyang*

Ch'unhyang in Yu and Yun's *The Tale of Ch'unhyang* represents the working class. The film begins with the heroine diligently weaving a piece of cloth on a loom. This differs from the typical opening in which she appears in a colourful dress and in a leisurely mood. Yu and Yun's Ch'unhyang evokes an opposite image, wearing a plain dress and working hard in a shabby house. Before she goes out for the *Dano* festival,[19] she finishes a work order from her neighbours and prepares food for her mother. As soon as she returns from the festival, she resumes her work in the kitchen. Even after she becomes Mongnyong's wife, she does not stop earning money for her family.

This Ch'unhyang is burdened with the anxieties and difficulties of everyday life. In spite of the grim economic realities, however, her character is positively delineated with sincerity and industriousness. She is not the type of a girl who dreams of marrying a *yangban* man to escape the miserable life of the lower class. Yu and Yun's film stresses Ch'unhyang's strength to endure the contradiction of the traditional class society. Although she is a woman, Ch'unhyang takes up the role of the provider of her family. With the meagre sum of money her deceased father left to her and Wŏlmae, she looks after her mother with diligence and dedication as a son normally does. The underlying message here is that the important filial virtue is not to be monopolised exclusively by sons. Although deprived of the luxuries of upper-class life, Ch'unhyang makes every effort to partake in the community as a full and respectable member.

Interestingly, Ch'unhyang's role as a provider is not found in the original text of *Ch'unhyangjŏn*. The obvious purpose of inserting this new element in this film is to widen the economic gap between her and Mongnyong and thus to foreground the theme of the 'contradiction' of class society. The depiction of Ch'unhyang here epitomises the so-called 'modelling' theory adopted by North Korean film-makers, according to which a good socialist film should provide a role model for the audience.

Ch'unhyang's resolute image as a self-confident working woman is reinforced by the camera 'eye' that is not aligned with the male gaze as in Shin's *Sŏng Ch'unhyang*. Throughout the film, she stays outside the range of Mongnyong's voyeuristic curiosity. When he intensely stares at her on the bridge, she does not stop. She simply walks past him and then out of his field of vision. In other films she usually freezes on the spot until he comes very close to her. Her intrepid action in Yu and Yun's scene seems to be well co-ordinated with her speech: 'Ch'unhyang, Ch'unhyang is the fragrance of a flower, but it blossoms in a deep inner room. Although a spring wind blows, it never sends for the fragrance to the outside!'. Ch'unhyang sounds more determined here than in her speech in Shin's 1961 film in which she likens herself to 'a flower on the street waiting for a butterfly'.

The absence of coquettishness in Ch'unhyang's attitude toward Mongnyong is related to her unyielding class-consciousness against the 'structural contradiction' of the society. When Mongnyong tells her of his imminent departure, she criticises his double-faced nature, which is characteristic of the *yangban* class. More surprising than her reproach is her determination to cope with the evil of the class society on her own terms. As a symbolic gesture, she changes her maiden hairstyle into that of a married woman against the custom of the man doing it for his bride. She then serves Mongnyong wine for the first time. In this scene they pledge an oath to each other that they will not break the news of their marriage to the public. By doing this, she puts him to the test of whether he can keep his word and ally himself with her against the wrongful pressure of society, which is flawed. Ch'unhyang's action clearly insists that passivity and obedience should not be fostered as female virtues. Her action dispels any possible hint that her marriage can be used to help to scale the social ladder and secure a comfortable life. It presents Ch'unhyang's marital bond as no more than an effort to level the social classes.

Along with Ch'unhyang's political consciousness, Yu and Yun's film provides us with insights into the great value placed on chastity in North Korean sexual morality. However, what is rather odd in the film is that, while it sharply criticises the 'proper' gender relations as they are prescribed by Confucianism, it exalts the value of chastity. As an ideal working-class woman, Ch'unhyang appears to know how to control her sexual desire. Although she is in love with Mongnyong, she is never swayed by an impulse on the spur of the moment. To be convinced of his serious intention to marry her, she makes him visit her house three times. Although the same motif is used in Pak's *The Tale of Sŏng Ch'unhyang*, it is Wŏlmae in the South Korean film, not Ch'unhyang herself that demands the repeated visits. Moreover, in Yu and Yun's film, Mongnyong is never left alone with Ch'unhyang during his visits. Unless Wŏlmae calls in her daughter, he cannot see her. He is at most allowed to see her from the entrance hall of the house, while she sits rather remote behind a rattan screen in her own room.

The emphasis on chastity turns Ch'unhyang's room into a

12   This scene shows the strict spatial segregation between Ch'unhyang and Mongnyong. On the extreme left, she is playing the *kayagŭm* while he is sitting on the extreme right. Members of the house are symbolically positioned between them. Yu Wŏnjun and Yun Ryongsgyu's *The Tale of Ch'unghyang* (1980)

kind of invincible sacred place. It is symbol of her virginity. As such, her chamber connotes an antithetical meaning to the more common use of it as a hideout for the ill-fated lovers' sexual freedom. It is indeed surprising that Ch'unhyang maintains her virginity even after her secret marriage. Thus, she continues to wear her maiden hairstyle, a public symbol of her virginity, until the critical news of their separation breaks.[20] Ch'unhyang's maintenance of her innocence is also suggested by the precious present sent to her by a rich family as part of their formal proposal to their would-be daughter-in-law after Mongnyong's departure.

Ch'unhyang's pure and virginal image is reinforced by Yu and Yun's tendency to locate her and Mongnyong in an outdoor natural setting rather than confined in the closed space of her room. Throughout the film, Mongnyong is never with her in her room. Yu and Yun's purposeful outdoor shots strengthen Ch'un-hyang's austere chaste image. Her stroll with Mongnyong in the forest supports this interpretation. When Wŏlmae leaves Ch'un-hyang and Mongnyong, the camera shows them going out for a walk. The camera carefully follows their trail. During this sequence, they walk through the woods with a certain distance maintained between them. In other words, no physical contact takes place between them. The idea of two lovers in the forest usually conjures up a romantic scene, but here it ironically under-scores their unwavering platonic relationship. As they proceed deeply into the forest, the screen shows only a seasonal change from spring to autumn; the flowery field is replaced with faded leaves scattered all over by the wind. The passage of time does not alter their stoic attitudes.

In terms of the narrative sequence, Yu and Yun insert a unique series of scenes that do not exist in other adaptations. The scenes are placed between Ch'unhyang and Mongnyong's initial encounter in the marketplace and his first visit to her house. The South Korean films tend to link the two events closely, creating an impression that they spend their first night together on the same day they meet, although Wŏlmae and Mongnyong's dialogues sometimes hint that an interval of several days exists between the two incidents. Yu and Yun's film, however, sets an extended period of time in between them. During this time, Mongnyong, full of desire to see her, cannot concentrate on reading. Contrasted with a restless Mongnyong, Ch'unhyang continues to work industriously with great deter-mination. Their self-restraint is relaxed only when Wŏlmae gives her final consent to their relationship.

The excessive emphasis on class issues results in various problems in this film. One of the serious flaws is the total removal of sexuality from its discussion of gender relations. The film certainly advocates a woman's right to be a full-fledged, pro-ductive member of society and control her own destiny. While criticising the denial of this right in feudal Korean society, the film selectively recycles its patriarchal values. One of the past legacies this film inherits is the extremely repressive sexual morality inculcated by Confucianism, which is not only unreal-istic but tantamount to moral hypocrisy. By promoting Ch'un-hyang's image as a worker, and, at the same time, denying her basic humanity, this film severely distorts the beauty and power of the original folk tale, which presents sexuality as the healthy and true basis of a marital bond. Ch'unhyang in the original text perceives her sexual engagement with Mongnyong as a form of commitment, which is as sacred and biding as a formal marriage.

The virtuous and class-conscious wife in Shin's *Love, Love, My Love*

Love, Love, My Love directed by Shin Sangok during his enforced stay in North Korea is another case of blending traditional Confucian with contemporary socialist ideologies. However, the tension between the two ideological forces is not successfully resolved in a dialectical fashion, and is thus less interesting in aesthetic terms than Yu and Yun's film. As a consequence, the film occasionally suffers from inconsistency in characterisation and theme. The competition between traditional and socialist perspectives concurring in Ch'unhyang's actions is clearly felt in the clashing images of the heroine as a *kisaeng* and simultaneously as the virtuous wife of a *yangban* man.

This film made in North Korea, interjecting the theme of class, is manifest from the outset, which takes place quite unconventionally near monuments that were erected to commemorate the benevolence of former magistrates, unlike many other adaptations. The camera focuses on Ch'unhyang standing before a monument that commemorates her deceased father, reciting a eulogy for his virtuous deeds. This supposedly peaceful scene, however, is full of tension: Hyangdan watches out for any possible passerby while her mistress bows before the monument. The uneasiness springs from the societal rule that decrees that Ch'unhyang, a *kisaeng* by her social class, is not allowed to visit the father's monument and publicly bow before it. Therefore, she has to hide herself at the slightest noise. This opening scene instantly lays out the major theme of the film: the absurdity of the traditional class system that denies Ch'unhyang the *yangban* status despite her father's belonging to the class. It is by this monument that Ch'unhyang meets Mongnyong for the first time. The theme of the problematic social hierarchy and Ch'unhyang's class-consciousness is brought to the fore later in the separation scene. As he leaves her, she attacks Mongnyong for his decision to obey his father, which, she claims, is based on both the 'contradiction' of the class barrier and the double-faced moral stance of the ruling class. Ch'unhyang's castigation of Mongnyong is carried out in the socialist rhetoric of denouncing the class distinction of the traditional society.

Shin's film, however, vacillates between the old Confucian and the present socialist frames of morality. Shin attempts to adorn Ch'unhyang's character with the familiar patriarchal wifehood as in his 1961 *Sŏng Ch'unhyang*. She is as shy and obedient as her South Korean counterpart. The self-sacrificing tendency has also returned. In the prison scene, she refuses to write to Mongnyong for help in spite of Wŏlmae and Pangja's

13   Myongnyong returns to rescue Ch'unhyang from her execution:
Shin Sangok's *Love, Love, My Love* (1985)

repeated imploring. She adamantly chooses to suffer rather than
to disturb his study with the startling news of her imprisonment.
Ironically, the motif of Ch'unhyang's self-sacrifice is more prominent in the North Korean version than the South Korean once.

A major drawback in Shin's portrayal of Ch'unhyang is his
oscillation between the image of a refined *yangban* wife and that
of a lowly *kisaeng*. As a contrast to Ch'unhyang's virtuous wife
side, Shin introduces her unexpectedly tolerant attitude toward
sexual morality. The pendulum of Shin's characterisation swings
back to Ch'unhyang's lowly '*kisaeng*' side, showing her engaged
in sex with Mongnyong the day of their first encounter. A sense
of discrepancy is created in the audience between her demure-
ness and audacity. Shin's depiction of Ch'unhyang's uninhibited
liberal response to Mongnyong's romantic temptation is the antithesis of her stolid attitude in Yu and Yun's film. Contrasted with
Yu and Yun's insistence on Ch'unhyang's virginity, even past her
marriage, Shin's openness about her sexual initiation can be interpreted as a gesture of rejecting the conventional Confucian ethics.

Considering that North Korea is known for its extreme gender
segregation, Ch'unhyang's sexual morality may not, at first
glance, appear to match the actual social reality. The majority of
the films about Ch'unhyang, including the other North Korean

work by Yu and Yun tend to describe the heroine's chastity and dignity, qualities associated with the nobility, which could be seen as the residue of the past class society reinforced by traditional Confucian ethics. Therefore, Ch'unhyang's daring premarital sex in Shin's film is a blatant violation of audience expectation. On the other hand, it can be read as an indication of a certain degree of flexibility that may exist in the North Korean government's policy on sexual morality, contrary to its alleged rigid approach. Even though the primary intent of the film lies in exposing the hypocritical Confucian standards for female sexuality, the problem of internal contradiction in Ch'unhyang's portrayal, on the whole, is not satisfactorily resolved in this film.

Ch'unhyang and patriarchal gender relations in Korean society

According to Ch'unhyang's images in these films, what defines male–female relations in both South and North Korea is still rooted in traditional Confucian ethics, which succour differential treatments of men and women. In Chosŏn society, gender distinction was maintained through the enforcement of an absolute hierarchy between men and women. All of the five films touch on the established gender relation in terms of domination and subordination. On the surface, the films recognise the problems of the unequal status between men and women, but at a deeper level, they insist directly or indirectly on the continuous primacy and even necessity of the old Confucian gender distinction in shaping contemporary Korean cultural identity. Their supportive view of the traditional family values can be reiterated in two specific aspects: marriage and sexuality.

As stressed in all the films, marriage is the only legitimate form of relationship allowed between men and women in traditional society. The premise of marriage, however, is possible only by parental approval. This restriction accounts for the enormous attention each pays to defining the precise nature of Ch'unhyang's relationship to Mongnyong. Married, a couple achieves a social status as mandated by the family-centred value system of the community. Among various roles expected of adult Koreans, those of parents have the supreme bearings on their community life and thus are protected by society. Men and women can participate in their community on a full scale only when they are married and undertake parental responsibilities. This means that only through marriage can men and women move to the next stage of their social identity with due authority and power accompanying them.

The Confucian patriarchal structure of traditional Korean

society honours male superiority in the domestic order. Accordingly, a conjugal relationship stands firmly on the husband's authority over his wife. Female submission was required in family life. The frequent idealised references to Ch'unhyang's self-sacrifice for Mongnyong testify to such gender-specific power distribution in the family-centred Confucian value system. The cult of female chastity derives from the same notion of men's right to control and own women. Although fidelity and respect are claimed to be the ethical foundation of a marital bond, these morals are not equally applied to husband and wife. For women, a violation of the prescribed 'virtues' can lead to a tragic situation, because their social existence is conceived only in terms of daughter, wife and mother; never as a lover unless the individual belongs to the *kisaeng* class. Given the inflated rhetoric of chastity and obedience, women's pre- or extramarital affairs pose a serious threat to the patriarchal system as well as to individuals' lives. This is why Ch'unhyang's 'first night' emerges as one of the most sensitive and controversial areas of interpretation in these films.

The principal function of marriage in traditional society is to secure the succession of a family line. A married couple's sexual life, therefore, always remains taboo in public discourse. It is simply not discussed and should be left to the privacy of the couple within the sacred boundaries of their conjugal life. The general tendency to omit the explicit scenes of Ch'unhyang and Mongnyong's consummation comes from an idea deeply ingrained in the Confucian ethical codes that sexual matters between a husband and a wife cannot be opened to an outsider. Despite the occasionally provocative scenes of Ch'unhyang's sensual beauty, the films in general observe the Confucian interdiction on marital sex.

Although marriage is virtually an exclusive channel for fulfilling sexuality in the traditional society, sexuality itself and other related subjects like romance and eroticism are left ambiguous and unexplained in Confucian discourse. For women in particular, sexuality is considered no more than part of the reproduction mechanism. The elimination of erotic scenes in the films is in keeping with the deprived opportunity of contemporary Koreans in reality to express their sexuality. By simply espousing the murky, repressive attitude to sexual morality, the films reinforce conservative family values. The absence of the visual representation of Ch'unhyang and Mongnyong's sexual relationship inculcates respect for their inviolable right as a married couple. In Korean film language, such a didactic message is translated into turning off the light in Ch'unhyang's room. In this suggestive scene, the audience is at best allowed to peep through a hole in the paper window of the room from the perspective of the mischievous servant, Pangja.

In relation to Confucian sexual morality, mention should be made of the social function of the *kisaeng*, another significant factor in discussing gender issues in *Ch'unhyangjŏn*. A *kisaeng* was classified as a state-owned slave during the Chosŏn Dynasty. Therefore, from a strictly legal point of view, Ch'unhyang's refusal to serve the new magistrate cannot be justified because she is identified as a *kisaeng* in terms of social class, and furthermore, her marital status is not clear to the public.[21] As an entertainer serving men at their drinking banquets, *kisaeng* were, in a sense, exempt from the established norms of sexual morality. The *kisaeng* class, with its relative licence from various moralistic social constraint, compensated for men's unfulfilled sexual desire in their marriage. The cult of virtuous wifehood put down women in this occupation, who, at the same time, could not be held up as 'immoral' due to society's double standards for sexual freedom. The impregnable male dominance in gender relations integrated the *kisaeng* class into society's moral fibre.

In principle, Confucian ethics teach both men and women to restrict erotic desire to conjugal life. In actuality, however, men were given an additional institutional outlet for their repressed sexual fantasies. Thus men could escape from the rigidly codified sexual morals and enjoy an extramarital relationship, openly in most cases. A tacit acceptance of this hypocrisy is found in the South Korean films, which do not present Mongnyong's affair with a *kisaeng* as a fatal hindrance to getting a government position. They implicitly acknowledge that once he passes the state exam and becomes a state official, his controversial relationship with Ch'unhyang will be legitimised. Women's obedience and chastity were cultivated and exploited as stabilising in the patriarchal gender politics. Such a fundamental contradiction in traditional sexual morality induces the differing images of Ch'unhyang and the interpretative variance among the contemporary adaptations of the tale.

On the whole, both North and South Korean cinemas take a positive stance toward the traditional womanhood epitomised by Ch'unhyang. Yet minor variations exist within each cinematic tradition in handling gender issues. Seen in the chronological order of production, the three South Korean films reflect society's increasing tolerance toward sexuality. Shin's 1961 film is more faithful to the conservative morals of the original story than the later adaptations by Pak and Han. At its release, it was rated permissible viewing for 'an underage audience' although it contained the motifs of the young couple's secret marriage without parental consent and of their nuptial bed. Shin's treatment of the latter motif relied on the old Korean custom of village women peeking into the nuptial chamber through the holes in the door. In Shin's film old women are replaced with Pangja. Compared with Shin's film, Pak's 1976 adaptation contains more suggestive scenes, including the shots of Ch'unhyang in her underwear and the extreme close-ups of her sensuous lips and seductive neck. Despite these scenes, Pak's film was available to audiences of all ages. With regard to Han's film, it cannot be said that his rendition dramatically departs from Shin's film in that both suppress Ch'unhyang and Mongnyong's 'first night' motif. However, Han's film more blatantly presents the heroine as the object of male sexual desire. These small changes, in a sense, confirm the gradual acceptance of sexuality as subject-matter for public discussion domain in South Korean society.

Han's film, which highlights Ch'unhyang's erotic *kisaeng* image, may appear to counter my argument that the contemporary Korean films favourably recast the traditional ideas of marriage and sexuality. Contrary to its seemingly liberal outlook, however, the film still holds true to the old Confucian dictum that sexual matters of a married couple should not be subject to outsiders' eyes. Han may take a more open-minded approach to the subject of sexuality at a conceptual level, but his camera-work turns out to conform to the old, familiar pattern that eroticism should not be visually presented. If there are sexually charged scenes, they are all related to the perverse-minded new magistrate. In this respect, all three South Korean films repeat what is essentially the same message, that marriage is the only means through which women can secure their privacy and dignity.

The two North Korean films seem to approach the subject of gender relations in *Ch'unhyangjŏn* differently from each other. As noted earlier, Yu and Yun's film praises Ch'unhyang's chastity with an austere tone, but Shin's work discards the traditional proscription about premarital sex. In a way, their polemic messages betray the existence of conflicting views within North Korean society concerning sexual morality. Yu and Yun, and Shin have different attitudes toward the traditional patriarchal gender relations. Despite their opposite approaches to sexuality, however, the two films commonly use Ch'unhyang as a mouthpiece for criticising the hypocrisy of the traditional institution of marriage. As will be demonstrated in the following section, they both attempt to identify Ch'unhyang's problem as an issue of class, rather than gender.

Class and traditional family values in *Ch'unhyangjŏn*

The key motif of *Ch'unhyangjŏn* is the low-born heroine's inter-class marriage to the *yangban* man. The volatile subject of class barrier amplifies the story's dramatic effect, and Ch'unhyang's ultimate overcoming of the barrier is considered the most inspiring element of the narrative. The five films investigated in this chapter all agree that Ch'unhyang and Mongnyong's marriage is an extraordinary challenge to the legitimacy of the traditional social hierarchy.

There is, however, a difference between the North and the South Korean films with regard to the specific thematic use of the marriage motif. The former group regards Ch'unhyang and Mongnyong's union as the premium instrument to expose the class conflicts between the ruling and the ruled and indict the structural contradiction of the Chosŏn Dynasty. Yet the latter group tends to avoid overgeneralising the traditional social order into the simplified dichotomy of the exploiting and the exploited classes. The North Korean films directly define Ch'unhyang and Mongnyong's problem as caused by the class conflicts. In other words, they attempt to connect the fictional world with the ideological needs of their present society. In contrast, the South Korean films ascribe the central conflict of the story to individual character traits rather than to collective class issues.

The North Korean films effectively use language and space to dramatise the opposition between the ruling and the ruled classes in traditional society. To accentuate the extent of the gap between them, the films assign distinct registers of language to Mongnyong and Wŏlmae, which clearly demarcate their social standing. To understand the outcome of this linguistic device, it should be noted that the Korean language has acutely developed registers of language. The choice of an appropriate speech level in a conversation depends upon a variety of factors, such as age, social position, degree of intimacy, speech situation, and so on. Among them, seniority and social position are usually considered the most influential criteria. In view of this, Wŏlmae and Mongnyong's dialogue poses an awkward dilemma, because Wŏlmae is lower than Mongnyong in social status, yet as his mother-in-law, she is higher than him in terms of the Confucian kinship system. From a socio-linguistic perspective, theirs is a complicated situation. In general, seniority overrides status in such a situation. South Korean films follow this general rule of register: Wŏlmae lowers her register from polite and formal to lower and intimate after her daughter's marriage to Mongnyong. Once he enters her family circle, she in fact addresses him more or less in the same style as she uses for her daughter. However, the North Korean films keep Wŏlmae's speech in the polite register, generating an impression that the class barrier between them is too high to eliminate. Her continuous use of the polite register toward her son-in-law, who in Korean culture, is fairly close to his mother-in-law, reflects the psychological and social distance she feels about Mongnyong, and vice versa.

The North Korean directors also organise film space between the protagonists and villagers as a means to direct the audience's attention to the theme of class solidarity. Ch'unhyang and Mongnyong are often shown surrounded by groups of commoners. The couple's spatial proximity to the masses alludes to their intimate social bond. Yu and Yun's film attempts to capture Ch'unhyang actively involved with her neighbours. She mingles with them, earning her livelihood from their work orders. Never alienating herself from the community, Ch'unhyang in Yu and Yun's film differs from her Southern counterpart who is generally removed from others. To highlight her popular image, Yu and Yun interject several scenes of the masses into the film. For example, when Ch'unhyang is summoned by the new magistrate, the camera cuts to the villagers who, enraged by the incident, vehemently criticise the magistrate. The camera then shows them following her to the magistrate's office. When she is finally put in jail, they meet again, expressing their fears about her future.

The South Korean films are not particularly interested in such mass scenes. Ch'unhyang is usually shown alone or with Mongnyong; rarely amidst the crowds, Ch'unhyang and Mongnyong's physical isolation from the public suits the tendency of the South Korean films to characterise the couple's troubles essentially as private, not communal. Ch'unhyang is always shown as resigned to the enclosure of her room. The only exception to this pattern is the brief opening scene in Shin's film where Ch'unhyang walks around the crowded open market. By detaching her from other people, the South Korean films turn her ordeal into an entirely personal matter. Similarly, Mongnyong rarely comes into direct contact with the local people. As a consequence, their love story stays aloof from the everyday concerns of the general public.

The films from the South attribute Ch'unhyang's suffering to social injustice whereas those from the North blame the fundamental structural contradiction of the class society. The South does not condemn the entire *yangban* class for Ch'unhyang's hardship. Instead, they point to the moral depravity of a particular individual – the new magistrate – as the cause of the problem. The South Korean films portray the ruling class as a mixed group with the good and the bad just as any other classes. They show that the upper class has respectable members like Mongnyong's father, whose rule as a magistrate was reportedly fair and generous. Villagers also say that during his administration there were no crimes or wrongdoing committed against the poor and powerless. But the new magistrate is the very opposite of Mongnyong's father, and the villagers hold this corrupt official responsible for their miseries. Their anger and grievance are, therefore, not targeted at the *yangban* class as a whole but at certain individual members of the group. Representing the venerable and morally sound mind of the *yangban* class, Mongnyong's father sheds contrastive light on the new magistrate's villainy and cruelty.

Kim *Chinsa* in Pak's *The Tale of Sŏng Ch'unhyang* is another good *yangban* man.[22] His is a character invented by Pak who does not exist in the source tale. Kim *Chinsa*'s role in the film is to plead to the new, vicious magistrate to rule the village with benevolence. He reprimands the magistrate's materialistic attitude and defends Ch'unhyang's tenacious resistance to his temptation and coercion as a virtuous act because it attests to her fidelity to her husband. As is corroborated by the confrontation between the two *yangban* men in the scene, the South Korean films generally argue that conflicts do not necessarily exist between the different classes, but that they can arise even within the ruling class. They further suggest that the relationship between the upper and the lower classes fluctuates with the times and with the different individuals. In other words, discord and friction between the classes are transitory, and when the villagers have a fair and benevolent magistrate, they will enjoy a peaceful life. From this point of view, Ch'unhyang is an unfortunate victim of the new magistrate's crude vulgarity.

Ironically, the flexible, individualistic approach taken by the South Korean film-makers enables them to evade subtly or displace serious socio-political problems raised by the story. For instance, by inventing such a character as Kim *Chinsa* that embodies the caring and conscientious side of the *yangban* class, the film in fact appropriates the voices of women, peasants and many other commoners who could have delivered their own testimonies directly to the audience against the social ills caused by the privileged class. By setting up a *yangban* man as a spokesperson of the oppressed minority against another member of his class, the film reduces the potentially multi-vocal narrative to a monological, self-enclosed text.

The familial rhetoric at the crux of the Confucian ethics also helps the South Korean films to divert attention from the class conflicts. The films use the traditional family values to promote the king's authority to stop the abuse of power by the *yangban* class. At the closure of *Ch'unhyangjŏn*, the heroine's ordeal is ended, and the villain is punished in the name of the king, the ultimate father figure of the people. Confucianism conceives society as a gigantic, extended family network with a king as its head. Every member of the society is expected to respect and obey the king as children would do their father. Hence the emphasis on harmonious family ties contributes to the sustenance of the existing social order. The South Korean films draw various strategies from the Confucian patriarchal rhetoric to suppress potentially subversive elements in Ch'unhyang's tale. They obfuscate some of the most sensitive and topical issues to the contemporary audience, including among others, the male-dictated order, domestic as well as social, the hypocritical double standards for *kisaeng* and the self-righteousness of the ruling class.

In comparison to the South Korean films, the North Korean works are explicit in their view of the traditional social structure. It is composed only of two classes: the exploiting and the exploited. Ch'unhyang's problem epitomises the unavoidable conflict between the two classes. In the North Korean films, the exploiting *yangban* class is represented by the new magistrate. Yu and Yun's film portrays him not only as turning deaf ears to the peasants' woes but also as maliciously scheming to extort more tax from them. He mixes sand and straw in the crops which the peasants have already paid as tax, and then falsely charges them with tax evasion. The magistrate's abuse of power and exploitation of the lower-class people ranges from such undue taxation to unjustified property confiscation from those who are opposed to his tyranny. His brutality is repeated in Shin's film, identified as a typical characteristic of the *yangban* class. The new magistrate in Shin's work is furthermore, a pleasure-seeking sadistic pervert. Throwing an endless number of banquets with numerous *kisaeng* girls, he indulges in a thoroughly decadent life, totally indifferent to the villagers' miseries. Yu and Yun's and Shin's films commonly point out materialistic greed and moral debauchery as the essence of the *yangban* class, which deserves retribution from the exploited masses. Mongnyong's father in these films is opposed to his son's marriage to Ch'unhyang because it will deprive his family of all the privileges, including their properties and government positions. The *yangban*'s repulsive portrayal is believed to enhance class-consciousness among the exploited in their effort to realise a classless society.

The class struggle is further encouraged as a historical imperative by the North Korean films through the scenes of the masses who, after enduring the magistrate's misrule for a long time, finally prepare for a showdown with their exploiters. As mentioned earlier, this type of politically charged mass scene is not found in the South Korean films. In the North Korean adaptations, Mongnyong, now appointed as a secret royal inspector, witnesses various signs of an imminent peasant uprising at the outset of his journey back to his hometown. There are similar scenes in the South Korean films, but they contain only a handful of people, not large crowds as in the North Korean versions. Mongnyong in the North Korean scenes is impressed by the ordinary peasants who openly and courageously denounce the class distinction. While the South Korean films describe Mongnyong as an officer who is recruited by the state and thus, carries out his duties as instructed, the North Korean versions elevate him as a leader of the oppressed populace, who anxiously wait for his return to realise their will to level the class division. Mongnyong, in the former case, is no more than a messenger dispatched by the king, but Mongnyong in the latter takes on a messianic air as one who punishes the corrupt local bureaucrats and restores order in the community. Without doubt, Mongnyong's image in the North Korean films reflects and at the same time, encourages the audience's revolutionary spirit. To exalt Mongnyong's heroic image, the North Korean films even mystify the character. His long absence from the screen in the mid-section of the film makes his homecoming all the more dramatic and longed for. In the South Korean films he is occasionally shown preparing for the exam; thus his return has no such mysterious and dramatic impact.

Mongnyong's uplifting image as a long-awaited liberator and comrade ultimately develops into that of a great father figure. As in the South Korean films, the North Korean film-makers employ the patriarchal rhetoric and the notion of filial piety. The positive images of fatherhood recur throughout the two North Korean films. Given the present socio-political reality of North Korea, it cannot be denied that the filmic image of the great father figure is closely bound up with the cult of Kim Il Sung and his son Kim Jong Il's hereditary leadership. While rejecting any historical continuity of their current 'classless' society to the past patriarchal class structure, the North Korean films constantly remind the audience of a visionary paternal figure and the masses' filial obedience to him.

This chapter examines gender and class, two pivotal factors in the Korean people's cultural identity, through the cinematic portrayal of Ch'unhyang. The folk tale *Ch'unhyangjŏn* raises several key questions about traditional sexual morality and class relations. What emerges from my film analysis is the time-honoured importance of the Confucian family values in Korean cultural identity, which overrides the shifting ruling ideologies of the states. Traditional family values still exercise crucial influence on how Koreans perceive themselves in the contemporary period when their society is ideologically split into capitalist South and communist North. The Confucian paradigm nurtures a hierarchical order in conjugal, domestic and communal lives of contemporary Koreans. Korean women, nowadays, may not wholeheartedly embrace the idolisation of a virtuous wife, as is illustrated by the teenager-like Ch'unhyang figure in Pak's film, or the sexually attractive Ch'unhyang figure in Han's film. Notwithstanding this, the basic perception of women's place in society and their role in contemporary Korean culture has been shaped largely by the patriarchal social order and the family-centred moral codes.

Even the North Korean films, with their socialist perspectives, echo the female virtues defined in terms of the old Confucian gender hierarchy, paying homage to Ch'unhyang's perseverance, abstinence and fidelity. Ch'unhyang in the North Korean films is a figure of dual nature as a respectable wife and a representative worker. Her wifely characteristics derive from the traditional ideal womanhood, whereas her working-class traits reflect contemporary Korean woman's role as expected in the communist society.

The treatment of class issues in the films are also closely related to the old family values. The concept of filial piety, which lies at the core of the patriarchal value system, is persistently used by both South and North Korean film-makers. Demanding unconditional submission to paternal authority, the notion of filial piety is useful in explaining the contemporary as well as the traditional social ethics observed by the Korean people. Ch'unhyang is forced to sacrifice her own marital bliss lest her selfishness should obstruct her husband's filial duty to his father. The couple's decision not only saves the face of the *yangban* family but also prevents a possible disruption of the established order of the society.

At the same time, however, it is noteworthy that South and North Korean films approach the overall subject of social class from their present viewpoints. The former is bent on individualism, and the latter on collective class interests. While the South Korean films interpret Ch'unhyang's inter-class marriage as a laudable achievement of the courageous individual, the North Korean works read it as an ultimate victory of the exploited people over the intrinsic contradiction of class society. Hence, the specific use of the concept of filial piety differs between the two groups of films. In the South Korean works, it is intended to conceal the tension between the classes, whereas in the North Korean films it is meant to intensify their antagonism.

The five Ch'unhyang films examined in this chapter project varying images of contemporary Koreans. Their changing assessment of the traditional values is clearly reflected in the ways they reconstruct the folk material handed down from past society. Their differences expose the conflict in contemporary Koreans' views of their society and culture at the present moment. While this chapter covers gender and class in film adaptations of *Ch'unhyangjŏn*, the next chapter concentrates on nationality, another critical element in shaping Korean identity in the latter half of the twentieth century.

Notes

1 To avoid confusion between the folk tale *Ch'unhyangjŏn* and its cinematic adaptations, the original source is referred to as *Ch'unhyangjŏn* and its adaptation as *The Tale of Ch'unhyang*.

2 Although there were foureen films made on the basis of *Ch'unhyangjŏn*, most of the prints, especially earlier ones, have been lost. This explains the small number of films available to contemporary viewers and critics.

3 Norman K. Denzin, *Images of Postmodern Society: Social Theory and Contemporary Cinema* (London, Sage Publications, 1991), pp. ix–xii. Among these factors, race and ethnicity do not seem to be applicable to the contemporary Korean society since no differences exist in the ethnic composition between the South and the North.

4 Chosŏn is the last dynasty in Korean history and the longest-lived in world history. It was established in 1392 and was ended in 1910 by the Japanese colonisation.

5 Sŏl Sŏnggyŏng, *Ch'unhyangjŏn-ŭi Hyŏngsŏng-gwa Kyet'ong* (The Development and Classification of *Ch'unhyangjŏn*) (Seoul, Chŏngŭmsa, 1986), pp. 9–35.

6 There are several versions of this story and minor details vary among them. According to one version, she killed herself because she could not marry. Another version says she was love-sick and died after seeing the son of a *yangban* family. And yet, it is also said that after having an affair with the son of a *yangban* family, she tried to maintain her chastity for him when he had already left her. In this version, she was killed by a new local magistrate who forced her to serve him.

7 Kim Dong-Uk, *Ch'unhyangjŏn Yŏn'gu* (A Study of *Ch'unhyangjŏn*) (Seoul, Yonsei University Press, 1985), pp. 5–68.

8 Cho Yunje, *Ch'unhyangjŏn* (The Tale of Ch'unhyang) (Seoul, Ŭlyumunhwasa, 1983), p. 166. Ch'unhyang's social class is one of the ambiguous elements of the narrative. According to studies on the origin of the tale, she is described as a 'low-born girl', 'young *kisaeng*', and 'daughter of a retired *kisaeng*'.

9 Yu Ch'ijin, '*Ch'unhyangjŏn* kaksaek-e kwanhayŏ' ('On adapting

Ch'unhyangjŏn'), in Ch'oe Ch'ŏl and Sŏl Sŏnggyŏng (eds), *Sŏlhwa, Sosŏl-ŭi Yŏn'gu* (A Study of the Myth and the Novel) (Seoul, Chŏng-ŭmsa, 1984), pp. 205–7; Chŏn Kwangyŏng, *Shin Sosŏl Yŏn'gu* (A Study of the New Novel) (Seoul, Saemunsa, 1986), p. 170; and Kim Ch'unt'aek, *Urinara Kojŏn Sosŏlsa* (A History of Korean Classical Narratives) (Seoul, Han'gilsa, 1993), pp. 352–67.

10 Kim Dong-Uk, A Study of *Ch'unhyangjŏn*, pp. 363–77.

11 Kim Sunam, 'A study of Yun', p. 57.

12 Kim Sunam, '*Mise-en-scène* yŏnghwa-ŭi taega, Shin Sangok' ('Shin Sangok Shin, the master of *mise-en-scène*'), in *A Study of Korean Film Directors*, p. 222.

13 Made in the same decade, Shin's 1961 *Sŏng Ch'unhyang* and Yun's work would have been interesting material for a comparative study.

14 The most important Confucian tenet defining women's status in traditional society is 'three ways of obedience': 'Follow your parents in youth, follow your husband in marriage and follow your children in old age'.

15 The concept of the domination of the male gaze was first proposed by Laura Mulvey. See Laura Mulvey, 'Visual pleasure and narrative cinema', *Screen*, 16:3 (1975), 6–18. For further detail of recent debate on this concept, see Linda Williams (ed.), *Viewing Position: Ways of Seeing Film* (New Brunswick, Rutgers University Press, 1994); and *The Sexual Subject: A Screen Reader in Sexuality* (London, Roultedge, 1992).

16 Han Sanghun introduces it only once when Ch'unhyang's mother mentions her strange dream. In Shin's *Love, Love, My Love*, the fortune-teller appears in both the market and the prison scenes, but the film does not use Wŏlmae's dream in this scene. Pak's, and Yu and Yun's versions have no supernatural motifs.

17 The Confucian ethics lays out seven grounds for divorce, which are commonly called 'seven evils': disobedience to her parents-in-law, inability to have children, adultery, jealousy, hereditary disease, verboseness, and stealing. It should be also noted that a woman cannot ask for divorce under any circumstances.

18 The gender segregation in terms of space division produced such principles as: 'Men and women cannot sit in the same place from the age of seven'.

19 *Dano* is a festival held on 5 May on the lunar calendar to celebrate spring.

20 In other films, her hairstyle is changed ritualistically in her nuptial bed in keeping with wedding ceremony traditions.

21 In this sense, the effort to identify her as a noblewoman may be unrealistic.

22 '*Chinsa*' is a title given to a person in the Chosŏn Dynasty who has passed only the primary state examination.

3 Nationhood and the cinematic representation of history

Who is responsible for the national division of Korea? This is the central question for contemporary Koreans in defining their identity as a nation. Contemporary Koreans have a strong sense of nationhood since the peninsula had been ruled by a single polity since being unified in 668 by Shilla, one of the three ancient Korean kingdoms.[1] Moreover, the boundaries of this single polity coincided with the linguistic and cultural homogeneity of the people, regardless of how individual Koreans of different class or status actually identified themselves in different historical periods. Koreans' firm belief in their single nationhood was, however, destroyed by the military partition of the North and the South at the end of the Second World War, according to the agreement signed by the Allies. As a consequence, two states emerged in one country during the USA–Soviet occupation period (1945–48). The ideological confrontation between the communist North and capitalist South finally led to war in 1950, which lasted for three years until 1953.

The division of the country as stipulated by the Allies at the Cairo Summit in 1943, became a part of the post-war global politics, even before the end of Japanese colonial rule. The primary concerns of the superpowers at the summit were to secure their own national interests in Korea under the circumstance of the power vacuum brought about by the Japanese withdrawal from the peninsula. Therefore, as the Yalta meeting in 1945 confirmed, the division of Korea came about through the occupation of the USA and the former USSR, but history was to prove that the peninsular became the first and the most significant testing ground of the Cold War.

The repercussions of this traumatic conflict would continue up to the present day.

The Soviet and US military occupation following the division entirely undermined Korean efforts to restore independence to the country. The nationalistic movements of Korea against Japanese imperialism failed to yield a significant unity for the future of the newly liberated country. Prior to the end of Japanese occupation, the divisions between the political left and right were evident. The post-war global politics further polarised the ideological conflicts between Koreans. However, despite the opposing ideologies, there was a clear consensus among the nationalists or political groups: they shared a strong belief that the most urgent task for the country was to establish an independent nation-state. The foundations of the Committee for the Preparation of Korean Independence, and the People's Republic of Korea shortly after the liberation, well evince the common goal of the people and the alliance between the left and right political groups, contesting the continued intervention of foreign powers. They formed numerous nationwide political organisations including the People's Committees, furnishing the organisational base for the People's Republic of Korea. However, they realised that all their efforts were in vain when the military occupation authorities refused it as a legitimate government. From this point of view, the military demarcation line along with the 38th parallel served to transform the ideological conflicts among the various spectrums of socio-political groups into a proxy war between the two states supported by foreign military forces in five years.

The Korean War was the most decisive turning point in modern Korean history. It was initiated by Kim Il Sung, yet the counter-attack by the United Nations' forces led by the USA, and the intervention of China altered its nature from a civil to an international war. However, as outlined above, the enormous importance and implications of the war for Korean society and the international community surpasses the facts of the war's three-year development. First of all, the origins of the war and its lasting consequences in contemporary Korean society should be examined in the continuity of the colonial and post-colonial experiences of the people. Along with the internal power struggles and the relentless desire for unification, the disputes between the North and South on the issues of class and the vestiges of Japanese colonial rule were decisive factors in causing the war. Consequently, the war was used by both regimes in the North and South to eliminate their political enemies and strengthen their political bases. They also implemented anti-imperialist or anti-communist policies as their respective state ideologies.

Second, the political complexity and ambiguities of the war for the international community need to be understood in light of the geopolitical, strategic significance of the peninsula to the particular foreign countries involved in the conflict of Korea. The opening of national archives in the USA, Britain and the Commonwealth in the 1980s, and in the former Soviet and the People's Republic of China in the late 1990s attests a vital role of the Korean War in the Cold War world politics. Furthermore, it tends to testify that foreign involvement in modern Korean history was to greatly affect social, political and economic developments in both North and South Korea under such authoritarian or totalitarian states for the next four decades.

This chapter examines the notion of nationhood held by contemporary Koreans from two interrelated perspectives, political and cultural. Until the national division in 1945, Korea had maintained both political and cultural unity for over thirteen centuries. This historical continuity contributed to consolidating a sense of oneness as a nation among the Korean people. The recent national division, therefore, resulted in enormous confusion and conflicts among them. What is to be noted about the experience of partition is that the majority of Koreans, both South and North, perceive the conflict as political. In other words, their fundamental cultural unity has not been questioned even after the division. The role of culture as a sustaining force of nationhood in the politically divided country is well elucidated by Andrew Heywood, who defines nation essentially as 'cultural entity, a collection of people bound together by shared values and tradition, for example, a common language, religion and history, and usually occupying the same geographical area'.[2] In contrast, the term 'state' indicates a 'political association, which enjoys sovereignty, supreme or unrestricted power, within defined territorial borders'.[3] Heywood's distinction between nation and state illuminates contemporary Korea, which has not lost its cultural homogeneity. The significance of the shared cultural root in Koreans' self-identity accounts for the common aspiration and determination between North and South Korea to restore their 'nation-state', although they disagree on the specific methods of unification.

Post-war Korean cinema is a cultural text that vividly exposes the coexistence of political discontinuity and cultural continuity in contemporary Koreans' perception of their nationhood. The conflicting self-identities between communist North and capitalist South are handled most acutely in the films about the

Japanese colonial period and the Korean War. Colonialism and war provide intense occasions in which the idea of nationhood manifests itself. As Heywood points out, the creation of a nation-state is closely related to liberation from foreign domination and achieving control over one's country.[4] The significance of war in establishing nationalism or nationhood is well explained by Michael Howard: 'in nation-building as in revolution, force was the midwife of the historical process'.[5]

To examine nationhood in contemporary Korea from a cultural perspective, this chapter analyses six films made between 1966 and 1989. Among them, three are from the North: O Pyŏngch'o *Ch'oe Hakshin's Family* (1966), Ch'oe Ikkyu's *The Sea of Blood* (1969) and Cho Kyŏngsun's *Wŏlmi Island* (1982). The other three films are South Korean: Yu Hyŏnmok's *A Stray Bullet* (1960), Im Kwŏnt'aek's *The Banner Bearer without a Flag* (1979) and Chŏng Chiyŏng's *Southern Guerrilla Forces* (1990).

The selection of these six films is based on their subject-matter, popularity and accessibility. All of these films have drawn not only large audiences but also critical acclaim since their release. Their importance in the history of Korean cinema can partly be glimpsed in the recognition they received at the major film festivals, domestic and international. In the case of the North Korean films, the official commentary by the Party was also taken into consideration. As for the accessibility of North Korean films, priority was given to films that are available overseas in video format. *Ch'oe Hakshin's Family*, *The Sea of Blood* and *Wŏlmi Island* have been distributed internationally as representative works of North Korean cinema. South Korean films pose far less problems in availability. Therefore, contents and aesthetic merits were the main criteria for selecting the three South Korean films.

This chapter is organised in two sections. The first section examines the films in relation to the conflicting ideological orientations of North and South Korea. In the North Korean films, anti-imperialism constitutes the core of their definition of nationhood. Two specific characteristics are observed in the ways in which the North Korean films treat subjects related to anti-imperialism. First, the recurrent theme of anti-imperialism is closely tied to a nationalistic opposition to the colonisers or invaders of Korea. The Japanese rule up to 1945 and US inter-vention in the ensuing years offer fertile narrative contexts in which the North Korean films tackle the issues of self-identity of contemporary Korea. Second, seen from a chronological point of view, the development of the anti-imperialist theme in the three films parallels the effort to mount Kim Il Sung as the ultimate definer of Korean nationhood. Hence, the apotheosis of Kim calls for a careful examination of the social and political implications of the colonial experiences as they are represented in each film.

The situation with the three South Korean films is more complex. Nationhood is approached from multiple angles. The three films commonly point out the forced division of the nation as accountable for many of the problems confronted by modern Korea. This attitude explains that two of the three films – *The Banner Bearer without a Flag* and *Southern Guerrilla Forces* – treat anti-communism as their thematic crux. One of them tends to advocate anti-communism, and the other attempts to dismantle its legitimacy as the state ideology. In *A Stray Bullet*, it is viewed as an irrelevant issue. The film focuses more on the cultural dimension of the Korean national identity. As will be discussed in detail later, these three films tend to show increasing scepticism about anti-communism as the basis of their nationhood. The renunciation of the antithesis of pro- and anti-communism reflects the changing perception of self-identity among the Korean people in the contemporary period, at least in the South.

The second section of this chapter examines the common cultural elements between North and South Korean films. Although the six films are all constructed around the ideological tension between South and North, they invariably touch on the Confucian notion of family and connect it with their ideal nationhood. Their reliance on traditional family values seems to suggest the enduring Confucian cultural root as a possible alternative to the current political ideologies to lay out an appropriate ground for establishing integrated nationhood.

Anti-imperialism in three North Korean films

North Korean films consider anti-imperialistic sentiments, class-consciousness and endless loyalty toward Kim as the most important elements in defining the national identity of the Korean people. Although in different proportions, all three components coalesce to form a distinct thematic pattern in *Ch'oe Hakshin's Family*, *The Sea of Blood* and *Wŏlmi Island*. This pattern shifts in focus in each film, according to the specific socio-political situations at the time of the film's production. In other words, each film reflects the pressing needs of the state in representing their history on the screen. These needs range from the historical necessity to establish a classless society and the consolidation of the rule of the Kims – the father and the son successively – to the legitimacy of a party-centred social structure. A chronological review of the three films enables us to infer the changes in North Korea's internal political situations, especially its increasing idolisation of Kim Il Sung and his son Kim Jong Il, along with the promotion of the *Juche* ideology formulated by Kim, the father.

Ch'oe Hakshin's Family

O Pyŏngch'o's *Ch'oe Hakshin's Family* is a good example of the close link between anti-imperialistic sentiments and the theme of nationhood in North Korean films. The story is set during the US attack on Northern Korea. The historical context is capable of instantly arousing antagonism in North Korean audiences, who believe that the US troops nearly massacred their entire population during the war. With this emotional dimension at the forefront of the narrative, the film develops its anti-imperialist theme through the downfall of the protagonist Ch'oe Hakshin and the brutality of the US occupation forces. Ch'oe is a priest who adores Americans in the same way that he worships God. His encounter with the US inhumanity, however, is an eye-opener. The 'real' picture of the Americans completely shatters the esteem in which Ch'oe had held them.

Ch'oe Hakshin's Family portrays the US occupation forces as ruthlessly pursuing their national interests only. They are portrayed as willing to commit atrocities at all costs for their selfish purposes. The film urges the audience to penetrate the ulterior motive behind their sweet words and hypocritical smiles. They pretentiously talk about philanthropy and liberty, ascribing their humanitarianism to their Christian belief. As the US commander himself points out, the purpose of the Korean War is to secure the peninsula as an American military base. For this purpose, the Americans justify their deceptive lies, even though such lies may result in the decimation of Koreans in their own land. In the course of the film, these 'despicable' imperialists indeed perpetrate savagery on Koreans. In their view, the slaughter of the innocent villagers is the inevitable result of US expansionism.

The moral depravity of the US occupation forces is represented most vividly through their commander's attempted rape and murder of Songok, Ch'oe's eldest daughter. US duplicity is also extended to Richard, who is the missionary living in the village and an old friend of the Ch'oe family. He has always shown deep affection for Songok, treating her as if she were his own daughter. After she is murdered by the commander, however, Richard attempts to hide the crime. He orders his henchman not only to throw Songok's body into the sea but also to kill her mother to cover up the treachery of his fellow countryman.

Later in the film, the missionary turns out to be a secret agent working for the US intelligence bureau.

Ch'oe Hakshin's Family sharply contrasts the ruthlessness of the invaders and the helplessness of the villagers. Along with this contrast, the film draws attention to the strong solidarity of the people who have fallen under US rule. In doing this, the film particularly stresses that solidarity is formed under the collective leadership of the communists. A series of scenes shows how the villagers enjoyed their lives in a free society before the arrival of the US forces. In the new, communist society, people's past – specifically their class status or ideological stand – did not matter. To project the positive images of the communists, the film suggests that they even allowed freedom of religion. When the villagers are faced with the impending attack of the US troops, the communists swiftly come to help them to escape. Even after the Americans take over the village, the communists continue their efforts to rescue people who refused to follow their advice to retreat earlier. The communists are generous and are able to relate to the masses without hierarchical order.

While the film praises communist humanistic attitudes, it also emphasises the critical insights of the masses into the crisis that their nation is undergoing. When Ch'oe visits the villagers in prison to dissuade them from sympathising with the communists, none of them listens to him. They are critical of Ch'oe's position toward the Americans. Their unsympathetic reactions to his daughter's death clearly display their disapproval of the alliance between the Ch'oe family and the foreigners. Songok is an intelligent woman who received a university education, but she does not have the revolutionary spirit of the masses. This is, the film implies, her detrimental character flaw, which brings catastrophe upon herself. The villagers view her death as the logical consequence of her blind fondness for the invaders. Two local women comment that she invited the tragic incident by attending the welcoming party for the US occupiers and conveying to them how she 'worshipped' them. Songok is, in a way, a scapegoat for the anti-imperialist war.

The title of the film is derived from the ironic turn of the protagonist's fortune. Ch'oe's son who serves in the South Korean army as a lieutenant confesses that he was trapped by the Americans and that when he realised their duplicity, it was too late for him to escape from them. The protagonist's family once enjoyed great respect from the villagers, yet they fail to become a model for the masses in the newly liberated communist society.

Ch'oe Hakshin's Family was made before Kim Jong Il began to engage himself seriously in the North Korean film industry from

14 Ch'oe Hakshin rejects his belief in God after his son's death: O Pyŏngch'o's *Ch'oe Hakshin's Family* (1966)

the late 1960s onwards, with the specific goal of materialising the *Juche* theory on screen, and thereby promoting the leadership of his father. This explains, to a certain degree, the absence of a direct message of loyalty towards Kim in this film. However, it explicitly asserts the significance of the *Juche* theory as a state ideology. For example, the film echoes the *Juche* theory, which maintains that everything should be centred on men, not God. This argument is realised in the film through the total destruction of the protagonist who used to preach that men cannot live without believing or depending on a figure greater and more powerful than themselves.

Ch'oe Hakshin's Family represents a relatively early period of North Korean history in which the cult of the individual leader was yet to be enforced. There is no trace of *Yuil* thought in this film as is often seen in other North Korean films that consciously foreground Kim Il Sung's absolute charisma over the factional rivals in the Party. Although a few scenes in the film implicitly refer to Kim Il Sung's leadership,[6] the overall camera work focuses more on the collective leadership of the communists. For instance, the film consistently uses low-angle images for the communists. The camera tends to highlight the whole group rather than particular individuals.

This film was made before 1967, the year in which the Party released new ideological guidelines to promote loyalty to Kim-centred party politics.[7] The two aspects of *Ch'oe Hakshin's Family* – overt messages on the *Juche* theory, which continuously recited by characters as well as the narrator of the film, and the absence of the cult of Kim Il Sung – appear to evince the earlier mode of the *Juche* theory. This is a common feature of early North Korean films produced before the '1967 anti-sectarianism struggle'. Instead of loyalty towards Kim, the film is more concerned with the grim social reality of the masses under the imperialists, and emphasises the close ties between the masses and the communists. In this way, *Ch'oe Hakshin's Family* provides a stark contrast to those films produced after the evolution of the *Juche* theory cultivated by Kim Jong Il into the present form. Furthermore, the film clearly demonstrates the historical transformation of North Korean films in the late 1960s when Kim Jong Il renounced the socialist realistic tradition led by the KAPF film-makers and advocated the 'Great Leader's literature' the sole theoretical basis of North Korean art and literature.

The Sea of Blood

Unlike *Ch'oe Hakshin's Family*, *The Sea of Blood* was produced in 1969 under the direct supervision of Kim Jong Il. The story is set during the Japanese colonial period. North Korean film-makers approach modern Korean history in terms of the class struggle of the masses, and in doing so, they find the anti-Japanese resistance activities led by Kim Il Sung to be the most effective and readily available material. Among the films drawn on this subject, *The Sea of Blood* is regarded as the best by the Korean Workers' Party, as it is a classic example of North Korean cinema art. It is praised for treating such important themes as the historical legitimacy of North Korea and the indispensability of Kim's leadership in the struggles of the masses. The film is commented upon as having achieved a higher level of artistic sublimation in form that helps the masses to develop a revolutionary world-view.

To understand fully the significance of *The Sea of Blood*, its political background should be examined first. In 1967 Kim Il Sung brought charges against the 'Kapsan' faction, one of the two rival groups within the then Korean Workers' Party, for alleged anti-party and anti-revolutionary activities and its nefarious ideological influence. Kim's charges led the other, military-based faction to monopolise the Party. This was the faction that had evolved from Kim's original anti-Japanese partisan group. In 1967, the Party held a meeting of the Supreme People's Committee. The goal of this meeting was to consolidate Kim's '*Yuil* thought' and to overhaul the Party structure by placing him at its centre.[8] '*Yuil* thought' emphasises unconditional obedience to Kim's monolithic leadership whose historical authority was based on his anti-imperialistic activities during the colonial period. To carry out this task at a popular level, the Party urged its members as well as lay citizens to study the revolutionary tradition in Korea and the historical goals of the Korean communist movement. The specific purpose of this campaign was to force the public to learn about the communists who played a major role in 'liberating' Korea from Imperial Japan.[9] This intention explains much of the outlook of *The Sea of Blood*, which glorifies the anti-Japanese militant struggles of KPRA (the Korean People's Revolutionary Army) in China in the early 1930s under Kim Il Sung's command.

The Sea of Blood is the prototype of the 'anti-Japanese revolutionary' films, which strongly adhered to the tenets of 'Great Leader's literature'. According to the Party's official comments, it truthfully describes how North Korean people were awakened to the idea of revolution and subsequently embarked on the path of class struggle.[10] Supposedly written by Kim Il Sung himself, *The Sea of Blood* is about a family that is transformed into revolutionary fighters. The film does not explicitly mention Kim by name, but his presence is strongly felt throughout the narrative. For example, the film has an active KPRA member constantly remind the audience of their 'Great Leader'. Although the Party's comments on the film stress the power of the masses as the real force to move history, it is not too difficult to find where their real emphasis rests: the critical impetus brought about by the leader to stir up the masses and instruct them about the need to be engaged in a revolutionary struggle.

The main character of *The Sea of Blood* is the mother of a poor family. The plot is woven around the process in which she is metamorphosed into a dauntless political fighter. As a member of the exploited class, she is illiterate and has suffered greatly from extreme poverty. At the outset of the film, she appears as an ordinary mother whose sole concern is obtaining food for her starving family. Politics is far from being a concern of hers. In fact, she is even unaware of Japan's annexation of Korea, asking her husband why the Japanese have come to her country. She simply does not understand the foreigners' presence in Korea. Her indifference to the world outside of her family life is not changed even after her husband is killed by the Japanese police for instigating a dispute between the villagers and their greedy landlord.

A critical turning point in the film, which brings a fundamental change in the poor and ignorant woman, is her encounter with a political activist. Her transformation is dramatically portrayed in a series of four scenes. The first three of these repeat the same dialogues, camera angle and action, yet the last one reverses them, signifying the change taking place in the mother. In the initial three scenes, a family member – husband, son and then daughter – surreptitiously enters the room at night, evoking a suspicion in the audience that he or she is involved in some kind of anti-Japanese resistance mission. The camera first shows the mother sitting in the room, filled with fear. It then cuts to her husband and child's stern faces as they come into the room. Their dread-stricken state of mind is vividly transmitted to the audience who, throughout the scenes, shares the mother's low-angle point of view. In these scenes, the scared mother occupies a corner of the room in the margin of the frame. Her husband or child walks across the centre part of the room. In the fourth scene, however, everything is inverted: the mother is no longer passively waiting for her husband and children at home. She herself is performing a secret task given by the KPRA. She enters the room from the outside, looking down at her daughter, who obviously has been waiting for her mother. The camera shows the mother in a higher position, in stark contrast to the previous scenes. This time, the camera places the audience in the daughter's position, from which they have to look up to the mother.

The movement of the mother's position from the lower to the upper part of the frame symbolically indicates both an internal change in her and, as she represents the masses, in them as both have been passive. To convey visually the theme of transformation, the film employs a mirroring technique between the first and the second halves of the narrative. A fine example of this is found in the scenes of the husband and son's deaths. The scene in the first half shows her husband brutally killed, while trying to save his friend from an inferno, which the police set to disperse the villagers from their demonstration. Witnessing her husband dying, the mother cries helplessly, totally perplexed. A similar scene is repeated in the latter half of the film; this time, she bitterly cries over the corpse of her 7-year-old son. Her reactions in the two scenes may appear to be similar, but their meanings differ in many respects. The death of her son is, in a way, a price she pays for her revolutionary task: the police kill her son

15 The revolutionary mother in Ch'oe Ikkyu's *The Sea of Blood* (1969)

because she refuses to inform them of the hideout of a wounded fugitive. This fugitive happens to be the political activist she met earlier in the film. By sheltering the patriot in her house, the mother attains heroic fortitude. Prior to this heroic moment, she already demonstrated her newly awakened political consciousness by sewing a military uniform for her elder son so that he could join the KPRA. The mother embodies the tenacious revolutionary spirit with which she can put the well-being of her nation before that of her family.

Reborn as a political fighter, the mother is expected to inspire the exploited masses, awakening their revolutionary potential. The film emphasises that she is not a unique case and that such a change can take place in anyone once he or she is exposed to Kim Il Sung's leadership. To elicit this conclusion, the film deploys several interesting scenes that allude to Kim's influence upon her. At an early point in the film, the mother happens to hear an old villager's account of the anti-Japanese struggle of the KPRA members under General Kim. When Kim's name is pronounced by the villager, a bright smile appears on the mother's face, and the sun comes out from behind a cloud at the same time. Later, the mother accidentally runs into Kim while looking for a new place to settle after her husband's death. This scene aims to elevate Kim's role in the revolutionary transformation of an ordinary person. By doing this, the film reiterates the importance of a close tie between the political leader and the masses as the initial step in the effort to break free from foreign rule and the old class system and to establish a classless society. If one follows this path, the 'sea of blood' can be transformed into the brightest place under the sun, that is, Kim.

While class issues are an integral part of the revolutionary struggle, they do not seem to receive a full treatment in this film. Since the source of the dramatic conflict is specifically located in the antagonism of colonised against coloniser, the film dismisses class conflicts among Koreans. The fact that the story is set in China underscores the theme of anti-imperialism at the expense of diffusing the tension of internal class struggle among Koreans. In fact, the issues of class conflict are only verbally touched on when the characters recollect the old days in their hometowns. The secret meeting of the villagers at the beginning of the film suggests an imminent strike against the landlord. However, their plan is discovered by the Japanese before the peasants are able to carry out the plan. The landlord does not even appear on the screen. The subject of class virtually disappears from the second half of the film. The superficial treatment of class conflicts in the film well verifies the weakness of 'anti-Japanese revolutionary' films in that they mainly stress the image of the 'Great Leader' as the saviour of the nation.

On the one hand, the omission of class-related themes in *The Sea of Blood* can imply that the classless North Korean society was achieved without class conflict. Interestingly, this reading accords with the historical development of land reform in the North after the Liberation. When Kim returned to Korea in 1945, he and other communists, with support from the Soviet Union, drew up numerous ambitious programmes to build a socialist state. By the end of 1946, all land had been distributed to those who actually worked on it. This measure was taken to terminate the exploitative landlordism. Also, most of the industries, banks and other financial institutions that had been previously owned by the Japanese were taken over by the communist state. Confronted with the land reform and the nationalisation of the industries and various economic institutions, many landowners, along with a small number of the newly rising capitalists had already left for the South. What is to be noted here is that these landlords lost everything to the new ruling power, not to the masses. Their 'defeat' was not caused by a class revolution initiated by peasants and workers. In other words, the current classless North Korean society is not the fruit of fierce class struggle. The problematic representation of the class conflicts in *The Sea of Blood* poignantly exposes the weakness of the Party's claim that North Korea has inherited the tradition of the class revolution.

On the other hand, the fact that Kim was the leader of one of the anti-Japanese guerrilla bands in Manchuria in the late 1930s could be reckoned as factual evidence for his leadership in the national liberation war since the Japanese colonial period. Yet this does not mean that the film's depiction of his activities is entirely faithful to the historical reality of the independence war that was waged against the Japanese. By displacing its geographical setting from Korea to an unnamed place in China, the film, to some extent, dismisses the abject conditions in which the overwhelming majority of Koreans lived as colonial subjects. This drawback undermines the film's realistic portrayal of the colonial period and its effort to uplift Kim's role in the class struggle and liberation.

Wŏlmi Island

Wŏlmi Island is considered by the North Korean authorities to be the best war film made in recent years, for its contribution to raising artistic standards in depicting the patriotism and indomitable fighting spirits of the masses with their endless loyalty towards Kim Il Sung. Set during the Korean War, the film depicts a three-day battle on the coast of Wŏlmi Island between UN forces and the communist coastal company, which attempts to secure a safe route for a strategic retreat of the North Korean army. On the surface, the dominant theme of the film appears to be the patriotic self-sacrifice of the company, but underneath it, the film discloses its real message: endless loyalty to Kim. This underlying theme is communicated mostly through the mouth of the protagonist T'aehun, who, as the company commander, repeatedly tells his followers as well as his superiors that their 'fatherland' *is* General Kim. T'aehun describes Kim as the one who saved their lost country from the Japanese. The reason for the company defending the island is to check the enemies from advancing to P'yŏngyang where General Kim resides. The content of the film supports T'aehun's claim that the war with the Americans is to defend Kim as much as their country.

What distinguishes *Wŏlmi Island* from the other two North Korean films is its exclusive concentration on Kim's importance in the Korean perception of nationhood. The film starts with the praise of Kim's eminent leadership and ends with it. The company's devotion to Kim is equated with patriotism, which has a universal appeal. To generate a mythical resonance in the company's heroism, the film liberally uses dramatic elements, although they contradict its claim that the story is based on historical fact. A typical exaggeration is the claim that the company, which was equipped with only four guns, could defeat

50,000 US soldiers who, led by General MacArthur, attempted to land at Inch'on. This unrealistic victory mentioned at the outset of the film is followed by a line from Kim's *Juche* theory: 'nothing is impossible for people with will-power'. This motto is amplified throughout the film, urging unconditional loyalty to the Leader.

The above sentiment quoted from the *Juche* theory is also used to mobilise the North Korean people for the economic development plan. North Korea began to be faced with a serious economic crisis from the late 1970s. Films made during this period often cite Kim's fatherly encouragement of workers to raise their productivity. A sergeant says that General Kim once visited his mine before the war broke out and told those who complained about the lack of equipment that manpower 'precedes' equipment. Kim is also said to have added that if the spirit of the working class is elevated, there is nothing it cannot accomplish. The theme of economic development is noted in T'aehun's speech to his soldiers: 'Our fatherland already gave us everything, and what is left to be done is show our endless love for our nation ... We should fight for our country and General Kim until we die so that we would not feel ashamed before our parents and brothers'. As T'aehun's lines illustrate, the film attempts to set an exemplary model for the audience with the heroic deaths of the young soldiers who do not flinch even in the hopeless situation they are faced with on Wŏlmi island. This effort is based on the so-called 'modelling theory', one of the three principles of film-making in North Korea.[11]

Another noteworthy aspect of *Wŏlmi Island* is its characterisation of the new class of military élite which was emerging in North Korea. T'aehun represents this group. As a graduate of the Naval Officer College, he is portrayed as fully qualified to serve as the commander of the company. His main function is to execute efficiently Kim's ideological instructions. The film catalogues several important attributes of this élite group. Above all, T'aehun demonstrates a profound understanding of soldiers' psychology. He sympathises with their difficulties, especially when their fighting spirit wanes. He is well aware of his responsibility to convince them of a victory so that they can perform their tasks successfully to the end even at the risk of sacrificing their lives. As the film visually demonstrates, T'aehun's commanding ability and stern personality are impressive. Besides T'aehun, Min'guk, a battalion commander, and T'aehun's lover, a military doctor, also belong to this élite class. They are all endowed with distinct class traits: a strong sense of commitment to their work, emotional strength and a fine sense of judgement. These élite also demonstrate classical military heroism. In the battle scenes, the

16   Soldiers ready to die for their nation express joy after scoring direct hits on UN ships: Cho Kyŏngsun's *Wŏlmi Island* (1982)

camera marks their leadership by positioning them in the frontal zone of the screen, with the soldiers in the background.

The film, however, prompts a vexing ideological question by singling out the small group of officers from the masses. To prevent such an ideological problem, *Wŏlmi Island* constantly draws attention to their class background. T'aehun and Min'guk not only come from the working class but were also anti-Japanese fighters. The film stresses that this class homogeneity between the officers and soldiers cements their emotional tie as comrades. T'aehun and Min'guk's anti-Japanese resistance, in particular, contributes to reminding the soldiers of their common experiences in the exploitative class system and slavery under foreign rule. By referring to their shared history, the film carefully suggests that the relationship between the new élite group and its followers is based on mutual respect and understanding, not conflicting interests between two different social classes.

The efforts to suppress any hint of class distinction, however, do not seem to be entirely convincing. A perceptive viewer cannot miss the irreconcilable gap between the military élite and the low-ranking soldiers. It is shown in their distinctly different appearances and behaviours, which are related to their different living standards. These external cues of their class backgrounds, coupled with the different positioning of the commanders and the soldiers on the screen, cannot handle satisfactorily the suspicion that a certain hierarchy exists in North Korean society. This undeniable oddity in its internal logic ironically confirms the film's function as a truthful mirror of social reality. In actuality, the loyalty to Kim shown by this emerging class did play a pivotal role in bolstering his control of power in the early 1980s.

Anti-communism in three South Korean films

Whereas anti-imperialism, class-consciousness and Kim's leadership are the controlling themes in the North Korean films, anti-communism serves as a basis for exploring nationhood in the South Korean films. The film industry in the South has always been in a vulnerable position due to political pressures from the government. The severe censorship during the military regime (1961–93) was an especially tough obstacle to film-makers who were interested in topical subjects.

Unlike the North Korean films, state ideology is not always indiscriminately exalted in South Korean films. At the same time, however, it should be mentioned that, to an extent, anti-communism has had a genuine emotional appeal to the audience who remember the tragedy of the civil war and suffer from the separation from their family members after the armistice. *The Banner Bearer without a Flag* thus offers anti-communism as the outright means to recover nationhood. However, the other two films – *A Stray Bullet* and *Southern Guerrilla Forces* – interpret the discontinuity in nationhood somewhat differently. Although they fundamentally agree that the forced division of the nation was the origin of the conflicts of contemporary Korean society, *A Stray Bullet* is more concerned with recording the impact of the political conflicts on those on the margins of their society rather than discussing abstract ideological issues. Its non-judgmental tone contributes to documenting the agonies of ordinary people during the post-war period. *Southern Guerrilla Forces* attempts an objective investigation of the so-called communist sympathisers, delimiting the power of anti-communism as a factor in characterising the nationhood of modern Korea.

A Stray Bullet

A Stray Bullet, although dealing with the aftermath of the Korean War, is not a typical anti-communist film where emotional appeal relies solely on the ideological opposition between North and South. Anti-communist film emerged as a distinctive genre during the US occupation period and enjoyed its heyday under Rhee's autocratic regime and the Parks' military regime. Produced in the short period between the 19 April 1960 Student Uprising and the 16 May military *coup d'état* in 1961, *A Stray Bullet*, however, does not make an ostensible attempt to condemn anti-government, subversive elements in South Korean society, as is often the case in anti-communist films. Furthermore, Yu's film also avoids accusing North Korea of being solely responsible for the war.

The film defines every Korean more or less as the victim of the fratricidal war and rejects a simple, schematic approach to post-war social problems. The film does not claim to offer a 'solution' to the problems, either. The absence of the didactic tone and moralistic perspective corroborates the film's conscious refrain from becoming a propaganda tool to legitimise the current social order which was rampant in the post-war film industry.

In *A Stray Bullet*, the question of nationhood is explored through the chaos between traditional and Western cultural values, and, through a sense of loss pervading society in the industrialisation process. These themes are efficiently handled in the film's depiction of the day-to-day struggle of ordinary citizens during post-war repression. As the film shows, the lives of the characters are all, one way or another, affected by the war, but their everyday concern is a far cry from political slogans. The characters are preoccupied with how to survive the economic and spiritual wasteland.

The plot of *A Stray Bullet* is woven around the tension between two brothers, Ch'ŏlho and Yŏngho. These brothers, with their opposite views of the economic situations, serve as foils to one other. Ch'ŏlho is a poor but hard-working 'salary' man. As a low-paid, public accountant, he cannot fully support his family. Nevertheless, he makes every effort to live honestly, according to his conscience. In the eyes of Yŏngho, an unemployed war veteran, his brother appears to be passive and even cowardly. As Ch'ŏlho advises him to look for a job and not idle away his time, Yŏngho responds that to be rich, one must give up one's conscience and morals. Yŏngho's indignation about social injustice, especially his discontentment with the ever-widening gulf between the rich and the poor ends in an attempted bank robbery.

The agonies of Ch'ŏlho and Yŏngho's family represent the range of problems faced by post-war South Korean society. The family cannot go back to their hometown in the North, but, at the same time, they cannot adjust themselves to the poverty-stricken and emotionally barren city life in Seoul, either. The war tragically alienated them from their environments in both places. Each member adds a different problem to the family. Yŏngho, the wounded veteran, feels that his country for which he fought so hard with his life has abandoned him. The film traces how he further and further drifts away from society to the point of complete self-alienation. The mother becomes insane from the shock of the war. Their younger sister, Myŏngsuk, prostitutes herself to foreigners, and their youngest brother quits school to sell newspapers. Moreover, Ch'ŏlho's wife suffers from severe malnutrition and eventually dies in childbirth. These family ordeals ultimately destroy Ch'ŏlho, the lone bastion of conscience in this calamitous society, who makes frantic efforts to cope with his duties as head of the family. The last scene of the film shows him as having completely lost his sense of direction. He gets on a taxi but does not know where he wants to go. He asks the driver to go to his house in Haebangch'on where his insane mother is. Next moment, however, he asks the driver to change direction and go to the police station for Yŏngho and then to the hospital for his wife. After much confusion, he at last gives up everything, shouting 'Let me get out! Let me get out!' Ch'ŏlho's desperate cry at the end overlaps with the shrieks of his deranged mother. The title of the film 'A Stray Bullet' thus refers to Ch'ŏlho, an anomaly in society in which moral integrity is not rewarded but derided. He is thoroughly lost in a world where human dignity is forced to subjugate itself to animalistic survival instincts.

Ch'ŏlho and Yŏngho's opposite attitudes toward their trying existential conditions epitomise schizophrenia from which the entire society suffers. Polar symptoms of the schizophrenia are acutely exhibited by the mother and her granddaughter (Ch'ŏlho's daughter). The spasmodic screams of the mother bring back the painful memories of the war to the family. The little daughter in the meantime pesters her father and uncle, constantly asking them to take her to a big department store, move to a Western-style house and buy her new clothes and shoes. Ch'ŏlho and Yŏngho nearly lose their minds between these two extreme, infantile forms of maladjustment to the social reality.

Schizophrenic symptoms are also visible in cultural values, which the film superbly incorporates into the question of national identity. The film portrays the clash between traditional Korean culture and the Western, or more precisely, US culture. To Myŏngsuk, selling her body to American GIs is not a sound but justifiable means to make a living in harsh times. She is not, however, free from self-hatred. While she knows her 'immoral' way of life, she raises sharp criticism of Korean men who dodge or fail in their social responsibilities. Her *fiancé*, a wounded war veteran like Yŏngho, forsakes his promise to marry her. Her brother Ch'ŏlho is also a failure as a son because he cannot provide adequate care for their sick mother. It is a potent irony that this 'despicable' GI girl voices the traditional Confucian morality on family life.

A pitiful comic irony also springs from Ch'ŏlho's contradictory

17   Yŏngho and family await Ch'ŏlho in Yu Hyŏnmok's
A Stray Bullet (1960)

attitudes toward his sister and her money. He ignores Myŏngsuk's complaints and suggestions about their family affairs. But when she offers him money to pay for his wife's hospital fees, he accepts it at the last minute with much reluctance. When he finds out that his wife has already died, however, he spends the money on having his rotten teeth taken out at the dentist's. The rotten teeth clearly symbolise the 'sick' society, the pain caused by the cavities implying the agonies of the people who have to live in such 'abnormal' society. While he stubbornly refuses the money that Myŏngsuk earns from US soldiers, it is after all, this 'tainted' money that relieves him of the pain.

The conflict between traditional and Western cultures is reinforced by sound effects as well. This technique is most effective when Ch'ŏlho spots Myŏngsuk from the inside of a trolley he is riding. In this scene, Myŏngsuk appears in a military jeep paralleling the trolley, wrapped in the arms of an American soldier. Both she and the GI are framed within the trolley window, through which Ch'ŏlho and other passengers stare at them. There is an explicit cultural disharmony in the juxtaposition of the soldier–prostitute couple inside the window frame, and the trolley passengers outside of it. The bitterness of the scene, which is doubled by the passengers' sarcastic remarks on Myŏngsuk, increases as the background sounds of *p'ansori* are slowly blended with jazz music from the trolley radio. The jazz begins in timely fashion when the jeep comes into view. The final scene of this sequence shows Ch'ŏlho despairingly sinking into the two incompatible soundtracks dancing around him in parallel.

A *Stray Bullet* contains other charged signs of Western culture, such as the sounds of church bells, hymns of the churchgoers and English phrases interspersed in the dialogues between Yŏngho and his girlfriend. These sounds reflect the contribution of Western religion and language to the frantic social scenery of post-war Korea. These alien sounds are used as background music throughout the film, against which the mother's outcries tragically rebound, generating bizarre psychological effects. The mother often shouts: 'Let's get out'. Once, however, she says, 'Let's get out, let's get out ... to follow a herd of sheep on the green pasture'. As the sheep is not an indigenous animal in Korea, her unconscious reference must be to a kind of eternal resting-place described in the Bible. Her mental state serves as an objective correlative for the cultural anarchy experienced by Koreans after the war.

Like the Western music, English phrases interjected into the film also feel totally out of place. They are a filmic means of indicting the unhealthy influx of Western culture into a country that has already lost its sense of identity through the war. When the couple expresses their private feelings, they switch to English expressions, such as 'OK', 'Thank you', 'Please', 'Goodbye', 'Sit down', 'I love you', and so on. Since Koreans hardly ever use foreign phrases in their everyday conversation, English sentences spoken by Yŏngho and his girlfriend create odd moments in the flow of the film.

Yŏngho and his girlfriend are both misfits in society despite the university education both have received. The film's message is clear. The new generation represented by this young, highly educated couple does not provide 'hope' for the future but increases despair. This theme is metaphorically conveyed in the artificial brightness created by 'Mona Lisa's smile', a nickname for Yŏngho's girlfriend. Her action manifests her blind admiration of superficial Western values. When Yŏngho visits her at midnight, she appears in a Western-style night-gown. Contrary to the traditional code of conduct for women, she willingly receives a nocturnal male visitor. Her body gestures, and especially her smoking, recall heroines of Hollywood films. In short, she epitomises the identity crisis of Korean society into which this film delves.

A *Stray Bullet* is an excellent social commentary. It raises a critical question on the role of culture in nationhood. Although it deals with a family tragedy, it in fact covers a wide range of people in post-war Korean society who grope for a direction amidst confusion and chaos. For this reason, the film is viewed as a masterpiece in South Korean film history by many South Korean film critics and scholars.

The film also deserves critical scrutiny for its treatment of the pervading sense of alienation as a by-product of industrialisation and urbanisation, which the military government began to pursue aggressively from the 1960s. Sordid urban scenes and arid emotional landscapes are notable in various locations in the film. The opening credit scene clearly establishes this theme. As the title of the film appears on the screen, the camera shows August Rodin's sculpture *The Thinker*. Simultaneously, it shows a lonely man in the background, surrounded by dazzling traffic lights and noises. The man could be any Korean who cannot properly adjust himself or herself to the changing society. The mechanical sounds, such as car noises, steam-train whistles, sirens and traffic signals that constantly interrupt the flow of the film register the individual's sense of loss. Also, the man's fixed position within the window frame transmits a sense of claustrophobia. Again, the man can be seen as Everyman or Everywoman who feels helpless within his or her own emotional cell, unable to grapple with the whirling speed of urbanisation and industrialisation. The credit scene adumbrates the shattered peace experienced by the characters in the film who are perpetually marginalised in the gigantic city.

The film poignantly exposes society's failure to meet its members' expectations and needs. It is full of people who are uprooted because of the war. They aimlessly wander the streets with an illusion of wealth. These marginalised people are denied the fruits of the booming national economy, and as their self-denial and sense of failure deepen, they are further kept behind the times. The only exception to this tendency is Ch'ŏlho who desperately clings to the old values of honesty and hard work. Many of the ugly urban scenes are thus presented through his eyes. He is overcome by humiliation when he passes by the dirty public toilets and unsanitary well in his neighbourhood. To him, the slums look like dead souls. While Ch'ŏlho feels nauseated about his stagnant neighbourhood, Yŏngho and his friend plot to rob a bank, a prime symbol of the modern economic system. The streets outside of the bank are, however, occupied by beggars, unemployed tramps and disabled war veterans, demanding that the government lessen their hardship. During the police chase of the bank robbers, Yŏngho brings the audience to the climactic scene of urban despair – a woman hanging herself from the ceiling of the underground pathway, with a crying baby abandoned next to her.

Although the film does not cast a cold eye on Yŏngho's problem, it does not approve of his 'solution', either. It signals in various ways that his attempt is doomed to fail. Most noticeable is the use of small objects that create the images of a prison. On the screen, Yŏngho is often placed behind iron bars, bed frames, a birdcage or an iron ladder. In one respect, he is already locked up in his own home. His crazy mother and his puerile niece create a living hell for him at home. He cannot find a haven from his sense of entrapment.

The use of deep focus effectively communicates the sense of estrangement and entrapment. For example, the depth of family conflicts is strongly felt in the scenes where the mother and her children are vertically separated in a deep-focused frame. The mother lies on the floor of the room, and other family members sit in the background. The deep focus in these scenes connotes the chasm between the mother and her two children and also the abyss of thoughts in which Ch'ŏlho and Yŏngho are sub-merged. The same camera technique is repeated when Ch'ŏlho escorts Myŏngsuk from the police station, after she has been arrested for prostitution on the streets. The deep-focused camera exposes the unbridgeable gap between them. He is placed in the foreground, she in the background. Not only the spatial composi-tion of the brother and sister but also the angle of their gazes contribute to the increasing sense of estrangement between them. Both Ch'ŏlho and Myŏngsuk face the camera, but they never look each other in the face. When they come out of the police station, they begin to walk with a certain distance between them. By placing them vertically on extreme sides of the frame, the camera implies that they will stay in parallel in their own emotional compartments, and their problems are going to remain unresolved forever. Through these scenes, the film suggests that the problems experienced by this family are indicative of the larger-scale crisis undergone by the nation. The family members are estranged from one another due to the problems of their society rather than their own character flaws. By presenting the family conflict as originating from society, the film reminds the audience of the crisis of Korean nationhood.

The Korean War furnished the South Korean economy with the opportunity to become incorporated into the world's capital-ist system. It is true that to rehabilitate the post-war economy, industrialisation was an inevitable measure taken by the govern-ment and in this process foreign aid was pivotal. However, by monopolising the distribution of the aid, the government aimed primarily to strengthen their political alliance with the industrialists and thus failed to create fundamental changes in the social structure. Driven by self-interest, the ruling élite did not attempt to ameliorate the economic situations of those living on the peripheries of society. For Koreans such as Ch'ŏlho's family, industrialisation appears to be a superficial imitation of the Western lifestyle, as is illustrated by Yŏngho's girlfriend. Hence, the film points out, the industrialisation of the nation is matched by a corresponding dilution of its cultural identity.

The Banner Bearer without a Flag

The Banner Bearer without a Flag represents what is commonly called 'anti-communist' films, which form their own genre in South Korean cinema on the basis of their distinct ideological content. In general, this type of film approaches modern Korean history from the binary perspective of pro- versus anti-communism. In addition, many of these films tend to advocate the dominant ideology of South Korean society, which combines anti-communism and capitalism.

The plot of *The Banner Bearer without a Flag* is essentially a reconstruction of the social and political unrest during the post-Liberation period through the eyes of a journalist. In content and form, it shares many of the generic characteristics with other anti-communist films. Above all, it singles out communism as the source of Korea's current political problems. By doing this, the film suggests that if Korean society purges itself of communist sympathisers, it will be able to restore stability. The condemnatory tone toward communism is evident in labelling communist sympathisers 'anti-nationalists'.

The Banner Bearer without a Flag was made at the end of the 16 May military government, which lasted from 1961 to 1979. This historical background explains the film's explicit ideological stance and also, its implicit intention to reinforce the historical legitimacy of the military rule. The leaders of the 16 May coup initiated a long period of military dictatorship. The military regime, however, abruptly ended on the night of 26 October 1979 when President Park Chung Hee was assassinated by his own intelligence chief. This incident, against the expectations of the majority of the Korean people, did not put an end to the military dictatorship but was immediately followed by another coup led by General Chun Doo Hwan in December 1979. The power succession of the military élite in South Korean politics lasted until 1993. During this period of military rule, numerous films were made that directly attack North Korea and its communist regime for their role in the national division and the suffering of the people that continues even today.

The film's polemical approach to the characters' ideological orientation is evident in the scene where the protagonist and his three friends are engaged in a heated debate on Korean politics. In the scene, the four characters are split into pro- and anti-communists. Later, they actually join political organisations that suit their ideological inclinations. Sunik, an idealistic pro-communist becomes a member of the Communist Party, and the character called Kom (a nickname meaning 'bear') joins an extreme right-wing terrorist group. Yun, the protagonist, and his best friend Hyŏngŭn are more or less in between their two extreme friends, yet, in reality, they tacitly lean toward Kom's side. Interestingly, these three characters who are opposed to communism happen to come from North Korea. They agree that people in the South, including Sunik are too naïve about communists. In their view, Sunik is misled by the rosy words of communists. When Kom mentions Russians' attack on local women, for instance, Sunik counters him by saying that Russia is Pushkin and Tolstoy. Sunik's romantic view of the Soviet Union and North Korea is further exposed throughout their debate.

The film is chiefly concerned with those who cannot choose a side between the right and the left wings, and thus remain grey on the black-and-white pole of ideological orientation. Yun and Hyŏngŭn are categorised as people of a grey persuasion, who are frequently denounced as 'opportunistic'. The main body of the film narrative is the actions taken by such grey intellectuals. Hyŏngŭn's course of action is rather simple: he commits suicide, unable to resolve the ideological tensions in and around him. Stark as it is, his action has various implications, the darkest of which is that those who cannot or do not want to take sides should rather stay away from the vortex of Korean politics.

The protagonist Yun handles his 'greyness' differently. He is forced into action when he happens to witness a group of communists lynching innocent people to death. The inhumanity of the communists not only disgusts him but makes him literally sick, as is seen in his bloody coughs. As is the case with Ch'ŏlho in *A Stray Bullet*, toothache is used in this film as a metaphor for the protagonist's painful process of coming to terms with his ideological standpoint. He develops toothache when he is under pressure to write an article about the conflicts of Korean society or when he sees Korean prostitutes with US soldiers. Through the psychological and physical illness, he finally comes to discover the origin of the current conflicts of Korean society and even a cure for the problems.

As is expected, Yun's 'cure' for the social problems is compared to pulling out the rotten teeth from his mouth. He believes

18   The agony and frustration of intellectuals in post-colonial Korea
in Im Kwŏnt'aek's *The Banner Bearer without a Flag* (1979): from left,
Kom, Hyŏngŭn, and the protagonist Yun

that by getting rid of communists from Korean society, he can be
freed from the intellectual agonies he has long suffered. He
finally locates his enemy in the famous communist leader Yi
Ch'ŏl. Yun investigates Yi's private life and brings the dark side
of this highly respected communist leader to light. Yi turns out to
be a shameless, hypocritical and immoral individual. He is widely
admired as a national leader for his compassion for the poor. His
alleged frugal lifestyle is an expression of his sympathy with the
underprivileged. A little boy whom Yun comes across in the
communists-initiated anti-trust strike, tells him that Yi worked in
a brick factory before the Liberation and still lives humbly,
having only a slice of bread and a cup of water for lunch. The
boy believes that Yi lives for the poor as Abraham Lincoln did for
blacks in America. However, what Yun finds out about this
heroic leader is far from his popular image. It turns out that Yi
studied in Germany during the Japanese colonial period and has
lived a luxurious life ever since. To dramatise this, the film shows
that Yun runs into Yi in a high-class Western-style restaurant.
His hypocrisy is exposed when he orders beefsteak in English.
Yun also uncovers that Yi is notorious for love affairs since his
college years, and he is in fact, having a secret affair with Yunim,
who lives with a high-ranking US secret agent. Yi uses her for
both pleasure and information.

Yun's determination to eliminate the poisonous elements in
Korean society reaches its peak with his dramatic assassination

of Yi in a hotel room where he is lying in bed with his mistress. In this scene, the camera captures Yi's collapse in slow motion against the opaque backside of a mirror. The mirror is an effective device to allude to Yi's action of unveiling the truth. The murkiness of its reverse side can be read as a metaphor for Yi's false identity and impurity behind the mask of the 'protector' of the poor. Yun's careful plan to expose fully the repulsive face of the communist can be seen even in his choice of the hotel room instead of an outdoor public place: catching him in the most private and secret moment is a pre-emptive measure for the possibility of Yi's uninformed followers to promote him to the stature of a political martyr.

Yun's final action is a patriotic one; nevertheless, a violent one. And as such, it invites comment. The film attempts to attenuate the violent ending by hinting that the killing is strictly Yun the individual's action, not the society's. The title, *The Banner Bearer without a Flag*, refers to a man who takes a lone action without the endorsement of his group (the 'flag'). A close reading of the mounting pressure on Yun, however, leads the audience to conclude that his action reflects the will of the majority who is antagonistic to North Korean communists and views their removal as contributing to purifying Korea. This is why Yi's murder cannot be seen entirely as the isolated individual's voluntary action but a kind of invisible scheme induced by the state's anti-communist ideology. From this point of view, Yun does carry the flag of 'public justice', which is bestowed on him by his own society.

This argument is supported by the political reality of the period, which the film portrays. During the occupation period, terrorist activities, including those by the extreme right-wing political groups got beyond control, exasperating the masses to polarisation of the left and right wings. In actuality, however, it is well known that the US military government condoned and even thought of the terrorism committed by the extreme right-wing organisations as the Korean people's self-defence from communist attack. The occupation government succeeded in turning the hatred of communism among the refugees from the North into a means to establish an anti-communist state firmly in South Korea. This historical context once again confirms the collective encouragement for the course of action Yun takes as an individual member.

Yun is an intellectual who cannot tolerate the brutality of the communist mob and the hypocrisy of their leader. *The Banner Bearer without a Flag* stresses the civic duties of the élite to enlighten the masses about the evils of communism. For this effect, the protagonist is delineated as having a piercing journalistic insight into their real and hidden 'intentions'.

However, the film's portrayal of anti-communist intellectuals is not without problems. To begin with, there is a danger in exalting the educated élite represented by Yun and his friends as the ideological safeguards of Korean society. The film implicitly tells the audience that only highly educated members of society can properly understand and handle ideological matters. In this film, the majority of ordinary citizens are presented as the politically uninformed or even ignorant masses who can easily fall victim to, or become scapegoats of, the antagonistic power groups in hegemonic conflict.

Another factor that mars the film's realism is its rather simplistic black-and-white approach to one of the most complicated and volatile transitional periods in modern Korean history. The film designates a handful of communists as the arch-devils responsible for the problems, while depicting the majority of citizens as naïvely deluded or easily terrified by them. Communists are depicted as the unabashed agitators of the nation's stability, always conspiring to take over the entire country. The film certainly lacks objectivity and balance in investigating the seedbed of the ideological conflicts among the Korean people. Anti-communism has dominated South Korean society since the Liberation. A powerful rhetoric as it is, its treatment in this film is rather superficial. Social reality is far too complex to be explicated in such simple binary terms. For this reason, *The Banner Bearer* demonstrates ironic affinities with typical propaganda films of North Korea that blindly glorify communism.

Southern Guerrilla Forces

Southern Guerrilla Forces is a humanistic story about the communist partisans fighting against the South Korean government in the 1950s. Tackling one of the forbidden subjects in South Korean cinema, this film marks a new phase in Korean film history. Through a serious and unbiased re-examination of the lives of the communist guerrillas, the film has raised the discussion of the ideological differences between North and South and their role in nationhood to an unprecedented level. Contrasted with *The Banner Bearer*, Chŏng's film stresses that blind antagonism for communism itself cannot be the key definer of nationhood. Thus, for the first time in South Korean film history, *Southern Guerrilla Forces* calls into question the legitimacy of anti-communism as the state ideology. This message is conveyed through a careful depiction of the human side of the communist resistance forces headquartered in the exacerbating war situation.

To explain the significance of this film in South Korean film industry, a brief review of the national security policies is in order. Roughly from 1988, unification emerged as the major issue in South Korean politics. This development was closely related to the 'Nordpolitik' policy of the Roh Tae Woo administration (1988–93), which, recognising the need to reduce tension between the North and South, began to pursue better relations with the socialist countries. This policy was a response to the changing climate of the international politics that had been brought about by the end of the Cold War era and the reunification of Germany, among others. Roh's government, which was the last leg of the military rule that had prolonged for over thirty years, finally allowed unification to be discussed as part of public discourse. Motivated by this change in policy, various sectors of Korean society began to redefine the North as part of one national community. With this shift in the public view of North Korea, a clearer picture of North Korean society, and some of the historical events that had been heavily suppressed by the South Korean government, came to light.

The overall changes taking place in the film industry at the time were in keeping with these new measures in the government policies on North Korean matters. Since the mid-1980s, a series of films was produced about the families that had been separated between the North and South since the war. Works such as Pae Ch'angho's *Warm It Was That Winter* (1984), Im Kwŏnt'aek's *Kilsottŭm* (1985) and Yi Changho's *A Wayfarer Never Rests on the Road* (1987) signalled a drastically different approach to issues related to national division, reflecting the popular unification movement of the late 1980s. They tend to focus on the psychological problems of the separated families, rather than the 'evils' of communism. Their specific subjects are the memories of the family members in the 'other' territory and the rift between those who have successfully joined the middle class and those who have fallen to the bottom of the social ladder due to the forced separation from their families. *Southern Guerrilla Forces* belongs to a group of films that looks at the national tragedy from the victims' point of view.

As mentioned above, the Southern communist guerrillas were for a long time a taboo subject. Their existence had been erased from official history. On the screen, they were usually portrayed as villains who fell into the trap of North Korean communists because of their naïveté. *Southern Guerrilla Forces* deviates from such a stereotypical treatment of the communist guerrilla warfare in the 1950s. First of all, the protagonist of this film is not an uninformed and uneducated believer of communism. As in *The Banner Bearer*, *Southern Guerrilla Forces* selects an intellectual as the hero of the story and interprets his acceptance of communism as a kind of fate in the turmoil of the war.

Southern Guerrilla Forces was adapted from Yi T'ae's auto-biographical essay of the same title. The plot of the film is based on the author's personal experience as a partisan during the war. Yi, the protagonist and narrator of the film, is a reporter who once worked for the *Haptong Press*, the leading news agency in Seoul. After North Korea took over this agency during the early stages of the war, Yi was sent to the South as a war correspondent by the Party. He joins the Southern communist guerrillas who were hiding in the mountains due to the sudden retreat of the North Korea army under the unexpected massive scale of counter-attacks by the UN forces.

As Yi himself narrates, his entrance into partisan life was not something that he planned consciously in advance. Rather, the precarious war situation drove him into the mountains when no other alternative was available, and there he found the guerrilla forces. His initiation into the group was more or less fortuitous. As the film shows, however, once people choose sides between North and South, they are put in ideological straitjackets and are not allowed to change the position even though their political beliefs alter. This problem is seen when Yi and his colleagues are branded as communists by the South Korean government simply because they escaped into the mountains. Although Yi was critical of the censorship imposed by the South Korean govern-ment while he was working for the *Haptong Press*, he never considered himself a communist sympathiser. His narration on the development of the war are too objective to be used as an index of his ideological stance.

An important point raised by this film concerning ideology and nationhood is the lack of hatred among ordinary Koreans no matter which side they happen to be on. It is inevitable that they kill each other for survival in war, yet deep in their psyche, they always view each other as brothers who unfortunately have ended up on the 'enemy' side. The film maintains that this is why the Korean War is such a tragic irony for the majority of Koreans. This irony is expressed by one of the partisans: 'What a contradictory situation we are confronted with! In order to live like humans in the future, we have to kill our own people in the present'. This film does not present the guerrilla forces as inhuman machinery of the 'Communist Party' as has been done in numerous anti-communist films. Their partisan activities are motivated by a sincere wish to put an end to the national division as soon as possible. The film portrays them essentially as the unfortunate victims of the ideological conflicts as everyone else who was caught in the tragic fratricidal war. The images of the fugitive guerrillas in this film drastically diverge from the one-dimensional, negative portrait of the communists in the propaganda films produced in the past. Various episodes from the guerrillas' past lives demonstrate that they are people of flesh and blood with whom the audience can relate, not dehumanised ideologues who are out of touch with reality.

While the film adds a human touch to the partisans by interjecting their personal stories in the plot, it does not lose sight of their unity as a group. Their brotherly bond and patriotism are highlighted throughout the film. Their emotional ties to their outcast community and their nation keep them together. This solidarity and patriotism help to convert Yi and many other like him who joined the forces with no conviction towards communism. Their respectable attitudes towards each other and towards villagers also promise the possibility of restoring unified nationhood among the Korean people after the war.

In war films produced before the late 1980s, the Southern communist guerrillas appear as brutal bandits who massacre their innocent neighbours and then run away into the mountains. By contrast, Chŏng's film draws attention to the brotherly warmth and disciplined attitude they display towards people living at the foot of the mountains. When the guerrilla forces attack the South Korean army or when they retreat, their main concern is the safety of the villagers, who have to continue their everyday lives regardless of the changing situations of the war. Hence, before launching an attack, the guerrilla forces ensure that all villagers move to a safe place. To reduce the casualties among the villagers, the guerrillas sometimes choose a less advantageous course of action for themselves, even though it could be fatal for them. The film attempts to realistically capture a deep emotional bond, which still continue to exist in the Korean people even in war-time devastation. Along this line, the film also stresses the guerrilla forces' strict moral standards. A battalion commander is ordered to kill himself by his superior for raping a village woman, who is the wife of a policeman and is suspected of informing the police of the guerrillas' activities in the village. Her information resulted in a large number of deaths. She deserves a severe reprisal by the guerrilla forces, but the partisan leaders determine that the battalion commander's crime is inexcusable and that the reputation of the entire forces cannot be slurred by pardoning him.

The villagers' attitudes toward the guerrilla forces in this film are also very different from those in anti-communist films. They often help the partisans although they are well aware of the punishment for such activities by the South Korean government. They feed the guerrillas and hide them from the South Korean army. The film emphasises that their help is purely a humane one and is not politically motivated. The villagers cannot turn their backs on their fellow countrymen who are in danger of starvation and death. The film's emphasis on humanism that transcends ideology is evident in many scenes. Although the positive portrayal of the guerrilla forces occasionally takes on an unrealistic note, it is on the whole, not excessive.[12] If it is, its main purpose is to rectify the mistaken view of the Southern guerrilla forces, which was fostered by the anti-communist policies.

Southern Guerrilla Forces occasioned a re-evaluation of the Southern guerrilla forces among the public in the South. They began to be seen as a group with its own vision for the nation's future, not a handful of rebellious people manoeuvred by the North. They gathered around the eminent historical person, Yi Hŏnsang, who had earned respect from people for his anti-Japanese resistance activities. Yi is also known as a legendary communist and nationalist who fought against the US military regime and Syngman Rhee's regime (1948–61) from 1945 until he was killed during the war.

Another important adjustment the film makes in official history is that communist sentiments were far more widely spread in South Korean during the 1950s than the government acknowledges. According to the official account, the Southern communist guerrillas were an isolated group of rebels living in the areas of the T'aebaek mountain range who mounted a 'mutiny'. *Southern Guerrilla Forces* challenges this explanation. The members of the guerrilla forces, including the journalist–protagonist, are not local residents. The film thus carefully avoids the regional dialect of the T'aebaek Mountains. The partisans came from all over the country, and their motives to join the group also differ from one member to another. Some wanted to escape from poverty, and some were driven by the patriotic impulse to fight for the country. Some were simply discontent with the South Korean government, and others indeed embraced the idea of a classless society as espoused by communism. Many other reasons exist besides these. Their diverse backgrounds successfully dismantle the long-held misperception that the guerrillas were reckless malcontents and 'traitors' of their country.

In essence, *Southern Guerrilla Forces* is an anti-war film. At the closure of the film, the guerrilla base is extirpated by the South Korean army. The majority of the partisans are killed and those

19 Yi T'ae and his comrades struggle for survival, trapped behind enemy lines: Chŏng Chiyŏng's *Southern Guerrilla Forces* (1990)

who survive leave the mountains by their own will. Some of the few survivors are eventually arrested by the government. Despite this terrible end, none of the surviving members consider themselves defeated. They believe that they did what they viewed as the best for their country at a given moment of history, although this will ostracise them permanently from society. Their ultimate heroism lies in this acceptance of the consequences of their action. The ending of the film reiterates that they did not waste their youth or abandon their lives for meaningless war. Given this unconventional treatment of the Southern communist partisans, it is not surprising that the film caused huge controversy when it was released in 1989.

An overview of the three South Korean films helps to tap into the changes in their interpretations of the impact of the national division on nationhood. One of the major shifts is the increasing scepticism about anti-communism as the ideological basis of national identity. Since the end of the Korean War in 1953, anti-communism has been enforced in every aspect of Koreans' lives in the South in the name of national security. At the same time, its has been appropriated as a rhetorical instrument by the military regime for its own political interests. Anti-communism has been used to control the public by engendering the fear of a possible recurrence of civil war and of the communists' total take-over of the South. The rhetoric appealed to the generation that experienced the tragic war. Yet as the socio-economic conditions improved over the years, the propaganda about a communist threat has lost much of its appeal for new generations. Consequently, the emotional power of anti-communism, which constituted the strong basis of Korean self-identity during the immediate post-war period, has been slowly eroded in recent years. The tremendous success of *Southern Guerrilla Forces*, despite the direct and indirect interventions of various conservative groups, such as the Censorship Committee, military, war-veterans' association and North Korean refugee organisations, clearly reflects the changing perception of the general public.[13] The rejection of the hackneyed Cold War ideology testifies to the shifting sensibility of the audience toward films dealing with the South–North political confrontation and their demands for a more mature discussion of nationhood in the 1990s.

Familyhood and nationhood

North and South Korean films follow different ideological frames for defining nationhood. The North Korean films tend to approach the issue exclusively in political terms, whereas the South Korean ones adopt more varied perspectives. Underneath these surface differences, however, both groups employ surprisingly similar motifs of Confucian familyhood. They commonly see the traditional family structure as the unchanging, fundamental frame of Korean nationhood. One noticeable difference between the two sets of films is that the North Korean works concentrate on patriarchal lineage, whereas the South Korean pieces are interested in the implications of the husband–wife union.

Throughout *Ch'oe Hakshin's Family*, *Sea of Blood*, and *Wŏlmi Island*, nationhood is defined in terms of the opposition between imperialism and the Korean people's resistance to it. This antithesis manifests itself in different forms in each film, but what remains common in all of them is their use of the old Confucian rhetoric of family. The three films present the Korean nation essentially as one large family. The relationships of the characters are defined in terms of the constituents of a family tree. In this extended family, Kim Il Sung takes the position of the father, who then looks after the rest of the members as his children.

North Korean films employ three strategies to promote paternal authority: the replacement of the biological father with the symbolic one; the elevation of maternal virtues as an alternative to the failure or absence of the biological father; and the foregrounding of the eldest son as the legitimate heir to the family line. The symbolisation of Kim Il Sung as the father figure is partly achieved by means of the contrast between true and false fatherhood. In all three films, the actual father is presented as a failed or false hero who is too weak to embrace the masses. The protagonist in *Ch'oe Hakshin's Family* typifies false fatherhood. His mistaken view of Americans leads his family and neighbours to death. His youngest daughter is the only one that bravely stands up to the father's misjudgements and criticises his reactionary attitude. Her search for a reliable father figure begins when she breaks off her filial relationship with her father and leaves her family to follow her communist fiancé Yŏngsu, much to her father's objection. When she joins a guerrilla unit later, she also forms a pseudo-filial relationship with her commander, a father figure, whom the film appears to relate to the image of General Kim.

In *Sea of Blood* and *Wŏlmi Island*, fatherhood is not fully handled. In the former, the family does have the father but he dies too early and thus fails to become a model revolutionary for his family. His untimely death leaves the unfinished burden of revolution on the shoulders of his family. The search for a true father figure culminates in *Wŏlmi Island*. The protagonist T'aehun is an orphan, and characters around him also have no memories of their father. Odd as it is, this phenomenon clears the ground for implementing Kim's symbolic fatherhood. As is shown by the film, Kim fills in the psychological void of the characters as the patriarch of the nation.

In relation to the symbolic substitution for the inadequate father figure, the North Korean films uplift the mother's role. In each film, the mother figure is portrayed as drawing her children's respect for her self-sacrificing dedication to them. In *Ch'oe Hakshin's Family*, the mother helps her youngest daughter to take care of her injured fiancé without her husband's knowledge. In *Sea of Blood*, it is the mother who, with her enduring strength and determination, brings up the children as anti-Japanese fighters. Her heroic qualities are strikingly contrasted with the untimely death of their helpless father. *Wŏlmi Island* does not contain a mother figure. However, the old soldier who works as a cook in the company embodies attitudes that are associated with the mother figure. His role can be safely said to be equivalent to the mother's. Maternal qualities in him are fully demonstrated by the care he provides for the entire company behind the bloody battle fronts.

At first glance, the positive maternal images may appear to undermine the promotion of Kim's stature as the benevolent father figure. But a close reading of the scenes centred on the mother figure clearly reveals that, while her virtues are glorified, she does not have any real authority or power over her children. The mothers in these films faithfully perform the maternal role prescribed by the Confucian ethics. Therefore the close tie between the mother and her children is not in conflict with the effort to consolidate Kim's 'boundless' love and absolute power as the ultimate Father. The mother is always in an inferior position to the father. Therefore the elevation of her virtues cannot pose a threat to the patriarch. In Confucian family life, respect for the mother does not mean obedience to her. With the father, however, these two attitudes go hand in hand. Any suggestions the mother makes for her children can be valid only if they are approved by the father. Therefore, no matter how noble they are, the mother's virtues cannot affect, let alone damage, the father's absolute authority over the children. One of the important responsibilities of the mother figure in the Confucian family circle is to ensure that her children serve their father appropriately with filial piety. *Sea of Blood* praises the mother's patriotic dedication of her own children to the father: she first sends her eldest son to join the KPRA and then sacrifices her second son for the anti-imperialist cause. In the last scene of the film, she presents her daughter, the only child left to her, to the communists. In *Wŏlmi Island*, the old cook believes that he can repay Kim's love by taking good care of the soldiers. He keeps telling the soldiers about Kim's great fatherhood as a mother would do in a Confucian family.

The last feature of the Confucian family values found in North Korean films is the respect displayed for the eldest son as successor of the paternal lineage. The films promote the eldest son of the family in lieu of an inadequate father. He can represent the entire family when his father is either dead or cannot perform his due function. These films commonly assign a special role to the son: instilling his family with the revolutionary spirit.

Without doubt, the positive images of the eldest son in North Korean films are directly relevant to the preparation for the power succession from Kim Il Sung to his son Kim Jong Il. This tendency becomes markedly noticeable in films made since the mid-1970s over which Kim the junior was designated the prospective successor to his father's position. The eldest son in *Sea of Blood* leaves his family to join the KPRA, and later, he returns as a saviour figure for the family when it is besieged by the Japanese assaults. In *Wŏlmi Island*, T'aehun acts like a typical eldest son, taking care of the soldiers in this family-like company unit. Brotherhood is a universal metaphor used to describe military personnel in action. Therefore T'aehun's fraternity with the other battalion members in this film does not seem to require further detailed explanation.

South Korean films also explain society in terms of the unity and responsibilities of family members. The use of the family metaphor is used largely in three patterns. First of all, the burden of securing family welfare is put on the shoulders of the male protagonists. By extension, any disorder in society, be it political or cultural, is attributed to the inability of the male adults to perform their functions in their home and society. Second, the South Korean films frequently use women's predicament as a metaphor for the troubled nation. Lastly, these films use the motif of marriage in relation to the possibility of the nation's regeneration. The betrayal of a marriage promise, therefore, often accounts for the problems faced by the characters. It can be further read as the society's uncertainty about or even pessimistic view of its future.

The protagonists of *Stray Bullet*, *Banner Bearer without a Flag* and *Southern Guerrilla Forces* are all male. As a father and/or son, they are responsible for providing for their family and establishing order in society. Therefore their confusion and drifting symbolise the quandary into which the entire society has fallen. In the last scene of *Stray Bullet*, Ch'ŏlho confesses in a monologue that he cannot cope with 'too many responsibilities' put on his shoulders as the eldest son, husband and father. As he wanders the streets of Seoul, his mind is never free from the family pressure, which only grows with the arrival of his first baby. In *Banner Bearer without a Flag*, Yun's decision to eliminate Yi is prompted by the misery of the little boy, a son figure, whom he meets in the anti-trust demonstration. Yun's 'fatherly' duty is also provoked by the son of his lodging house who is savagely killed by the communists. In *Southern Guerrilla Forces*, the guerrilla members provide paternal care for teenagers who joined the forces but are too young to be engaged in battle. Responsible and reliable in the isolated mountain community, the guerrillas embody the respectable attributes of male adults as expected in traditional family life.

Compared with these male protagonists, nearly all the female characters are depicted as defenceless victims of forces beyond their control. The ordeals that they undergo figuratively stand for the plight of the entire country. Aside from poverty and insanity, prostitution and rape serve as particularly acute metaphors for the country's traumatic experiences of humiliation and helplessness. Typical examples are: Myŏngsuk in *Stray Bullet*, Yunim, Yi Ch'ŏl's mistress, in *Banner Bearer without a Flag* and the policeman's wife in *Southern Guerrilla Forces* who is assaulted by the battalion commander.

The miseries of these women are partly brought about by the failure of their men in their social role. In *Stray Bullet*, Ch'ŏlho's loss of a sense of direction contributes to the worsening of his mother's illness and the death of his wife. The mother and the daughter of the lodging house in *Banner Bearer without a Flag* suffer from the father's political ambition, especially his involvement in the communist activities during the Japanese colonial period. The father's misjudgements in action – betraying his communist comrades and the subsequent efforts to overcome his guilt – result in the death of his son, which leaves a deep scar in the two women's lives. In *Southern Guerrilla Forces*, the stories of three women partisans also evidence the influence of the old patriarchal values on women's lives. One of them joined the forces to revenge the villagers who killed her father and attacked her mother. The second woman became a partisan out of compassion for the wounded soldiers who reminded her of her dead brother. The third character entered the partisan life, led by her love for the student–poet who was in the guerrilla forces.

The emphasis on a stable patriarchal order in the South Korean films is more or less akin to the persistent reinforcement of the family rhetoric in the North Korean films. In their films, traditional family values are commonly treated as the most powerful cultural force that provides the Korean people with a sense of 'oneness' as a nation. An ability to extend familial affection and responsibility toward non-family members in society is stressed in both groups of films as an important factor for Koreans in maintaining their nationhood. These films even suggest familialism as the moral foundation for restoring a unified nation in the future. In this sense, the representation of nationhood in South and North Korean films can be seen as an extension or variation of familyhood. In other words, nationhood is simply a form of familyhood amplified to a societal level.

In handling the familial aspect of nationhood, however, one distinct difference exists between North and South Korean films: while the former puts the accent on the father–son relationship, the latter has the motif of marriage as an indispensable element in a plot development. As marriage often signifies a successful restoration of the lost order of a community, the broken dream of marriage indicates the difficulty of resolving the conflicts of society. In *Stray Bullet*, the broken engagement drives Myŏngsuk out to the street. Her loss of trust in men is comparable to a suspicion about society's moral basis. Similarly, Yŏngho's attempted bank robbery is caused by the unexpected death of his girl friend. Unlike in *Stray Bullet*, the motif of marriage introduces a note of hope in *Banner Bearer without a Flag* and *Southern Guerrilla Forces*. In the former, Yun's subtle proposal to the daughter of his landlord allows the audience momentary relief from the oppressive tension pervading the film. Their dialogue about marriage is perhaps the only moment in this tragic story when the protagonist is shown cheerful and happy. In *Southern Guerrilla Forces*, the prospect of a happy marriage is part of the humanistic portrayal of the guerrilla members. The protagonist promises Pak Minja, a fellow partisan, to marry her when the war is over. Their idea of a happy union means domestic peace based on the traditional patriarchal order. Their dream of a new family life recapitulates the hope and vision that the guerrilla forces have about the future of their nation.

The analysis of the six films confirms the existence of differences between North and South Korea in their perceptions of nationhood. Given the wide range of ramifications of their ongoing confrontation in nearly every aspect of their society, we can safely conclude that their conflicting self-identities are the results of the 'politics of the division'. The North Korean films lucidly illustrate this point. In North Korea, there are party guidelines that film-makers are mandated to follow from choice of subject-matter through to the distribution of their finished works. The late Kim Il Sung has left an instruction to this effect, according to which each film should be well balanced in incorporating the elements of the anti-imperialist struggle during the Japanese colonial period and those of the 1950–53 national liberation war. The proportion of these elements, Kim stresses, determines the attitude of the film towards nationhood. Faithful to this instruction, North Korean films interpret the current national division as the consequence of the foreign interference in Korean politics since the late nineteenth century. In their view, the US troops stationed in Korea epitomise the continued intervention of the superpowers. For North Korean film-makers, Korean nationhood has been moulded through the Korean people's strife against foreign imperialists. For this reason, South Korea cannot claim historical legitimacy and is not regarded as the counterpart to North Korea: their 'real' opponent is the USA. This view is translated into their film language: North Korean films scarcely portray South Koreans in depth because they do not represent a *separate* political entity that deserves meaningful attention.

The partition of North and South Korea is a product of the Cold War, and the Korean people perceive themselves as its victims. Until the early 1970s, both sides had denied that there were two Koreas, and there had been no direct contact between the two governments. Since the end of the Korean War, their ideological confrontation had only intensified. However, signs of change, feeble as they were, were discernible from the 1970s. They were largely owing to the changing mood in the international community, general trends toward a *détente* in North East Asia and the Sino-American *rapprochement*, in particular. Encouraged by these developments in the arena of international politics, the North and South Korean governments began to negotiate the possibility of recognising the existence of two Koreas. The initial phase of their discussion was not fruitful, yielding only nominal recognition of the status quo. Toward the late 1980s, however, both sides began to make efforts to legislate actual policies that would materialise the idea of two Koreas. *Southern Guerrilla Forces* can be counted as a concrete reflection of this change. At least in the South, films began to express doubts more openly on the political approach to the question of national identity. On the one hand, they reassess the validity of the Cold War ideology as the basis of their nationhood. On the other hand, they admit that any sincere attempt to discuss nationhood cannot but be overshadowed by the reality of the political confrontation. This dilemma is not irrelevant to the fact that the antagonistic rivalry between North and South has not much abated despite their occasional peace talks. The two governments still hold on to their mutually contradictory diagnoses on the causes of the national division and to their incompatible plans for a future reunification. All these differences fundamentally stem from the legitimacy problems of the current regimes.

This ongoing tension does not mean that there is no vision for a broad and more integrated version of nationhood in Korean films. As has already been pointed out, the long-standing values of Confucian family relationships, which are commonly present in North and South Korean films, can provide a model for restoring cultural continuity and rebuilding unified nationhood. Benedict Anderson maintains that nation is an imagined political community and that nationalism invents nations where they do not exist.[14] He also argues that the central factor in the conception of nationalism is a cultural system rather than a self-consciously held political ideology.[15] Despite the obvious existence of two polities on the peninsula, the majority of Koreans do not recognise the idea of two Koreas in the cultural realm. Their conviction of ethnic and cultural homogeneity is so strong that the unification of the country is viewed as historically inevitable.

Having been a single nation for the most part of their history, the Korean people in both South and North interpret the last fifty years as an unwanted arrangement forced upon them by the superpowers and, as such, as a temporary phase they should and will overcome in time. This aspiration to retrieve unity and solidarity as one nation is manifest in the persistent theme of treating neighbours as one's own family members. The fostering of familial ties among the community is widely found in *Ch'oe Hakshin's Family*, *Sea of Blood*, *Wŏlmi Island*, *Stray Bullet* and *Southern Guerrilla Forces*. Even in *Banner Bearer without a Flag*, a true hero is defined as one who has courage to take action against hidden vice in one's neighbourhood. These films commonly emphasise empathy and respect as necessary conditions for the Korean people to achieve a sense of community. It would operate like a family, transcending the current internal dissension, and the films attempt to find a model for this in their pre-war cultural tradition.

Notes

1 In this book, the term 'nation' is defined as 'a group of people who have some common ancestry, history, culture and language, which figure as a focus of loyalty and affection'. See Andrew Vincent, *Modern Political Ideology* (Oxford, Blackwell Publisher, 1995), p. 239. It is generally understood that 'nation' and 'nationalism' came to be accepted terms in Europe from the late eighteenth century. Their definitions are, however, applicable to an earlier period in case of Korea, because it shows general characteristics of a nation since the unification by Shilla in the seventh century.

2 Andrew Heywood, *Political Ideologies: An Introduction* (London, Macmillan Press, 1992), p. 141. In contrast to Heywood, scholars such as Max Weber and Anthony Giddens put more weight on political factors in defining a nation. According to Weber, 'national' affiliation does not need to be based on a common language, a common religion or a common blood. Similarly, Giddens argues that 'a nation only exists when a state has a unified administrative reach over the territory over which its sovereignty is claimed'. Max Weber, 'The nation', in John Hutchinson and Anthony D. Smith (eds), *Nationalism* (Oxford, Oxford University Press, 1994), pp. 21–5; and Anthony Giddens, 'The nation as power-container', in Hutchinson and Smith (eds), *Nationalism*, p. 34.

3 Heywood, *Political Ideologies*, p. 141.

4 Heywood, *Political Ideologies*, p. 148.

5 Michael Howard, 'War and nations', in Hutchinson and Smith (eds), *Nationalism*, p. 255.

6 The agreeable characterisation of the head of the village can be interpreted as hinting at Kim's leadership. However, given several scenes that do not consciously elevate his authority, the connection between the character and the cult of Kim's personality can be said to be, at best, tenuous.

7 Jae-Jean Suh, 'Theoretical revision of *Juche* thought and nationalism

in North Korea', *The Korean Journal of National Unification*, 2 (1993), p. 20.

8 Kim Il Sung, 'Let us embody the revolutionary spirit of independence, self-sustenance and self-defense more thoroughly in all branches of state activities: political programme of the government of the Democratic People's Republic of Korean announced at the first session of the fourth Supreme People's Assembley of the DPRK, 16 December 1967', in *Kim Il Sung Works 21* (Pyongyang, Foreign Languages Publishing House, 1985), p. 414.

9 Ch'oe Ch'ŏkho, *Pukhan Yesul Yŏnghwa* (North Korean Art Film) (Seoul, Shinwŏn Munhwasa, 1989), p. 125.

10 *Korean Film Art* [no page number is available].

11 For the 'modelling theory' and the other two principles of filmmaking in North Korea, see Chapter 1, p. 33.

12 For example, when a little boy runs across the battlefield, chasing after his dog, both the guerrillas and the South Korean army stop crossing-firing. As soon as the boy gets out of the danger, they shout at each other to elicit a surrender and later even sing together, instead of resuming shooting.

13 The commercial failure of *The T'aebaek Mountains*, Im Kwŏnt'aek's 1993 film which deals with the same materials as *Southern Guerrilla Forces*, testifies to the change in the public opinion. The failure is generally ascribed to the anti-communist resonance that reverberates throughout the film.

14 Benedict Anderson, *Imagined Communities* (London, Verso, 1991), p. 6.

15 Anderson, *Imagined Communities*, p. 12.

4 Class and cultural identities in contemporary Korea

Class is one of the foremost factors in the formation of cultural identities of contemporary Koreans living as a divided nation. Class conflict was a major contributor to the breakout of the Korean War,[1] and the ongoing confrontation between North and South is, arguably, the manifestation of their fundamentally irreconcilable stances on class issues. Class defines Koreans' selfhood in both personal and social domains through such economic indicators as occupation, income and ownership as well as through their relationship to the modes of production. As will be demonstrated below, however, the concept of class in Korean society depends on not only the economic system, but also on the cultural legacies of the Confucian occupational order from the traditional period.

In cultural criticism, a widely cited Marxist definition of class is 'categories based on the economic resources of different groups of people in a given society'.[2] For Marxists, then, 'normally only *two* classes are permitted' because class is defined in terms of ownership or non-ownership of the means of production.[3] The problem with this dichotomy is noted by Marx himself, who admits that 'not everybody in capitalist societies necessarily belongs to one of the two great classes'.[4]

Class is a cultural phenomenon resulting from the interplay of multiple factors. In the case of contemporary Korea, history plays a decisive role in the construction of social classes. From this point of view, E. P. Thompson's emphasis on the historical dimension of class provides lucid insights into the cinematic representation of the ways in which contemporary Koreans relate class issues to their cultural identities. In the preface to his book *The Making of the English Working Class*, Thompson maintains that class is 'a *historical* phenomenon', not 'a "structure" nor even a "category"'. It is 'something which in fact happens (and can be shown to have happened) in human relationships'.[5] In other words, class is 'a social and cultural formation, arising from processes which can be studied as they work themselves out over a considerable historical period'.[6]

Class issues are at the core of the ideological foundation of North Korea; therefore, it is not surprising at all that they have remained major preoccupations of North Korean film-makers throughout film history. Nearly all North Korean films, in fact, deal with class issues in one way or another. Their treatment of the subject is invariably driven by the motivation to indoctrinate North Korean citizens about the superiority of their worker-dominant socialist society. As their cultural products are under state control, the self-identities of North Koreans cannot be conceived separately from the class-consciousness defined by Kim Il Sung and the Party for their specific political purposes.

A solid working class was an economic as well as an ideological exigency for North Korea as a nascent socialist state. On the one hand, the nation-building during the post-liberation period necessitated a large-scale drive for labour force. On the other, a working class was an ideological foundation of North Korea's statehood, whose supreme premise is the proletariat dictatorship of society. Unlike a capitalist society in which a working class gradually forms itself in the process of industrialisation, North Korea was under severe internal pressure to establish this class for the legitimacy of its own *raison d'être*. Therefore, it can be maintained that the working class in North Korea was, to a large extent, deliberately 'created' rather than 'naturally' formed as a by-product of industrialisation.

As a preliminary step towards its constitutional mandate to 'transform the entire population into a unitary class of workers', North Korea began to prepare a plan to classify all its citizens from the late 1940s. When a more consolidated form of communist social structure was emerging in the late 1950s, the initial concept of the unitary class of workers became further categorised into three strata, which have continued in a basic structure up to the present day. These societal levels are comprised of the core, the unstable and the hostile (or ruling, basic and complex).[7] The core (or ruling) stratum constitutes about 25 per cent of the entire North Korean population. They are comprised of revolutionary fighters, war veterans, party members, office workers, labourers, military officers and all of their family members. This stratum also includes those who were servants in traditional society as well as the so-called 'new' generations of intelligentsia that appeared after the Liberation. Members of the core stratum are qualified for higher education, Party memberships, military careers and important governmental posts. They are also given privileges in medical care, food distribution and the choice of residence.

The unstable (or basic) stratum accounts for approximately 50 per cent of the population in a wide variety of occupations, ranging from ordinary factory workers, low-ranking office workers, farmers, artisans and waitresses to small-scale merchants and industrialists. Intellectuals from the pre-Liberation period also belong to this stratum. There are limitations for members of this stratum in terms of residence, travel and career development. For example, they are not allowed to travel without permission beyond certain districts.

Lastly, the hostile (or complex) stratum that makes up roughly 20 per cent of the North Korean population consists of anti-revolutionaries, factionalists, sympathisers with Japan or America, wealthy farmers, landowners, criminals, political prisoners, spies, capitalists, members of religious groups, and so on. The family members of these people are automatically categorised as hostile. Such groups are consequently subject to various forms of social discrimination and severe restrictions. They are forced to live in designated areas invisible to outside visitors, virtually quarantined from people of the other strata. They are under the tight surveillance of the Party. Most of them are in fact sent to forced labour camps. Throughout their lives, they are denied opportunities for education and are prohibited from applying for Party membership.

To follow the orthodox Marxist doctrine, a socialist country should be classless, because, in theory, no private ownership of productive property can exist.[8] Of course, reality is far from this ideal. Recent studies on North Korean class structure and the testimonies of North Korean refugees show that the self-claimed 'classless' North Korea in fact suffers from growing tension and conflicts within its unitary class system.[9] According to the refugees, the antagonistic sentiment of the ordinary working masses against the state has become more intense over the years. This is due to a noticeable gulf in living standards and other social and political opportunities between the masses and Party members or other high-ranking officers and their families. Their discontent has also deepened due to the economic stagnation of the whole country since the 1980s and the strict control of the central government over their social mobility.

The above problems reflect a change over the decades in the class composition of North Korean society. Recent sources suggest that the socio-economic divisions in North Korean society still appear to be sharply defined. This tendency seems to reflect the growing social inequality: for instance, the middle class has risen from 6.2 per cent in 1946 to around 17 per cent in 1987.[10] The increase consists mainly of intellectuals, technicians and office workers. The new middle class, whose key members are highly educated professionals, forms technocrats in the Party and is expected to substitute the old partisan generation. As the recent North Korean films show, the Party has become seriously concerned with various ideological and social consequences of the newly emerging power élite groups, along with the increasing aspiration of the working masses for upward social mobility and white-collar jobs.

In South Korea, the class situation is more complex. As a capitalist society, South Korea has a more varied and flexible class division, starting from the traditional landed ruling class; old and new bourgeois; peasants; proletariat and so on. These classes can be conveniently grouped into four: the working, new middle, old middle and capital classes. This categorisation has been the result of the industrialisation since the 1960s, which significantly altered the social fabric of the country. This period witnessed the transformation of peasants into the working class, the rapid rise of a new middle class and the replacement of the old landed class with the newly formed capital class. As of 1995 the ratio among the four classes was 41.6 per cent working class; 30.9 per cent new middle; 20.9 per cent old middle; and 6.6 per cent capital.[11]

Given the open possibility of social mobility, class does not affect South Koreans' cultural identities as deeply as is the case with North Koreans'. Nevertheless, class issues have begun to attract attention from the general public since the 1970s; largely in connection with the increasing number of cases involving labour disputes and coupled with the influx of the rural population into urban areas. This was the period in which the first full-scale economic development plan was carried out. The all-out drive for industrialisation was possible under President Park's dictatorship. However, the tight censorship of the film industry during the 1970s did not allow film-makers to treat subject-matter related to class.

Due to the all-out drive for industrialisation, the capitalist economy took off in subsequent decades in South Korea, but at the same time, its politics was restrained and restricted by the successive military regimes. Witnessing various social ills from the growing gap between the rich and the poor and spurred by the oppressive political atmosphere, young directors began to analyse class conflicts from the 1980s as the most pressing concerns of their society.[12] Using cinema as a medium for social criticism, they addressed the inequity in cultural opportunities and material conditions among different population groups. It is the dark side of the economically prospering country that triggered these film-makers to demystify the 'Miracle of Han River'. Some of their representative films are: Yi Changho's *A Nice Windy Day* (1980), *Children of Darkness* (1981), *Widow's Dance* (1983), and *A Declaration of Fools* (1983), Yi Wŏnse's *A Little Ball Launched by a Dwarf* (1981) and Pae Ch'angho's *Slum Dwellers* (1982). These films generally focus on the anxiety and despair of the urban poor struggling for survival. In terms of formal characteristics, these works follow the realistic tradition by attempting to mirror social realities in the manner of verisimilitude.

With the emergence of the cinema of social criticism, the government intensified its ideological and political control over the film industry.[13] The escalating censorship of 'undesirable' films was justified by the rationale that they would 'lower' the morale of people at the peak of the industrialisation process. Some films were even banned from export for fear of discouraging foreign investments. One of the unexpressed yet vital concerns of the government was that these films might draw public attention to class problems latent in South Korean society. Raising a class issue during this period was considered an ideological offence similar to treason because the country was, technically speaking, still at war with the North.

Despite the government intervention, new generations of directors continued to make films on the social chaos and political turmoil in the late 1980s and throughout the 1990s: Pak Kwangsu's *Ch'ilsu and Mansu* (1988), *Black Republic* (1990) and *A Single Spark* (1996), and Pak Chongwŏn's *Kuro Arirang* (1989). Some directors took a drastic direction in the 1980s and the early 1990s and led the National Film Movement. Centred around a film group called 'Changsan'gonmae', these film-makers approached film as a socio-political text of the masses and a medium for protest. Their primary aim was to expose the 'structural contradiction' of capitalist society and appeal to the public on the necessity of a class revolution. They claimed that film is neither a commercial activity nor mass entertainment and thus must be produced and distributed separately from the existing systems. They maintained that to accomplish their revolutionary goals, their works should attract working-class viewers. However, their total rejection of the existing systems and purposeful treatments of labour issues resulted in alienating the majority of the viewing public. Among a series of films they made, *The Night before the Strike* (1990) is the best known. Of the latest South Korean films bent on social commentary, Chang Sŏnu's *A Petal* (1996) and Yi Ch'angdong's *Peppermint Candy* (2000) are worthy of note. Both deal with the deep psychological scars left by the 1980 Kwangju Uprising, one of the most violent democratisation movements in modern Korean history.

Class provides engaging yet controversial materials for the Korean film industries on both sides. As discussed above, contemporary Koreans have generally suffered from the fear of class-labelling, a form of political stigmatisation. Once a North Korean is labelled 'reactionary', his or her class-consciousness is declared impure. For Southerners, the expression 'red' means pro-communist thereby anti-social and worse yet, pro-North Korea. Keeping such a political climate in mind, the central concern of this chapter is to describe the ways in which the class structures in the North and the South infiltrate the daily lives of ordinary people. Broadly speaking, North Korean films show a tendency to defend the security of the existing social structure, whereas those from the South tend to challenge it. Film as a cultural text unveils the complex workings of the notion of class in social interaction. It inevitably exposes problems of the established social structure through textual interstices, which are often hidden under an ideological rhetoric. For example, the North Korean films examined in this chapter reveal that the self-claimed 'classless paradise' of North Korea is troubled by the discontented workers and farmers. They are dissatisfied with their social positions and yearn for a more privileged place in the class system. Similarly, the rather seedy slums portrayed in the films make a stark contrast with the glittering modern buildings in the South Korean urban topography.

A discussion of contemporary Koreans' selfhood would not be complete without an appropriate examination of the cultural manifestations of the idea of class. The six films analysed in this chapter were made between 1980 and 1990. The texts from North Korea are: O Pyŏngch'o's *The Untrodden Path* (1980), Ch'ae P'unggi's *The Brigade Commander's Former Superior* (1983), and Cho Kyŏngsun's *Bellflower* (1987). The corresponding South Korean films are: Yi Changho's *A Nice Windy Day* (1980), Pak Chongwŏn's *Kuro Arirang* (1989) and Pak Kwangsu's *Black Republic* (1990). These six films commonly concern the life of the working class by portraying various consequences of the social dislocations and cultural confusion of contemporary Koreans.

Class conflicts in three North Korean films

The Untrodden Path

Set in the post-Liberation period of North Korea, O Pyŏngch'o's *The Untrodden Path* dramatises the process of establishing a working class in the newly emerging socialist state. The process takes the form of journey by the protagonist Kim Ch'ŏljun, who, as a former anti-Japanese fighter, is now determined to continue his patriotic work for his liberated country. Upholding Kim Il Sung's doctrine of 'an independent national economy', Ch'ŏljun does his utmost to build heavy industries amidst a severe dearth of resources. He believes that self-reliance is the only way to overcome the shortage of materials and technology. In this way the film symbolises the values and ideologies behind General Kim's revolutionary economic theory. O's film covers the initial phase of the period in which the North Korean authorities endeavoured to organise society according to their vision of a proletariat dictatorship.

The Untrodden Path presents Ch'ŏljun as an exemplary worker who has successfully risen to a group of power élites, with his background in anti-Japanese activities and with his invincible class-consciousness. Because of this status change, he functions as an ideal mediator between the state and the masses. The film consists of a series of journeys he makes to distant corners of the country, delivering Kim Il Sung's message on how to build industries with the limited resources, and addressing the importance of the working class in achieving that goal. His call for hard work aims to bring disparate pockets of labour forces in remote areas under the central state control.

The camera-work reinforces Ch'ŏljun as an embodiment of the 'inseparable tie' between the working class and the Party. Two contrastive compositions are noted in the scenes of public meetings. When a conference is held among factory officers, the protagonist is placed in between General Kim's portrait, which is in the upper zone of the frame, and the factory managers and supervisors who are seated in the lower zone. In keeping with the hierarchical positioning of the characters, the camera alternates between low and high angles, indicating Ch'ŏljun's perspective on the factory leaders and vice versa. Conversely, scenes in which Ch'ŏljun mingles with ordinary factory workers tend to position everybody on the same level. The horizontal alignment of the masses is accompanied by the camera's tendency to shoot the scenes through panning rather than craning the camera.

Ch'ŏljun's mission as a party messenger is partly to gather information from all sectors of North Korean society as a preliminary phase of the Party's classification of the population. One of the hidden agenda behind his visits is, therefore, diagnosing each category of North Koreans. The upshot of the film is to justify the Party's intention to integrate the majority of citizens into one unified working class. In the process, however, the film inevitably deals with the problems of industrialists, capitalists, intellectuals and technicians, who do not easily fit in the new system envisioned by the Party but are useful in their economic development project. The broad picture of the social strata suggested by the film squarely matches the actual class system, which came to be stabilised forcibly by the Party in the subsequent years. As mentioned in the introduction, North Korean society was divided into three strata in the late 1950s: the core, the unstable and the hostile. In O's film the three strata are represented by a factory worker Kim Ch'ungil, an old-time intellectual Yi Pyŏngch'an, and the unnamed director of the arms bureau, respectively. In screening and selecting people for each stratum, Ch'ŏljun considers their economic and social backgrounds together with loyalty towards Kim Il Sung and the Party to be the two most important criteria.

The film portrays Ch'ungil, a steel factory worker, as a role model for the core stratum. He has a sound class background, as is revealed by his painful memories of his two brothers killed in industrial accidents when the factory was under Japanese control. The film repeatedly emphasises that the Japanese never cared about the safety of Korean workers. Ch'ungil is well aware of this danger because he himself worked for the factory during the colonial period. This is why he loathes working there after the Liberation. However, he ultimately volunteers to return to the factory out of sheer patriotism; he feels that he should participate in the nation-building by producing much-needed steel. He deeply impresses Ch'ŏljun with his enthusiasm for work and his absolute belief in Kim Il Sung's vision. When the General later orders the factory to be closed for safety reasons, he praises the leader's 'deep concern' for the workers, in opposition to the managers who complain about the loss of the precious resources in the middle of their intensive endeavour for industrialisation. After the demolition of the factory, Ch'ungil even proposes to introduce a new method of processing steel with granulated iron. Due to his positive and aggressive attitudes toward the post-war reconstruction, Ch'ungil is put forward by Ch'ŏljun to attend an engineering college. On receiving formal education, he is finally appointed to the top manager position in an arms-manufacturing factory.

Ch'ungil is sharply contrasted with those who do not accept

the idea of self-reliance in technology. The director of the arms bureau, for example, looks down on Ch'ungil for his 'lowly' class origin and lack of professional knowledge on automatic rifles. Having studied engineering abroad, the director openly ridicules and insults the 'upstart'. As is expected, Ch'ungil succeeds in achieving the goal of producing automatic rifles without the aid of foreign technology and thus fully proves the potential of the working-class people. His achievements convey that the core stratum has easy access to higher education and mobility in the social ladder. This kind of political *Cinderella* is recycled in numerous North Korean films, legitimising the class structure of the closed society and effectively mobilising the masses into forced labour.

The Untrodden Path presents Pyŏngch'an, the assistant director of the industrial bureau, as the representative of the unstable stratum. O's characterisation of Pyŏngch'an is based on colonial intellectuals and industrialists who enjoyed prestige as the ruling class and who thereby made fatal 'errors' for their socialist country. Pyŏngch'an's problem is precisely his collaboration with Japanese colonialists in the past. Interestingly, the film's overall approach to the unstable stratum is rather positive: it suggests that the state generously gives the members of this stratum the opportunity to prove themselves as useful and faithful to the working class. Quoting General Kim, Ch'ŏljun states that their new society embraces every walk of life, including those who have questionable political backgrounds.

The term 'unstable', however, clearly evokes general hostility of the North Korean authorities towards colonial intellectuals whose political orientation is judged as beneficial to the traditional ruling class, and thus can be easily manipulated by the enemies of the Party. They are politically 'unreliable' and therefore 'unstable'. When their experiments of steel production fail, Pyŏngch'an betrays his general scepticism about communism and, furthermore, his doubt about the Party's economic policy. His 'undesirable' attitude culminates when he irresponsibly resigns his post without helping the authority to find the causes of the failures of their experiments. He is only concerned with his own safety and totally indifferent to the interest of the nation, although he is indebted to the Party and the working class, which have pardoned his past and even put him in an important position. The film shows that the lack of faith in the Party is a serious flaw in intellectuals, and Pyŏngch'an is a prime example who never fully trusts communists, thinking that they will eliminate him once he becomes useless to them.

According to the film, the North Korean government does not

20   Chŏljun proudly inspects the production of the automatic rifles:
O Pyŏngch'o's *The Untrodden Path* (1980)

entirely rule out the possibility that intellectuals can play a useful part in society. Indeed, the government needs their professional knowledge and experience to carry out its development
plans. Their official policy is that the government involves every
citizen in the nation-building even though it may cost extraordinary time and effort. Concerning intellectuals, the Party
classifies them into two sub-groups: old-time intellectuals and
new/labour intellectuals. Old-time intellectuals such as Pyŏnch'an
belong to the unstable stratum. Because of their suspicious political proclivity, this category of intellectual is constantly inculcated with the socialist ideas, and especially with the legitimacy
of the dictatorship of the working class. Through the mouth of
Ch'ŏljun, the film stresses that despite their lack of class-
consciousness and revolutionary spirit, the Party has secured a
place for old-time intellectuals in their new society and, at the
same time, trying to persuade the other classes to accept their
'reborn' comrades.

Contrasted with old-time intellectuals, labour/new intellectuals are young breeds untainted with feudalistic or capitalist
ideas and well armed with North Korea's communist ideology.
As mentioned earlier, these intellectuals are assigned to the core
stratum.

In *Untrodden Path* the director of the arms bureau embodies
the traits of the hostile stratum, the so-called 'anti-working class'
or 'public enemy'. Among its members are intellectuals who

studied abroad and regard themselves as superior to others. With his arrogant attitudes, the director of the arms bureau illustrates several characteristics of this class. First of all, his political background is devoid of anti-Japanese resistance. He is also described as a factionalist who tends to break unity among people. Moreover, he relies on foreign powers for his authority and is, therefore, an opponent to the philosophy of 'self-reliance'. When Ch'ungil fails in his first experiment to make an automatic rifle, the director bitterly criticises the idea of self-reliance in technology and capital.

The factionalist issue touched on by the film is based on Kim Il Sung and his anti-Japanese guerrilla group's 1956 attempt to purge the pro-Chinese Yenan and the Soviet factions from the Party politics. Because of this incident, factionalists were once considered the prime enemy of the state. The overall unsavoury portrait of the director in *Untrodden Path* echoes the antagonism mounted toward those who had formed their power base outside of North Korea. From this historical perspective, the film can be read as an attempt to rationalise Kim's political struggle with and his final elimination of the rival factions within the Party.

In North Korea those branded 'hostile' are virtually social outcasts. After all, what determines one's life path in North Korea is his or her social and class origin, which is inherited and not acquired through one's efforts. In this respect, North Korea is not far from feudal society where one's social status is predetermined and where there are limitations or a social ceiling to one's ascendance. For example, a career of anti-Japanese fighting is one of the most favourable qualifications for an individual to be placed on the upper echelon of the North Korean class system, but, for many, it is not a matter of choice but a historical fate beyond his or her control.

Untrodden Path, whose Korean title literally means 'the first journey', employs the metaphor of road for the theme of integrating everyone into a new community. But what the film really addresses is a restructuring of the class system that Kim Il Sung and his newly formed Korean Workers' Party inherited from the thirty-six years of Japanese colonial rule. The economic motivation behind the establishment of the new social structure clearly anticipates the *Juche* theory that was not formulated until the 1960s. Thus, *Untrodden Path* is a retroactive application of the *Juche* theory to the nascent stage of North Korean economy.

Given that O's film was made in the 1980s, its slogan of a self-reliant economy directs our attention to the early symptoms of the failure in North Korea's agricultural production and light industries whose nefarious effects have surfaced recently in the form of food shortage. As the North Korean economy has dwindled drastically, there has been escalating criticism since the mid-1970s concerning its policy centred on heavy industries and weapons production. In this light, *Untrodden Path* appears to be an attempt to clarify the historical circumstances in which the economic policy was made and put into effect in the 1940s. By doing this, the film can boost the morale of today's working class beleaguered by dire economic crisis. The film urges North Koreans to go back to their humble yet confident beginning and reflect on how they transformed a poor agrarian society into a modern industrialised nation without basic technology or capital. The North Korean regime still denies its need for foreign aids; at least on the surface. The film stresses mental power as the only solution to the financial and technological problems under the euphemism of 'human capability'. This is the 1980s vantage viewpoint on the 1960's *Juche* ideology whose ground-work was laid nearly a half century ago during the post-Liberation period. The film conveys an inspirational message for the workers of present North Korea that they are capable of achieving an economic miracle through their own efforts as they once did with fewer resources during their nation-building. O's work, therefore, can be understood as a revival of the foundation myth of the People's Democratic Republic of Korea as an independent modern state, for the 1980s audience.

The Brigade Commander's Former Superior

The Brigade Commander's Former Superior, which is the latest of a series of films awarded the People's Prize Winner in North Korean film history, is a story about a heroic military truck driver who refuses to succumb to the lure and pressure of social climbing. If *Untrodden Path* is a film about class formation in the early days of North Korean history, Ch'ae P'unggi's *The Brigade Commander's Former Superior* concentrates on a subtle conflict experienced by ordinary North Koreans between class and social status and between the abstract notion of class consciousness and their practical need for social recognition. Through the moving story of Chu Hyŏnch'ŏl's dedication to his demanding yet unappreciated job, the film shows the triumph of the noble creed over the earthly desire.

Hyŏnch'ŏl is a sergeant major who has served the People's Army as a truck driver for over thirty years since the Korean war. Although he received a discharge order from the military service at the end of the war, he decided to remain in his humble but important position for the rest of his life. After helping an inexperienced recruit, Kim Chŏngmin, to repair a truck on a rugged mountain road, Hyŏnch'ŏl realised that the army needed skilled hands like himself. The film opens as Chŏngmin arrives many years later in his new post as a brigade commander and re-encounters Hyŏnch'ŏl who has not changed in his enthusiasm for work and in his post. The reversed hierarchy between the two men poses a dramatic conflict as the new commander now attempts to release the sergeant major from the army out of respect for his former superior's old age. Realising that his decision has caused Hyŏnch'ŏl immense distress, the commander, in the end, yields to the sergeant's wish to continue to serve his country as a low-ranking soldier until, according to this seasoned war veteran, the American army completely withdraws from the South and national reunification is achieved.

The central problem tackled by Ch'ae's film is that Hyŏnch'ŏl's lofty intention is not fully understood by people around him, who tend to measure one's success or failure in life in terms of his or her social status or position. Their role model is a person like the brigade commander who makes a glorious return to Paeksŏl Bridge Hill where he started his career as a struggling novice truck driver. Hyŏnch'ŏl's wife, daughter and son suffer from his stubborn refusal to retire and enjoy a peaceful life with them. They are frustrated by the fact that he does not gain much respect from others despite his total devotion to his work. The film shows that, although nobody expresses it openly, people do not consider his job to be as significant as those of high-ranking officers. His wife is embarrassed by the passing comment made by a young girl in her work place about the 'funny' scene of the old soldier marching in the field side by side with young recruits. For his family, it is painful to watch him engaged in tough physical labour, carrying heavy stones for a road construction and transporting supplies to outposts in the mountain.

The film presents Hyŏnch'ŏl as a champion of the virtues of the working class. He has all the qualifications to be the most respectable member of North Korean society. He is, above all, the son of an extremely poor farmer, who was killed by the Japanese during a revolutionary struggle. His mother and the rest of his family perished in the hands of US invaders during the war. On top of this, Hyŏnch'ŏl is married to a retired soldier who is herself from the working class and who has also lost her parents to US soldiers. Such an immaculate class origin, combined with his genuine sincerity for his duties and, most importantly, with his unperturbed attitude toward the temptation of social mobility qualifies Hyŏnch'ŏl as an ideal folk hero.

It is quite ironic that Hyŏnch'ŏl's children enjoy prestige thanks to their father's class background but, at the same time, complain about his low social standing. His son, Tongsu, graduated from an air-force academy and became a bomber pilot, and his daughter, Suok, is always seen at her desk at home, obviously studying for a college (or, she may already be a college student). Their future is secure because of their working-class lineage inherited from their father. However, Tongsu and Suok are more concerned with others' perception of their father's title. It is precisely this conflicting view of class and social status that generates dramatic tension in this film. Why do Hyŏnch'ŏl's children who receive all the benefits from society as members of the working class still aspire to attain higher social status? This dilemma points to the problematic self-perception held by the working-class people in their 'proletariat paradise'.

Chŏngmin plays the role of a foil for Hyŏnch'ŏl and also that of an observer–narrator of the old hero. In the eyes of the world, Chŏngmin has successfully risen to the top. However, the film constantly reiterates that the commander may be higher than the sergeant major in rank, but not necessarily in merit as a citizen. The commander visually pays homage to the old man in the plain soldier's uniform, which he has been wearing for three decades. Through their mutually respectful attitudes towards each other, the film sustains a delicate balance between public power and private ethic as accepted in the North Korean political culture. It should be noted, however, that the film does not deny the necessity of ranks in society. Ranks are defined more or less as different roles to be played by different members of society: so long as individuals perform properly the role as assigned by the state, they are all equal in statuses. In other words, rank is treated more or less as a system of convenience.

On a more practical note, the film stresses that, although one's rank may not always appear to be commensurate with one's social status, the gap should not cloud the importance of national unity for which the system exists. As a solution to the class–status conflict, the film emphasises harmonious inter-dependence among people in different positions as is demonstrated by Chŏngmin and Hyŏnch'ŏl. The opening scene shows that without the sergeant's experience and knowledge, Chŏngmin, as an inexperienced driver, would not have been able to get out of the trouble of his truck being stuck in the mud. Correspondingly, Hyŏnch'ŏl is as obedient as other soldiers to the young commander despite his seniority in age and his superiority in their past relation. The positive impact of their co-operation on society is seen when Hyŏnch'ŏl asks Chŏngmin to help one of the soldiers in the brigade to go to a university after he finishes his military service. This is the soldier Hyŏnch'ŏl scolded for becoming negligent of his duties as his discharge was approaching. The soldier's discovery of the sergeant's warm, private side beneath the stern public image leads to a renewed resolution to perform his duties conscientiously. The underlying message of this episode is unequivocal: earnest and unselfish dedication to one's work, no matter how insignificant it may appear to be, ultimately brings respectful recognition from others. This theme is reinforced by Chŏngmin's remark to Tongsu and Suok who still do not fully appreciate their father: 'Stars [military ranks] or duties indicate a division of roles in serving our Leader and Party, not the dignity, look or even loyalty to the country of an individual member of society ... Our Party taught us earlier that sincerity is the highest standard with which to judge people, not their ranks or duties, didn't it?'. Chŏngmin's point is dramatically confirmed when Hyŏnch'ŏl surprises everybody, including his family, new daughter-in-law and her parents by appearing before them with his uniform fully decorated with illustrious medals received from the Party. For Hyŏnch'ŏl's awe-stricken children, the didactic effect is double because Tongsu's father-in-law, a high-positioned navy officer, is witness to Hyŏnch'ŏl's extraordinary display of public honour. This climactic scene closes the drama, Tongsu's upcoming wedding transmitting the final symbolic message, that a familial tie can dissolve the positional difference between two groups of people. As is pointed out in the earlier chapters, the rhetoric of 'family' transcends blood relations in Korean society.

Although *The Brigade Commander's Former Superior* advocates that ranks in the liberated socialist country means nothing more than role-division in the workplace, it sharply divulges the problem of a gap between theory and practice in the North Korean class system. Nearly three decades after the class revolution, North Koreans still gauge their social standing through others' eyes, not through their own. As in the capitalist South, ordinary workers in North Korea tend to prefer white- to blue-collar jobs, aspire upwardly in the social scale and judge others in terms of their occupation. There is an undeniable discrepancy between what they are told by the state and what they *feel* about their positions. Rank and wealth still serve as a major yardstick in North Korean perception of social identity. Otherwise, Suok would not be concerned so much about the difference between her and her sister-in-law's families, and Tongsu would not have purchased a new suit for his father to replace the soldier's uniform. A cultural explanation for these behaviours can be found in Suok's remark to her father: 'You should think about the position of my brother's father-in-law and our *face* as well'. This

21   The proud and much-decorated hero Hyŏnch'ŏl in Ch'ae P'unggi's
The Brigade Commander's Former Superior (1983)

statement evinces that North Koreans are not free from the
traditional Confucian notion of 'face', a critical factor in Korean
social interaction. From this observation, it can be concluded
that in North Korean social life the force of traditional cultural
values still outweighs the decades of socialist indoctrination
about class equality.

Given that this film was made in the early 1980s, its target
audience seems to be the young generations of North Koreans
who have never experienced class struggles or contradictions
because they were born and grew up after the so-called unitary
class system had been already implemented. From Tongsu and
Suok's superficial understanding of their father's rank, it is implied that seeking a position of 'power' is undesirable when the
state endeavours to accomplish the goal of the abolition of class.
The film thus urges contemporary North Koreans to revisit
definitions of class, social stratification and occupational orders
in communist society.

Bellflower

Made by one of the most representative of North Korean film-
makers, Cho Kyŏngsun, *Bellflower* tells a story about a peasant
girl Chin Songnim who devotes her youthful life to the

reconstruction of a mountain village during the post-war period. By highlighting Songnim's self-sacrifice for the noble cause of the state, the film pays tribute to the ambitions and frustrations of the first-generation North Korean citizens who were caught in the fever of rebuilding their economy in the 1950s and 1960s. At another level, however, the film tackles one of the serious problems in today's North Korean society: the aspiration of the young rural population to social mobility and urban exodus. The film attempts to justify the rigid social stratification system by denying individuals the freedom of choosing occupation and residence. Despite the great efforts in addressing this intended message, *Bellflower*, on the other hand, reveals the problem of the idea of a unitary working class.

As is alluded to by the title of the film, Songnim is a girl who grew up in a remote countryside. She is engaged to Pak Wŏnbong, a young man in the same village. Unlike Songnim, her fiancé dislikes the simple mountain folk and dreams about city life all the time. He eventually leaves his hometown and his fiancée for a city. He urges her to go with him, but Songnim refuses his persistent proposal. She believes that it is her duty to stay where she was born and grew up. After Wŏnbong's departure, Songnim overcomes the pain of separation by dedicating herself to transforming her poverty-stricken, desolate village into an affluent, fertile farming community. On one stormy night, she dies heroically trying to rescue a herd of sheep in the villagers' collective farm. Twenty seven years later, Wŏnbong and his son Seryong show up in the village where Songnim's younger sister Songhwa still lives with the painful memories of her sister's tragic love and untimely death. Unaware of the past history between his father and Songhwa's sister, Seryong wants to settle down in the village according to his father's wish. He is, however, faced with the villagers' hostility. He later learns of the 'sin' his father committed against them. Seryong asks for their forgiveness by becoming a respectable comrade. Wŏnbong, however, is not given a chance for atonement till the end when he humbly accepts his destiny as an outcast from his community and remains a failure in society permanently. The villagers commemorate Songnim's love for her hometown by calling her 'bellflower', a flower whose beauty can be truly appreciated in the deep mountains.

Bellflower belongs to a series of 'hidden hero' films produced in North Korea in the 1980s and 1990s, featuring young country folk dedicated to developing barren lands and wild forests. These films glorify those who remain in their rugged places and work quietly for the nation. The purpose of political propaganda is evident in the way the films incorporate into their plots all sorts of speed campaigns for mobilising forced labour. They include the *Ch'ŏllima* working movement (1958), the Speed campaign (1974), the Three Revolutionary Red-Flag movement (1975), the 100-days battle (1978), the 1980s Speed Creation movement, the 1990s Speed Creation movement and so on. Although these films generally treat the early days of North Korea's nation-building as their main subject-matter, their ideological message is clearly targeted at the audience of the 1980s and 1990s who have been struggling desperately to survive the long economic depression. Given this socio-economic context in which they were conceived and produced, it can be said that these films are intended primarily to boost the morale of ordinary North Korean citizens.

Compared with other films, however, Cho's *Bellflower* intro-duces a relatively new theme: issues related to a personal desire for a more respectable occupation and comfortable urban lifestyle. At the core of this desire we can find the problematic notion of a unitary class system. During the post-war reconstruction years, North Korea conducted rapid structural changes and established a class system that denied a wealth-based hierarchy. Since then, this system has been handed down to each generation of North Koreans without its legitimacy or adequacy being seriously chal-lenged. From the point of view of young North Koreans, this class system has a fundamental problem in that it cannot accommodate the changing needs of society. Even though the existing social order has noticeable flaws, they cannot initiate a corrective. It is the state that devised and has maintained the social stratification system, therefore, the state has an exclusive right to locate individuals within the system as they see fit. The increasing discontent with the system is caused by the fact that it operates just as another form of hierarchy, contrary to the state's claim to be otherwise. Although the state's selection process for assigning individuals to different positions is intrinsically hier-archical and discriminating, it is always claimed that the system stands on the consensus of the people on the necessity of national harmony. Each member of society is, therefore, expected to accept his or her given position as the best for him- or herself as well as for others. In this way, the state forfeits ground for social mobility among their citizens.

The forceful nature of the North Korean social stratification system severely restricts opportunities for individuals to create their own lives. In *Bellflower*, individual freedom to choose his or her occupation is condemned as an idea corrupted by Western capitalism. Through the negative portrayal of Wŏnbong, the film warns against the tendency among today's North Korean youths to prefer white- to blue-collar jobs. The film draws attention particularly to the vile influence of those who shirk hard manual work to others who are faithful to their given posts.

In attempting to foster self-pride in the rural youths by emphasising that their status equals urban industrial workers', the film also addresses an important contribution of the farming industry to the national economy. This theme reflects a recent change in the population control policy. In the past, the Party accused strong attachment to one's native place as regionalism, claiming that it causes only internal dissension in their society. Consequently, the Party encouraged a migration of the population throughout the country. The industrial development in the early stages of the socialist reconstruction period created an array of new positions, and the rural youths were mobilised to fill these positions. Transformed into industrial workers, these rural youths later came to form the majority of the urban population.[14] However, as the rural depopulation and the decline of the farming industry became serious in the 1980s, the North Korean government had to call for a counter measure to the population migration policy.[15] The government's new policy on residence control now focused on maintaining a balanced occupational structure.

To reinforce the significance of farming, *Bellflower* foregrounds a tie between man and nature. Songnim is depicted as a natural beauty and, as such, an ideal, enlightened farmer. The opening scene of the film shows Wŏnbong returning to his hometown with his son. As he watches the beautiful landscapes of the village from the top of the hill, Wŏnbong expresses deep remorse for having abandoned it. When Seryong discovers a bellflower plant without a flower to his great disappointment, Wŏnbong comments: 'It blossoms for its root; so does it for us'. As bell-flower roots have been part of the traditional Korean diet, the plant serves as an effective metaphor with a dual meaning of beauty and utility. In addition, the plant clearly reminds the audience as well as the characters of the importance of being rooted deep in the soil even after its flower withers. In this way, the film identifies the existing social structure as a natural order.

A close reading of the film, however, exposes various contradictory messages undermining its surface text. Above all, the violent aspect of nature should not be dismissed. The villagers are shown struggling against a severe storm that eventually claims the heroine's life. The geographical and temporal settings of the film are also so far from being real that the village cannot be seen as representing typical rural communities in North Korea. Surrounded by steep mountains, the village is totally isolated from the outside world. Except for the Great Leader's 'heavenly' supplies of basic farming equipment and daily goods, there is no interaction between the villagers and outsiders. In fact, the residents of the village are antagonistic to the idea of social mobility itself, treating outsiders as unwelcome intruders. To Seryong, who plans to settle down in the village, Songhwa's daughter, whose name is taken from another edible plant, Tallae, quotes an old saying circulated in her neighbourhoods: 'Do not let a passing bird build a nest in the Pyŏkkyeri village'.[16]

Interestingly, Cho's film is set in the period in which every sector of North Korean society undergoes radical changes due to intensive industrialisation efforts. Of course, no mention is made in the film of the social upheavals sweeping through the entire country because the outside influence is completely shut out from this village. Given this historical context, it is quite odd that the people confined in this small, isolated world succeed in modernising themselves so quickly without the aid of outside agencies. In other words, the utopian messages intended by this film are so contrived that they provoke suspicion about the subtext of a dystopia. Indeed, the bridge scene, in which Tallae runs after a calf on the loose, invites an ironic reading. As the only exit to the outside world, the bridge is laden with symbolic meanings. This is where Seryong, a city boy, encounters Tallae, a country girl, for the first time. The calf, completely out of control, can be interpreted as rural youth driven by the desire to run away from his or her difficult and monotonous life in the backwoods. Ironically, it is Seryong who attempts to stop the calf but fails. So, he jumps into the river, along with the animal. His effort to hold off the reckless movement of the calf – that is, the frustrated young farmer's venturing out from his or her bounds – turns out to be useless. Through this bridge sequence, however, the film attempts a possible resolution of the old conflict between Songnim and Wŏnbong; their ill-fated romance finds a happy ending in the growing intimacy between Tallae and Seryong.

Obviously, the rosy ending implied by the film supports an ironic approach to Wŏnbong as a victim of the rigid social stratification system. He suffers simply because he does not fit the post at the village's collective farm to which he was allocated. He is criticised as a daydreamer who cannot be content with what was given to him. But the film, ironically again, describes him as a talented man; especially good at drawing. He designed the town hall and has drawn a picture of the village. In this way, the film in fact divulges the state's coercive, authoritarian way of enforcing the social stratification system without considering individual differences in abilities and preferences. Here lies Wŏnbong's and many other similarly creative and adventurous North Korean youths' existential agony.

As a way of preventing the audience from sympathising with Wŏnbong's inner conflict, the film interjects a sequence of the village youths' outing to a new film in town. The motif of a film within a film is specifically to show the gaiety of P'yŏngyang's urban scenery: city folks spend their holidays in parks or on the seaside in a leisurely mood with their families, enjoying various cultural programs in grand theatres. To its spectators the inside film only confirms a conspicuous gap between big cities and rural areas in terms of their occupational and educational opportunities, social and cultural environments, and not to mention their supplies of consumer goods. The propagandic function of this inner film may be applied to the role of North Korean cinema in general. The spectators from the Pyŏkkyeri are not only delighted by the seemingly 'happy' life led by the citizens of their capital city, but also inspired to 'work harder' to transform their hometown into the kind of modern city they saw on the screen. All of Wŏnbong's friends vow to pursue this plan. But, unlike them, Wŏnbong simply opts for a flight to a big city, stating, 'Everyone has the right to choose her/his own life. In this deep, backward mountain village, there is no life. There are no cinemas, and if I have new clothes, there is no occasion to put them on ...'. Hence, he is branded a 'deviant' in the group who violates a spirit of solidarity and who challenges the idea of the unitary working class. Interestingly, the fact that the inner film fails to communicate its intended message to Wŏnbong presents a disturbing implication for the spectators of the outer film *Bellflower* itself. They may act like Wŏnbong in their perception of the fictional treatment of their social realities. They may not accept the propaganda theme of the film at face value.

It is well known that, despite the Party's insistence on the unitary working class, North Korean society has functioned as a hierarchical structure. As in many former socialist countries, highly skilled workers enjoy higher positions in North Korea than lower or unskilled workers. They are treated differently in terms of status and material compensations. Obviously, the individual's social status cannot be determined by his or her class alone; it depends on various factors, such as occupation, level of income, education, lifestyles, patterns of consumption, and so on. From a traditional Marxist point of view, peasants are lower than factory workers because of their purportedly 'weaker' political consciousness.[17] As peasants are in 'need' of guidance from factory workers, they are also assigned to a lower rank in the stratification structure. In view of the Marxist distinction between the two types of workers, the film's emphasis on equality between urban workers and rural farmers and between industrial centres and rural outposts contains an element of ideological contradiction.

The upshot of an ironic reading of *Bellflower* is that the North Korean government aims to muster popular support for its outmoded political system to break through the socio-economic crisis of the 1980s. As the film reiterates, the first generation of North Koreans achieved great success in handling the calamity of the war in a short period of time through a rapid modernisation of the country. For today's North Koreans, however, the early success story may be too distant and too idealistic. Nevertheless, *Bellflower* faithfully serves the government's purpose to renounce youth's 'frustrating' aspiration to social mobility, trying to justify the coercive nature of the authoritarian society, which dictates individuals' lifestyles in the name of the collective benefits or the true comradeship.

Class dynamics in three South Korean films

A Nice Windy Day

A Nice Windy Day (1980) is the first work by Yi Changho, one of the most popular directors in Korea, after an enforced four-year hiatus in 1976 as a penalty for smoking marijuana. His resumption of film-making coincided with the political chaos and social unrest into which the whole country was catapulted with the assassination of President Park Chung Hee in 1979. The sudden upheaval of Korean society led Yi to declare the coming of a new era in South Korean film history in which film could engage in social criticism. Starting with *Nice Windy Day*, Yi made a series of works that treat the day-to-day struggles of the urban poor: *The Children of Darkness* (1981), *Widow's Dance* (1983) and *A Declaration of Fools* (1983). After these four pieces, Yi left the forefront of the cinema of social criticism.

These four films generally befit Yi's professed commitment to a new direction in Korean film, yet they lack the focused analysis of class issues that were one of the central concerns of the new cinema. It is, therefore, difficult to draw from these works Yi's concrete ideas on film's function as a medium for social commentary. This ambiguity seems to be related to the strong commercial tendency of his films. Despite this ambiguity, however, Yi left an undeniable influence on young film-makers, sensitising them to one of the underrepresented subject-matter in South Korean film: the suffering masses behind the bright slogans of the rapidly developing country.[18]

Nice Windy Day addresses the polarisation of the urban population into *nouveau riche* and poor masses during the state-led industrialisation process. The film is pervaded by the latter's anxiety about a widening gap between the rich and the poor and their relative sense of deprivation. The film's dominant perspective is set on those who move from rural areas to the peripheries of Seoul and supply cheap labour for the booming economy but who were ultimately denied their share in the newly accrued national wealth. The film successfully conveys a tragic sense of failure mixed with indignation in the way in which they are pressured to transform themselves from rural folk into unskilled urban drifters on the labour market. As they make a desperate effort to adjust themselves to the fast-changing social structure, they at once become totally lost in the countryside and in cities. This sense of loss is well expressed in the opening credit scene. As the discontented face of a little boy slowly recedes, along with a passing train, the image of an old man next to the boy comes into view whose gaze is fixed on an empty green field. With this signalling of a massive rural exodus, *Nice Windy Day* unfolds the stories of three uprooted youths in Seoul.

Tŏkpae, Kilnam and Ch'unshik leave their respective hometowns in the countryside for a dream of becoming 'citizens of Seoul'. After shifting from job to job in the city, they temporarily settle down as assistants in small shops in a wealthy residential area. Soon they notice their similarities as the rootless in the impersonal big city and become friends, sharing their loneliness. Although their life in the urban gutter is unbearable and even humiliating, they keep their spirits up as each of them finds a love. In the end, however, they are betrayed by the women they secretly admire, and their innocent dreams are also destroyed by money, which has dictated their lives. They have lost everything, as if a gust of wind blew it up in the air. The three young men have to separate, pledging not to break their friendship.

Nice Windy Day was produced during military terrorism under General Chun who took over the power vacuum after Park's assassination. The tightened film censorship during this period did not allow an open discussion of the deepening gap between the classes and the helpless position of the masses in society. Consequently, Yi reduced the heavily socio-political material to the personal misadventure stories of the three unfortunate youths, adding a tragicomic touch to their misguided dreams as city dwellers. The film contains no direct reference to the notion of class, and it tends to evade criticism of the structural problems of contemporary Korean society. Nevertheless, the audience can discern in this film an emerging pattern of ideological confront-

22   From left, the three country boys, Ch'unshik, Tŏkpae and Kilnam at the local bar, sharing the loneliness of their alienated urban life in Yi Changho's *A Nice Windy Day* (1980)

ation between the people and the government with regard to the growing economic disparity between the classes.

Among the various cinematic devices that Yi employs to deliver the hidden message on class inequality, the calculated use of sounds is especially noteworthy. Yi's deliberate manipulation of background sounds is immediately suggested by the opening credit scene in which cicadas' singing is sharply contrasted with the whistling of a train, and the folk rhythms of a farmers' band is blended with a contemporary Korean popular song (the film's title music). The juxtaposition of incongruent sounds serves as a primary metaphor for the confusing state of the people who are uprooted from their land and are transplanted into a new, inhospitable soil. The disparate strands of sounds also allude to the multiple layers of stories about the three characters and to the tension between different groups in the class system whose hierarchy is determined by an individual's buying power.

The film begins with a shot of a grand-looking church and an opulent house on a peaceful Sunday afternoon. As the church bell sounds overlap with light piano tunes, the camera focuses on Tŏkpae trying to collect empty dishes, which the family of the house ordered from the Chinese restaurant where he is working as a delivery man. Soon the piano tunes are mixed with a dog's barking, and the camera shows Tŏkpae first with a big German shepherd dog and then with the family. The camera changes position vertically from the family's viewpoint to Tŏkpae's. The dog stands on the stairs between the gate and the entrance hall, eating the leftovers from the plates that Tŏkpae needs to pick up. From the garden on top of the stairs, the family looks down at Tŏkpae and the dog's fight over the plates, giggling and making silly comments. As he is finally leaving the house, Tŏkpae also barks like a dog.

The piano music parodies the ostentatious lifestyle of the newly rich. For them, the instrument is an expensive piece of furniture and thus, a status symbol, which they believe displays their 'high living standards' and 'elegant taste' for Western classical music. The easy *études* played in the sequence are associated with the idea of 'a dream of a sweet home' and are especially popular among middle-class Koreans. The director's cynical view of their pretentious materialism is clear in the piano player's monotonous and even apathetic tone and repeated mistakes. By having the dog's barking periodically interrupt the metallic piano tunes, the film ridicules the upstarts' extravagant lifestyle, which adds to social disharmony and cultural incompatibility between the different classes. For those on the fringes of society, both the piano music and the church bells are suggestive of the world from which they are barred. Whenever Tŏkpae encounters Myŏnghŭi, a carefree, spoiled brat who lives in the area, her appearance is signalled by an electric doorbell or a car horn and then by clumsy piano music of various sorts. Myŏnghŭi and her friends embody a strange wonderland for Tŏkpae and his gang.

The one-sided interaction between Tŏkpae and Myŏnghŭi, who represent the two extreme classes, results in a crippling linguistic effect on him. This process takes place while Tŏkpae slowly succumbs to Myŏnghŭi's seduction game. As he is enticed into her childish yet cruel flirtation with his innocent heart, he is struck dumb, often surrounded by piano notes, Myŏnghŭi's hysterical laugh and the dog's barking. His feeling of absurdity is manifest in his stuttering, a new habit he develops since he starts living in Seoul. The strange deprivation of language as a result of displacement is also observed in Kilnam and Ch'unshik. While Tŏkpae stammers, Kilnam and Ch'unshik become noticeably silent. They speak properly only among themselves. Even then, their conversation is occasionally arrested by the dog's barking. Ironically, they feel free when the barking starts. The implication of their strange emotional relief at barking is evident: as humans, they are mute, but once they are identified with an animal, they can at least howl at the unfair society even if such an action is futile.

Although Yi carefully avoids amplifying Tŏkpae's story into an explicit indictment of the broad structural problems of Korean society, a keen audience will not miss the passing reference to them in a street wineshop scene. In the scene, Ch'unshik is asked about his hometown by Kim, the shop owner. Reluctant to reveal his peasant stock, Ch'unshik answers that he grew up in an orphanage in Seoul. While Kim is trying to find an appropriate response to Ch'unshik's unexpected, nervous statement, one of the drinkers in the background passingly is heard saying: '... is just like the atmosphere in your novel. You are also interested in such a social structure as ... aren't you?'. Incomplete as it is, this remark mentions a class problem that is not to be openly stated during the period in which the film narrative is set. Therefore, it is buried in the loud background music so that it becomes almost inaudible.

In *Nice Windy Day* sound effects are also used to convey the violent aspect of class conflict. Car sounds and piano tunes are often combined in the film to connote middle-class philistinism. Until the 1970s, cars were perceived as an indispensable status symbol for the middle class in Korean society. One of the street scenes in the film shows Myŏnghŭi and her boyfriend Ch'angsu driving their cars just like children playing with toys. Ch'angsu's car nearly hits a little boy playing in the sidewalk. Although the boy sprawls on the street, Ch'angsu does not stop but keeps chasing after Myŏnghŭi's car, which in turn hits Tŏkpae. Neither Ch'angsu nor Myŏnghŭi is concerned about the victims of their irresponsible playfulness. Throughout this sequence, the audience hears 'Vienna Waltz' played on a piano. The sounds become increasingly disturbing with wrong notes, abruptly stopping and repeating some of the same bars over and over again. This sound pattern and the visual content in the sequence anticipate violent confrontations among the characters of different classes in the later part of the film.

Along with the immoral behaviour of the *nouveau riche*, Yi introduces prostitution as another symptom of the problematic class relation in a materialistic society where the strong preys on the weak. The idea of the body for sale becomes part of the survival game for destitute slum people, such as the girl working in the same barber shop with Ch'unshik. Unaware that Ch'unshik is in love with her, she goes out with a middle-aged, married man, another upstart who made a big fortune through land brokerage. When Ch'unshik attacks him in a hotel room, the frightened girl reveals in tears: 'Now, what can I do for my father who is dying without even seeing a doctor?'. While the audience is not allowed to condemn easily her shady transaction or Ch'unshik's naïve and reckless reaction, his Seoul dream vanishes at once before his eyes as he goes to prison for attempted murder. In a way, Ch'unshik's action reflects the collective anger of the impoverished mass towards the unsavoury moral values of the *nouveau riche*. A vagrant old man who appears prior to Ch'unshik's attack scene represents the innocent victims of the selfishness of the rich: he is said to have lost all his properties to land speculators and then to have been institutionalised in a mental asylum. Through Ch'unshik's story, therefore, the film seems to warn that the self-destructive struggle of the powerless masses may be unavoidable in society, which turns a blind eye to the strained class relation behind its economic prosperity.

At the end of the film, Kilnam and Ch'unshik are forced to leave Seoul, their beloved city of dreams. Tŏkpae is irreparably broken-hearted by Myŏnghŭi's ridicule, and Kilnam is betrayed by Chinok, whom he believed to be his future bride but who runs away with all his money. Just as Ch'unshik is put in jail, so is Kilnam going to be enlisted by the army. Although Yi's treatment of women is too simplistic in this film, *A Nice Windy Day* can be seen, on the whole, as a parody of social realism in South Korean cinema that claims to raise a voice on the growing conflicts between different classes in contemporary Korean life. The film presents today's Korean society as producing essentially two types of people: one that has nothing but money to fill their empty lives and so, are always hungry for pleasure, and another that has nothing but their body to trade for survival. The film indirectly maintains that the class problems are ascribed to the ill-balanced socio-economic structure, which is a due consequence of the political leaders' blind faith in a wealthy and strong nation. *Nice Windy Day* focuses on the confusion among the rural population about the abrupt structural changes in society and their misplacement of their aspiration for upward mobility in the urbanisation effort, rather than on their subversive political action against the government's rush for the economic modernisation of the country.

Kuro Arirang

Pak Chongwŏn's *Kuro Arirang* (1980) is based on Yi Munyŏl's novel of the same title. Set in the 1980s in the Kuro industrial complex in Seoul, Pak's film depicts the awakening of political consciousness among the South Korean proletariat through the metamorphosis of a timid young girl into a self-confident factory worker. Compared with *Nice Windy Day*, *Kuro Arirang* is more outspoken about class issues, attempting to capture the anger, fear and frustration of factory workers in a Zolaesque manner. The main characters of the film are Chongmi, a female worker at a clothing factory, and her co-worker Hyŏnshik, a university student hiding his educational background and real name and employed as a plain labourer.[19] The film narrative consists of a series of loosely connected episodes on labour disputes, industrial disasters and sexual harassment in the complex. Exposing the ugly scenes in the workplace that rarely come to public attention, the film highlights a lonely battle of the young female workers against their physical and emotional exploitation by the class that profits from their toil. By tracing the changes taking place in Chongmi's self-perception as a factory worker, the film appeals to the audience for a sense of alliance and moral support for people like her who are abused and treated like machines in inhumane working environments. In this sense, Pak's *Kuro Arirang* can be said to be an exemplary case of the cinema of social criticism.

In handling the subject of class conflict, *Kuro Arirang* offers a fresh angle by pointing out a discriminatory view of blue-collar workers in Korean society as the fundamental cause of the problematic class relation. Rooted in the Confucian privileging of mental over menial labour, the disparaging perception of the working class is still prevalent among contemporary Koreans. By looking at issues relating to the female worker's doubly confined position in society in terms of her occupational and gender roles, the film attempts to expose the serious psychological and political ramifications of the long-standing prejudice against the working class in the country, which pursues industrialisation and modernisation as its prime goals.

Korean women had played an indispensable role in constructing or reconstructing national economy even before the country launched its ambitious economic development plans in full scale.[20] Despite their significant contributions to the industrialisation process, young factory girls are hardly accepted as respectable members of society. The discriminatory attitude towards them is contained in the widely circulated pejorative expression '*kongsuni*', which literally means 'a factory girl'. This term was coined along the same lines as '*shiksuni*' (kitchen maid), a traditionally humble position in a household. In the film, the lowly view of women workers is translated into the high-angle shot of the rows of young girls in dark-grey uniforms in the workroom. The camera eye is identified with those of the male factory manager who constantly monitors the crowded room as if it were a prison. Indeed, seen through the window frames of the factory owner's office, the girls do not appear to differ from prisoners: they are often shown behind the metal bars of the factory gate or under the dim fluorescent lamps dangling from the low ceiling of the workroom.

Although these girls are overworked and underpaid, it is not, according to the film, the physical or financial hardship that is most unbearable to them: it is the humiliation and contempt with which mainstream society treats them. Chongmi and her friends lament their miserable lot of being regarded as the lowest class in society simply because they are factory workers. They self-consciously call each other 'kongsuni'. Referring to a girl whose boyfriend is a college student, the workers taunt her with a sarcastic comment: 'A college boyfriend for a kongsuni!'. Their use of the derogatory term indicates an internalisation of society's condescending view of their status. The film presents such an inferiority complex as one of the most alarming yet pitifully neglected damages that society at large has perpetrated on the psyche of young female factory workers. The unfair stereotyping of factory girls and their self-deprecating reactions to the degrading label are noticeable in the film in such statements as: 'I'm not a kongsuni type'; 'Do you think I became a kongsuni because I wanted to?' and 'Even a kongsuni drinks beer?'. As is expected, these girls try to conceal their occupations and refuse to admit their identity as workers outside the industrial complex.

Just as she quietly accepts her disadvantaged position as a factory girl, Chongmi is reluctant to take political action to solve the problem of social injustice at the beginning of the film. She shows indifference to the efforts among her co-workers to organise a labour union. She even expresses cynicism about their collective action, considering it a self-degrading demand for a petty raise in wages. Idealistic about inter-class communication in a setting like the industrial complex, she detests her fellow workers' monetary preoccupation, the 'sole' motivation to unionise themselves. When Kyŏngmi suggests to her to consider joining the labour movement, she answers: 'I came to night-school to study, and I don't even want to think about work outside of the factory ... If we have a union, what difference would it make? Would it make us happy working at the factory, or would our salary be raised ten times? ... They might give us a few pennies as if giving a rice cake to a crying baby, but I cannot humiliate myself like that'.

Chongmi's scepticism of the union directs attention to another reason for the general passivity of the South Korean working masses in seeking their own interests in the hostile social atmosphere surrounding a labour movement. Once engaged in union activities, one is immediately labelled as 'threatening' the harmonious 'familial' tie between labourers and managers and disturbing the 'normal' operation of the industry. The real danger of being involved in a labour movement lies in that, not only does it cause friction with one's employer but it also provokes political repercussion from the government because it is viewed as a denial of their authority. The government's harsh renunciation of labour unions tends to border on an ideological condemnation in the name of national security: it claims that social disturbances instigated by radical unionists would result in checking the rapid economic growth of the country and also encouraging North Korea's communist agitation for a class revolution in the South. The so-called 'black list' serves as the most powerful deterrent for the coalition of the majority of ordinary workers. The film, therefore, characterises the workers' resistance as double-edged against the unfair pressure of the company and the absolute patronage of the government for the employer.

Pak's film conveys the public fear of the occupational and political reprisal in a brief scene where a group of factory workers distribute leaflets urging their co-workers to help to organise a union. As soon as the riot police approach them, the leaders disappear. Chongmi and Hyŏnshik who happen to receive the leaflets are arrested and taken to the police. This incident, on the one hand, occasions them to meet each other and create an immediate bond. On the other, it begins to attract unwelcome attention to them from their co-workers as well as managers regardless of their personal thoughts on the union.

Following the unwanted exposure to the political spotlight, Chongmi undergoes a dilemma between her previous naïve attitude toward the abusive class structure and her emerging sense of social activism. The development of the heroine from this point of the narrative shows that the director's perspective does not dwell on the pessimistic self-denial or self-hatred of the female workers. On the contrary, *Kuro Arirang* stresses the process in which they overcome the lowly opinion of themselves wrongly ingrained in them and, moreover, search for a new self-identity as proud members of society who deserve due respect and compensation. The possibility of the changing self-perception is hinted at earlier by Chongmi, who confides to Hyŏnshik: 'Until I met you, I never thought that female workers are equal with the factory owner's daughters or female university students ... You don't know how we feel about ourselves ... When we enter the office of the factory or walk in the street, we are always terrified that people might notice our dirty oily fingernails or threads on our hair'. The heroine's newly gained self-confidence soon evolves into political insight into the broader social context of her position as a worker. This change is demonstrated by her recognition of their need for a labour union.

After the first, aborted protest sequence, a series of industrial accidents – Manbok's injury from an electric shock and Kyŏgmi's death – brings a critical turning point for Chongmi's view of the union. Chongmi has consistently maintained that their deteriorating working conditions are as equally serious an issue as is their low wages because the former is the real cause of their work-related distress and is directly pertinent to humane treatment of the workers by the company. She tries to communicate this point to her colleagues in a public speech that she gives in the later part of the film: 'Don't talk about money ... There is a more important thing. Why do they always deceive and lie to us? Why do they always look down upon us, poor workers? ... We are human beings like them. We should demand that they treat us equally'. After Manbok's injury, she learns about the company's neglect of the safety rules and deceitful policies of handling his accident compensation insurance. Instead of reporting the case to the proper authorities, which is required by law, they attempt to deal with Manbok privately. Watching Manbok and his wife's suffering, Chongmi is finally convinced of the helpless position of the workers *vis-à-vis* the ruling class and concludes that they need a proper channel to deliver their collective voice to the company and to society. She learns that a poorly organised protest without an appropriate representative only vulgarises their causes into uncoordinated, chaotic queries about unpaid wages, never addressing long-term measures to improve their status. Her final resolution to participate in the labour movement is spurred by Kyŏngmi's death. As with the majority of the factory girls, Kyŏngmi had to work ninety hours a week, regularly resorting to chemical stimulants to stay awake at night. Under circumstances of virtual slavery, Kyŏngmi's fragile body eventually breaks down. Her tragic death provides a momentum for the factory workers to break out of their 'prison' and take to the street. The tragic loss of her best friend leads Chongmi to realise that she is a member of the working-class community, and whether she likes it or not, she shares a collective identity with the masses.

Through Chongmi's ultimate self-empowerment, the film materialises its central theme of the workers' resilience in the face of the societal repression of their demand for humanity. While many of her friends are forcefully eliminated from their jobs for dubious reasons, Chongmi survives all the labour-related troubles at the factory and eventually witnesses the major strike set up by the union, a climactic moment of the film. As her understanding of the social realities and class relation deepens, she discovers a new self-image based on pride and confidence as a person and as a worker. Through her final embrace of her self-

23   The workers' march to Kyŏngmi's funeral is blocked by riot police
from Pak Chongwŏn's *Kuro Arirang* (1989)

identity, the film celebrates the potential power of the working class to challenge the unjust obstacles to their dignified existence in society.

In the course of Chongmi's maturing, Hyŏnshik plays an invaluable role and thus merits brief discussion. Hyŏnshik represents a number of college students deeply involved in the South Korean labour movement for the last few decades. Some of these students disguised themselves as uneducated youths and worked in factories for first-hand experience of a worker's life and also for the education of the masses. They ran various forms of night-schools for factory workers like Chongmi who had to forfeit educational opportunities for reasons of poverty. Their impact on young urban workers has been considerable, helping them to open their eyes to their human rights. This is well illustrated by Hyŏnshik's positive influence on Chongmi: she is greatly indebted to his warm heart and sense of social justice for gaining a healthy self-perception.

While Yi's original story places much weight on Hyŏnshik's role in altering Chongmi's outlook on life and society, Pak's film adaptation shifts the focus from his to her own efforts to bring such a change. In the film, for instance, their relation is reversed towards the end. She convinces him that school is where he belongs. And he eventually returns to college, following her advice. The factory workers attempt to put him up as their representative to negotiate with the company in their unsuccessful initial protest. However, Chongmi quickly finds out the terrible consequences to befall him once he takes up the position. She eventually persuades him to leave the factory just before an imminent violent clash with the police. Her action demonstrates that workers are able to manage their own destiny by resisting the oppressive class structure. Pak's film thus suggests that an initiative to ameliorate the conflict-ridden class relation in Korean society lies in the hands of the working class and that intellectuals like Hyŏnshik can assist them in discovering such latent ability. Instead of portraying the poor, undereducated factory girls as innocent victims who need paternalistic protection and leadership, the film emphasises their inner strength and self-respect.

Today, South Korean film-makers enjoy more freedom to deal with class issues than during the last lag of the successive military regimes when social protest films such as *Kuro Arirang* were made. The unprecedented amount of 'scissoring' of the final version Pak submitted to the Censorship Committee attests to the degree of pressure with which 'socially conscious' film-makers had to cope to explore the cultural identities of contemporary Koreans in terms of class relations. Although the subject is now less of a taboo in the film industry than it was for decades, the residual bitterness of censorship still exists. Retrospectively, therefore, *Kuro Arirang* occupies a seminal place in contemporary Korean film history and, especially, in the development of the cinema of social criticism, in spite of its rather fragmentary narrative structure and monotonous conventional camera-work.

Black Republic

Pak Kwangsu is among the best-known South Korean film-makers to critics outside the country, along with Im Kwŏnt'aek, Chang Sŏnu and Hong Sangsu. Starting from his first work, *Ch'ilsu and Mansu* (1988), which won the Third Prize of the Youth Critics at the 42nd Locarno Film Festival in 1989, most of Pak's films were presented at international film festivals and received recognition from the juries. *To the Starry Island* (1993) was funded by British TV, Channel Four. This international exposure enabled Pak's films to reach a broad audience beyond language barriers.

Pak's key to success lies in the effective combination of serious social issues and melodramatic conventions. Through familiar types of character and predictable development of their relationships, his films unearth political violence and social injustice concealed in the everyday lives of ordinary people. As he pointed out in an interview, the dominant subjects of his films were drawn from the 'realities of Korean society', such as the national division and class conflicts.[21] Pak's box-office success evinces that the director considers the pleasure of film viewing as important as the serious themes. The formula of casting political issues in a melodramatic mode is well illustrated by *Black Republic* in which a tragic love story, family conflicts and a scandalous murder case are presented against the backdrop of the stark landscape of a mining village and the 1980s democratisation movement. In a similar vein to *Kuro Arirang*, *Black Republic* revolves around the relations between a well-educated labour activist and social outcasts, focusing on the tenacity of the down-and-trodden to keep up hopes for a better future in spite of their precarious day-to-day lives.

Han T'aeyun represents a group of college students involved in the South Korean labour movement who 'plunge into' the realities of the masses, disguised as undereducated workers. *Black Republic* is based on T'aeyun's journey into the lives of miners, one of the most alienated population groups in South Korean society. As he leaves home for a place far away from his city life, the camera shows the agonising young activist constantly ruminating on the meaning of the labour struggle of which he has partaken. Once in the mining village, T'aeyun slowly discovers the social and political realities as experienced by the villagers within their own community as well as in Korean society at large. His interaction with different members of the community becomes a test ground for his understanding of the needs of the working class and his ideas on social reform. In this sense, the film is about an urban intellectual's experiential education in the social realities of the alienated masses.

The plot of the film is simple. A wanted labour activist, T'aeyun comes to a declining coal-mining village, looking for a job with a false name (Kim Kiyŏng). Instead of mining, he ends up working at a small briquette manufactory. There, he makes friends with a lonely boy, Taeshik, and a tea-room waitress Yŏngsuk. He becomes a big-brother figure to Taeshik whose father is in jail for having led a miners' strike and whose mother has run away from the village. Yŏngsuk works at a 'ticket tea-room' as a call girl. She meets T'aeyun through Sŏngch'ŏl who is a wayward son of the factory owner and who indulges in women and liquor. Sŏngch'ŏl is violent and full of hatred towards his father who has abandoned his mother. Under T'aeyun's influence, Yŏngsuk gradually becomes ashamed of her job. One day T'aeyun happens to see Sŏngch'ŏl mercilessly beating her up for refusing his 'ticketing'. T'aeyun cannot control himself and intervenes. This incident takes T'aeyun to the police, where he is faced with the grave danger of his fugitive status being exposed. As he skilfully eludes

24   Yŏngsuk in police custody after her attempted murder of Sŏngch'ŏl in Pak Kwangsu's *Black Republic* (1990)

the interrogator and is released from the police station, T'aeyun decides to leave the village. Having found out about T'aeyun's departure, Yŏngsuk wants to go with him. However, she is caught by Sŏngch'ŏl at the last minute, and in fear of losing T'aeyun she attacks Sŏngch'ŏl with a knife. In the meantime, with Taeshik's help, T'aeyun barely evades the police hunt and arrives at the train station. Unaware of Yŏngsuk's arrest for attempted murder, T'aeyun is anxiously waiting for her. But the train arrives, and T'aeyun is forced to leave alone.

To evoke a vivid sense of political realities surrounding the protagonist, Pak deploys clips of newspapers, TV news broadcasting and computer screens in several places of the film. Their immediate function is to situate the narrative in a proper historical context. On a night shift, T'aeyun accidentally catches the headline of a newspaper article in the office that reads 'Underground Working-class Organisation Uncovered'. He also happens to watch TV news in a hotel room about the formation of the National Council of Korean Trade Unions in 1990. These media scenes add a documentary touch to the film. These devices also betray the internal conflicts and tension of the protagonist, reminding him of his shady status as a 'dangerous offender' of public security.

Through the different relationships that T'aeyun develops with villagers, the film examines the problematic alliance between intellectuals and workers, which has been the major driving force behind the South Korean democratisation movement since the 1980s. The coalition was based on their common view that the continued military dictatorship benefited only the capital class and similarly privileged groups that relentlessly pursue their interests at the sacrifice of the hard-working masses. But their collaboration was not always effective in actuality. As is alluded to by T'aeyun's bar conversation with his friend Namjin, the so-called 'June 1987 Uprising' could have succeeded if the efforts from the two camps had been better co-ordinated.

As is suggested by T'aeyun's momentary break away from the student activist circles, class conflict can be misconstrued as a purely political agenda by radical ideologues, who tend to use it as an excuse to deny the legitimacy of the existing social order.[22] Despite their enthusiasm and sincerity, young urban intellectuals often fail to relate to the day-to-day needs of the masses, taking the leadership of the labour movement upon themselves. Living the depressing working-class realities, T'aeyun, for the first time, learns the difference between what he conceived to be class struggle and what it actually means to each individual worker. T'aeyun's education in the social realities of the working class culminates with his discovery of the moral strength in Taeshik, who is an innocent victim of the socio-economic inequity. Taeshik quit school and works at the factory. He earns very little but never forgets to send money to his father in prison, never giving up a dream for a family reunion. Society, however, brands him a 'fatherless boy', the worst condemnation in Korean culture. Having a father convicted for instigating a labour dispute means a life-long social stigma for the boy. Therefore, class struggle means a normal home for Taeshik. One of the most touching moments in the film is Taeshik's confession to T'aeyun on his imprisoned father. Throughout the scene, the dark screen is divided into two by shelves, and Taeshik is shown posing like his father who is behind the bars.

T'aeyun's realisation of the strength of the masses leads him to reject Namjin's request to return to the front line of their urban struggles. What T'aeyun wants is to experience the 'wretchedness of reality' rather than remaining blinded by the romantic ideal formed in his and other activists' minds in abstract intellectual terms. Through T'aeyun's decision to stay in touch with the workers themselves, the film poses a question to the intellectual activists' lofty yet imagined sense of calling for saving the masses from the 'systematic oppression from the capital class and the power elite'. Until he decides to 'go into' the masses in the remote mining village, this sense of calling has dictated T'aeyun's conscience. Stripped of his privileges as a college student and thrown into the pit of the dismal life of the miners, T'aeyun descries their strong instinct for self-preservation and their will to challenge unfair society without resorting to the ideological 'guidance' of urban intelligentsia. In some sense, T'aeyun is a victim of the 'contentious society' which tends to put its members in oppositional terms to others.[23] From this point of view, he is not that different from the exploited workers. Their difference is that his suffering is due to his political belief whereas the miners' is due to the socio-political conditions. Nevertheless, they are common in that they both reject the problematic present and envision a more democratic future. This theme is reflected in the original Korean title of the film *Them, Like Us*.

The film presents a collective action by the masses as a logical consequence of the mounting tension between the miners and the company owner who has threatened to shut down the mines without providing an emergency measure for their livelihood. T'aeyun witnesses the action when he returns from a day trip with Yŏngsuk. The villagers' powerful expression of their anger is contrasted with and at the same time, complements T'aeyun's timid and resigned attitude. The powerful image of the outraged villagers marching to the company and Taeshik's inner strength complete the portrait of the workers in the film. Struck by the hidden power of the demonstrators, T'aeyun appears to be nearly pious in his attitude, recalling his earlier remark to Namjin: 'After all, those who failed are not "*minjung*" [the mass or the people].[24] It is only intellectuals ... We must be reborn with new ideas ...'.

Black Republic employs the metaphor of a tunnel to indicate the change in T'aeyun's perception of the masses. At the beginning of the film the camera shows a bus carrying T'aeyun through a long tunnel and then spinning down to the bottom of a mountain where miners live. He shifts from the bright, urban scenery to the coal-dark mining areas. The closure of Taeshik's confession sequence also contains a tunnel. This is, however, a reverse movement as the scene shows T'aeyun and Taeshik coming out of the dark tunnel into the bright world with big smiles on their faces, together with other healthy-looking miners. An uplifting note is evoked by this scene.

Despite the hopeful message conveyed by the effect of chiaroscuro in the tunnel scenes, the film as a whole does not promise a naïve optimistic vision for the future of the oppressed. This point is based on the terrible ending Yŏngsuk meets after her desperate effort to escape from her dreary life in the village and especially from Sŏngch'ŏl's grip. Although she learns to resist Sŏngch'ŏl's violence by rejecting his money, her tragic fate only confirms her helplessness. Sŏngch'ŏl embodies the evil of ruthless industrialism allied with political corruption. He dictates his black republic with his father's money, entirely estranged from the people. He is always alone, apart from the people: he rides a motorcycle all over the place but never mingles with the villagers. He represents the morally degenerate capitalist class whose destructive materialistic values target the most vulnerable members of society such as Yŏngsuk and Taeshik.

Made in 1990, the last days of the most violent period in the history of the South Korean labour movement, *Black Republic* dramatises the class problems from the perspectives of both intellectual and worker. Through the experience of hope and despair, T'aeyun learns that his is, after all, an unfinished journey as far as complex problems such as Yŏngsuk's remain in society. This theme is summarised by his narration at the end of the film: 'whatever we call it today, the change has already started. Those who must fade away are in despair with the darkness of today, but those who live in the brightness of tomorrow call it a hope'. In this way, *Black Republic* demands that the audience of the early 1990s be engaged actively in mapping out a path to their society's bright tomorrow, not remaining idle spectators of today's darkness.

Class experience and cultural tradition

According to Thompson, class experience is 'largely determined by the productive relations' whereas class consciousness is 'the way in which these experiences are handled in cultural terms: embodied in tradition, value-systems, ideas, and institutional forms'.[25] Seen in light of Thompson's claim, the above six films seem to suggest that class experience in contemporary Korean society is affected as much by cultural tradition as by productive relations. They show that productive relations expose the masses to the prevailing ideology of their society, which is intricately linked with the inequality of wealth and power among the different groups. However, what distresses the characters at a deeper level than the economic system is the legacies of the traditional perception of social hierarchy, which do not accord with the class distinction based on the productive mechanism. Wealth and social respect are two elements that account for the duality of the idea of class held by contemporary Koreans. This is why class issues recur in North Korean cinema even after they have allegedly been eradicated. According to the three North Korean films reviewed in this chapter, the working-class members are envious of those in managerial positions. This anti-revolutionary attitude is expressed by the unnamed director of the arms bureau and Pyŏngch'an in *Untrodden Path*, H'yŏnch'ŏl's children in *The Brigade Commander's Former Superior* and Wŏnbong in *Bellflower*. Their problem with the working class does not stem from physical toil or material hardships but from others' disrespectful attitude toward menial jobs. This psychological phenomenon cannot be adequately addressed by their communist ideology. Their class experience only confirms that North Koreans still subscribe to the hierarchical view of the occupational order inherited from a by-gone feudal society.

The persistence of the residual pre-modern class division is also discernible in the South Korean films. The prejudice against factory girls and their self-effacing reaction to society's skewed perception of their social status do not differ in essence from the frustration exhibited by the North Korean workers. Ironically, the new middle class in South Korean society is equally despised as upstarts, although they occupy an upper stratum in the productive relations. The rich youngsters and land brokers in *Nice Windy Day*, the factory owner and his associates in *Kuro Arirang* or Sŏngch'ŏl and his father in *Black Republic* hardly find self-esteem because they have climbed on the economic scale; not on the social one. They are characterised as cunning and abusive of naïve workers, pursuing only their own material success. Morally flawed, they embody the evil of exploitative capitalist society. Their contribution to dehumanising society is signified by a death or murder that closes the films.

In handling class issues, the films directly or indirectly discuss the significance of education in Korean society. In both the North and South, higher education is a pivotal factor in upgrading a person's social status. In the North Korean films, the first reward that the Party gives 'exemplary' citizens and their children is an opportunity to study at a university. This suggests that college education is part of the mechanism that maintains the strict stratification of North Korean society.[26] Ch'ungil's status change in *Untrodden Path*, and Hyŏnch'ŏl's pride in his children and even Ch'ŏngmin's successful career in *The Brigade Commander's Former Superior* are all attributable to their educational achievements. The role of education in social mobility is greater in South Korean society. In *Kuro Arirang*, many factory workers study at nightschool, and some girls are shown dreaming of marrying university graduates as a way of escaping their ghetto lives. Chongmi even sacrifices herself for the schooling of her young brother. The Korean tendency to place high values on education and their general reverence for the learned are based on old Confucian teachings.

Education, however, is more than an effective means of rise in social status. In the South Korean films and, to a lesser degree, in the North Korean ones as well, intellectuals are assigned a privileged place in society as a role model for the undereducated masses. Their image as social reformers reflects the heritage of Confucian scholar-activists in Korean history. Modern-day college students who are involved in the underground labour movement can be said to carry on the long tradition of social engagement by intelligentsia in Korean culture. Students have been one of the major forces of changing the course of history in modern Korea as is illustrated by the 19 April Student Uprising that toppled the corrupt dictatorship in 1960 and by the Kwangju Uprising in 1980 and the June 1987 Uprising. The scholar-activist is a culture hero in Korea whose conscience is viewed as the bulwark of social morality.

In three of the six films, the narratives are unfolded from the point of view of a young intellectual. As an honours graduate of the North Korean military academy, Chŏngmin's role in *The Brigade Commander's Former Superior* parallels Hyŏnshik's and T'aeyun's in *Kuro Arirang* and *Black Republic*, respectively. As a representative of the so-called new intellectuals in North Korean society, Chŏngmin serves as a link between the Party and the masses in the way Ch'ŏljun, the ex-partisan power-élite in *Untrodden Path*, has done in the early years of North Korean history. Similarly, the protagonists of *Kuro Arirang* and *Black Republic* are driven by a sense of mission to enlighten the masses and realise social justice.

Despite their positive images, however, the use of intellectuals as the dominant perspectives of the narratives results in diffusing the intensity of the theme of self-empowering ability of the masses. College students belong to the future middle class. By experiencing the working-class lifestyle, Hyŏnshik and T'aeyun can further their education in social realities. Their identification with the workers is momentary and mediated by their idealism, not by the kind of existential necessity of destitute workers. Consequently, they are bound to be outsiders to the masses in the long run. Their relations with the working-class women are suggestive of their fundamental class gap. For instance, Yŏngsuk's romantic feelings toward T'aeyun in *Black Republic* stop at the level of fantasy. A meaningful and socially acceptable union between them is infeasible within the given narrative structure. In this sense, T'aeyun's lonely departure at the end is in line with the overall realistic import of the film. Although more subtle, Hyŏnshik and Chongmi's developing friendship in *Kuro Arirang* also does not lead to a dramatic resolution.

Given the profiles of the three South Korean film-makers whose works are examined in the present chapter, it can be said that the role of the young intellectual in their films is somewhat analogous to the directors' own position towards the viewing audience. Through their educated protagonists, these film-makers challenge the dominant social order and instruct the public on the critical function of the film as a cultural text. The situation is the reverse in North Korea where film is expected to serve faithfully the government's purpose to legitimise the status quo. Even in such a stringent milieu as North Korea, however, film exists as a cultural text with its own internal logic. Its complex function and interpretative possibilities cannot be controlled by the government. This explains the contradiction that the audience notices between the workers' subjective views of their status in society and the Party's official position on the issue. Such self-contradictory messages draw attention to the textual ruptures in the North Korean films that invite an ironic reading. This is an inevitable consequence of repressing the mechanism of meaning production in a cultural text as is often seen in the films from North and South.

The notion of class in contemporary Korea has been formed in differing ideological soils between the communist North and the capitalist South. In a society embroiled in rapid industrialisation, a discussion of class issues is bound to excavate its contradictions. In the case of Korea, the situation is more complex because contemporary Koreans still adhere to the values associated with the old feudal class system, which has not been completely replaced by the modern concept of class based on productive relations. The above six Korean films attest to the fact that the perception of class held by contemporary Koreans is not determined merely by their present position in the economic system. The richness of class-related themes in the cinematic texts lies in the very fissures between the traditional cultural values and the modern industrial social structure. Contemporary Koreans are not content with their economic positions unless they are supported by culturally determined social respectability. This seems to be true of both the socialist and capitalist systems on both sides. So long as the cultural and economic perspectives on class continue to conflict with one other, the popular perception of its meanings will continue to challenge and deconstruct its official definition in contemporary Korea.

Notes

1 For example, Bruce Cumings defines the Korean War as a civil war caused by class struggles. Bruce Cumings, *The Origin of the Korean War: Liberation and the Emergence of Separate Regimes, 1945–47*, vol. I; and *The Origin of the Korean War: The Roaring of the Cataract, 1947–50*, vol. II (Princeton, Princeton University Press, 1990).

2 Arthur A. Berger, *Cultural Criticism* (Thousand Oaks, Sage Publications, 1995), p. 47. For detailed discussions of the Marxist definitions of class, see Michèle Barrett, *The Politics of Truth: From Marx to Foucault* (Cambridge, Polity, 1991); T. B. Bottomore, *Classes in Modern Society* (London, George Allen & Unwin, 1965); Pierre Bourdieu, *Distinction: A Social Critique of the Judgement of Taste* (Cambridge, MA, Harvard University Press, 1984); Anthony Giddens, *The Class Structure of the Advanced Societies* (London, Hutchinson, 1973); Stuart Hall, *The Hard Road to Renewal: Thatcherism and the Crisis of the Left* (London, Verso, 1988); Karl Marx and Friedrich Engels, 'The communist manifesto', in David McLellan (ed.), *Karl Marx: Seclected Writings* (Oxford, Oxford University Press, 1977), pp. 219–47; Frank Parkin, *Marxism and Class Theory: A Bourgeois Critique* (London, Tavistock, 1979); and Nicos Poulantzas, *Classes in Contemporary Capitalism*, trans. David Fernbach (London, NLB, 1975).

3 Richard Scase, *Class* (Buckingham, Open University Press, 1992), p. 2.

4 Peter Saudners, *Social Class and Stratification* (London, Routledge, 1990), p. 15.

5 E. P. Thompson, *The Making of the English Working Class* (London, Victor Gollancz, 1980), p. 10.

6 Thompson, *English Working Class*, p. 11.

7 It is said that the final classification began to appear frequently in official documents roughly from 1971. For further information on the historical process of this classification, see North Korea Research Institute (ed.), *Pukhan Ch'ongnam* (A Survey of North Korea) (Seoul, North Korea Research Institute, 1980), p. 528.

8 Frank Parkin, *Class Inequality and Political Order: Social Stratification in Capitalist and Communist Societies* (Frogmore, Granada Publication, 1972), p. 137.

9 Sŏ Chaejin, *Pukhan Sahoe-ŭi Kyegŭpkaldŭng Yŏn'gu* (A Study of Class Conflict in North Korea) (Seoul, National Unification Institute, 1996); Kyŏngnam University Far-East Research Institute (ed.), *Pundan Pansegi Nambukhan-ŭi Sahoe-wa Munhwa* (A Half-century of North and South Korean Societies and Cultures) (Seoul, Kyŏngnam University Far-East Research Institute, 1996); and Yun Tŏkhŭi and Kim Tot'ae, *Nambukhan Sahoe Munhwa Kongdongch'e Hyŏngsŏng Pangan* (Towards Formation of North and South Korean Social and Cultural Community) (Seoul, National Unification Institute, 1992).

10 *Chosŏn Chungang Yŏn'gam 1988* (Chosŏn Chungang Year Book 1988), ed. Chosŏn Chungang (P'yŏngyang, Chosŏn Chungang T'ongshinsa, 1988).

11 According to *Annual Report on the Economically Active Population* published by the National Statistical Office (Kyŏngje Hwaldong In'gu Yŏnbo, 1972, 1985 and 1996), the percentage of the primary sector workers in the total work force declined from 80.6 per cent in 1958 to 12.5 per cent in 1995. In contrast with this, those of the secondary and the tertiary sectors increased from 4.6 per cent and 13.8 per cent in 1958 to 23.6 per cent and 64.0 per cent in 1995, respectively.

12 These directors were also involved in academic film circles during their college years, and some went abroad later to study film-making. Many of them spent their twenties in the vortex of the violent democratisation movement in the 1980s.

13 The film authorities strictly prohibited using a labour dispute as the subject-matter of a film. Because of this, films that came out during this period typically dealt with the urban poor who were not directly related to labour issues. A good example is Yi Wŏnse's *A Little Ball Launched by a Dwarf*, which is based on Cho Sehŭi's famous novel of the same title. Cho's novel is set in an industrial site on the outskirts of Seoul, but Yi had to replace the setting with a seaside village in his film adaptation.

14 As a result, the North Korean industrial structure also underwent a change. The ratio between agriculture and industry was 59.1 per cent to 23.2 per cent in 1946 but changed to 21.5 per cent to 60.6 per cent in 1963.

15 For example, the farming population made up approximately 74.1 per cent of the entire population in 1946, when the land reform law and nationalisation of industries were implemented, but it decreased to 43.8 per cent in 1963 when the system of co-operative farming was introduced, and finally to 25.3 per cent in 1987. Contrasted with the continuous dwindling of farmers, the population in the industrial sectors increased from 12.5 per cent in 1946 to 42.0 per cent in 1963 and then to 57.9 per cent in 1987. Since the 1980s, the focus of North Korean economic policy has drastically shifted from heavy industries to agriculture, light industries and trade.

16 This phrase reveals Wŏnbong's selfish attitude toward his hometown. His old friends ridiculed him by calling him 'cuckoo'. This nickname derives from his mimicry of the cuckoo sounds when he calls out Songnim. The way he leaves her later also reminds the audience of the cuckoo having its own eggs hatched in the nest of other birds. This analogy is brought up by one of the characters in the film.

17 Kim Jong Il, 'Sahoejuŭi kŏnsŏl-esŏ kun-ŭi wich'ŏ-wa yŏkhal' ('The army's position and role in the socialist reconstruction'), in Kyŏngnam University Far-East Research Institute (ed.), *Kim Jong Il Chŏjaksŏn* (Selected Works of Kim Jong Il) (Seoul, Kyŏngnam University Far-East Research Institute, 1991), pp. 1–34.

18 During the 1970s and 1980s, Yi enjoyed great commercial popularity with a series of conventional melodramas about women's private lives, adolescents' growing pains, and tragic love stories: *Home of Stars* (1974); *Between Knee and Knee* (1984); and *Ŏudong* (1985). On the other hand, Yi continued to show his concerns about social problems in such films as *Wayfarer Never Rests on the Road* (1987) and *Myŏngja, Akkiko, Sonya* (1992). Recently, he was actively involved in the boycott movement regarding the direct distribution of US films in Korea. He played the role of a mentor for young directors, such as Pae Ch'angho, Chang Sŏnu, Park Kwangsu and Shin Sŭngsu.

19 The expression '*wijang ch'wiŏpja*' means 'students who conceal their high educational backgrounds and enter companies as menial workers to incite labour unrest'. The definition of this newly coined term well demonstrates the long history of the involvement of university students and intellectuals in the South Korean labour movements and the political orientation of industrial disputes.

20 According to a memoir written by a former government official who was in charge of promoting export by small- and medium-sized

companies in the 1960s, 'all the labour forces needed in the export line were the weak hands of young girls. It was poor girls who sold their hair, and it was also they who made wigs with the hair they had sold. It was also they who stayed up nights making tie-dyed fabrics ... The country was so poor ... [and] there were no jobs for men.' *The Chosun Ilbo*, 1 November 1999, p. 23.

21 Yi Chŏngha, 'Pak Kwangsu interview', in Yi Hyoin (ed.), *Han'guk-ŭi Yŏnhwa Kamdok 13 In* (Thirteen Korean Film Directors) (Seoul, Yŏlrin Ch'aektŭl, 1994), pp. 239–50.

22 Ch'oe Changjip, 'Minjujuŭi-roŭi ihaeng-gwa nodong undong' ('Transition to democracy and labour Movement'), Chang Ulbyŏng *et al. Nanbukhan Chŏngch'i-ŭi Kujo-wa Chŏnmang* (The Structures and Prospects of North and South Korean Politics) (Seoul, Hanul Academy, 1994), pp. 136–70.

23 Hagen Koo, 'Strong state and contentious society', in Koo (ed.), *State and Society in Contemporary Korea*, pp. 231–49.

24 For detailed discussion of *minjung*, see Koo (ed.), *State and Society*.

25 Thompson, *English Working Class*, p. 11.

26 According to Parkin's observation, this was a common phenomenon in the early period of reconstruction in most socialist countries. He pointed out, 'In pre-war Eastern Europe, as in most of Western Europe today, the universities were largely the preserve of the middle class and upper classes. In the period of socialist reconstruction this situation was dramatically changed by the introduction of selective systems designed to favour students from proletarian families'. Parkin, *Class Inequality and Political Order*, p. 142.

Conclusion

The film industries of North and South Korea adopt totally different production and distribution systems under opposite state
ideologies: communism and capitalism. This is manifest in the
representation of ideology in their films. The comparative analysis of the selected films from South and North Korea divulges a
complex relationship between the political and economic bases,
and the cultural forces of society in shaping the self-identities of
a nation. The present study demonstrates the function of cinema
to embody the conflicting perceptions of society and nation held
by the Korean people who live under the two different political
and economic systems. Under the observable differences between
South and North Korean films, however, my analysis also uncovers the sustaining power of cultural homogeneity among the
Korean people, which has not been entirely lost despite their four
and half decades of political confrontation.

Film as a cultural text dynamically unfolds the ways in which
people interpret their social world. It shows their various concerns about society as they are actively engaged in the process of
understanding themselves and, at the same time, communicating
with one another. To delineate the meanings of these concerns –
that is, to provide a 'thick description' in Clifford Geertz's terms,
we should approach ideology as operating broadly 'in service of
power' in the specific contexts of everyday life.[1] Culture reveals
the extensive workings of ideology on multiple levels. In the
context of contemporary Korea, the importance of cultural tradition lies in that it mediates the conflicting views on society and
nation between North and South. Culture, understood as a
mechanism of mediation, has its own terrain formed over the

course of history. To unearth implicit meanings enveloped in a film text, any cultural force should be gauged within its own context. Although it tends to be defined as primarily Confucian in the case of Korea, it could be argued that there are continuous reinterpretations of the salient social values inherent in traditional ideals. It is especially the case when new, contentious values, such as individualism, notions of equality or other ways of thinking relating to socially acceptable human relationships tend to undermine the ideological bases of the society. These changes tend to occur in response to the process of rapid industrialisation and/or democratisation.

The seventeen films examined in this book treat unique historical experiences of the Korean people, which are directly pertinent to their understanding of the country's division in the present. Simultaneously, however, these films also disclose the unceasing belief of the Korean people in their 'oneness' as a nation. Each text confirms the coexistence of tension and reconciliation and of political discontinuity and cultural continuity at the core of the Korean people's conflicting self-identities since post-Liberation.

In 1903, Koreans came into contact with motion pictures for the first time. For the majority of the Korean public, the introduction of motion pictures meant a serious encounter with Western cultures with all the connotations of their economic prosperity and technological progress. Film entered the Korean cultural scene as part of the propaganda efforts of the superpowers at the time: Japan, the USA, Britain, France and Russia. The beginning of Korean film history, therefore, differs drastically from that of its Western counterparts. French and US films originated from the experiments of the Lumière brothers and Thomas Edison, respectively. For Koreans, however, film was not the fruit of scientific research or artistic endeavour as it was the case in the West; it was no more or no less than a useful instrument which foreign companies, diplomatic corps and religious missionaries employed during the late Chosŏn Dynasty to win public favour for political and economic profit.

In such circumstances, it was inevitable that Korean cinema would suffer from political exploitation from its inception. The colonial government produced a large bulk of propaganda films from the early 1920s until 1945. More than 160 films were made in Korea during this period, most of which were either heavily melodramatic or pro-Japanese in content. In this oppressive milieu, however, a feeble yet distinct embryo of nationalistic cinema came into existence. Today the early anti-colonial resistance films and 'tendency' films which remarkably grew out of this precarious ground are regarded as the origin of the nationalistic film movement in South Korea. Film historians also acknowledge their contribution to the development of North Korean cinema.

Ironically, political censorship and economic intervention continued in the Korean film industry even after the Liberation. This historical context accounts for the rationale of this study to analyse the ideological underpinnings of contemporary Korean films. The five adaptations of *Ch'unhyangjŏn* epitomise how South and North Korean films tailor the common legacy of Confucian sexual morality and class distinction differently. The imagery patterns of Ch'unhyang in the three South Korean films suggest mutually complementary facets of an ideal female figure constructed in a male fantasy: a virtuous and yet sexually attractive woman with childlike vulnerability. Whereas the South Korean films present the heroine as remarkably adaptable to the male-centred gender dynamics, the North Korean films focus on her class background, depicting her as the representative working-class woman whose foremost merit consists in her courage to challenge the contradiction of the traditional class structure.

Similarly, the six films dealing with the Korean War expose the deep chasm between South and North in their perception of Korean nationhood. In the three North Korean works, a discernible correspondence exists between the development of anti-imperialist themes and the effort to mount Kim Il Sung as the ultimate definer of Korean nationhood. Viewed in chronological order, the three films reveal a parallel between the increasing glorification of the anti-colonial guerrilla activities allegedly led by Kim and the gradual consolidation of his power base in North Korean politics. The films' ideological emphasis, therefore, accords with the official Korean history promoted by the North Korean Workers' Party. According to the Party authorities, history takes the path of justifying the indispensability of Kim's leadership in the masses' goal of reaching the current North Korean society, the 'classless paradise on the earth'.

Compared with the North Korean works, the three South Korean war films are more complex in the treatment of the ruling anti-communist ideology. All three works stress the notion that the forced division of the country was responsible for the many problems facing modern Korea. On the other hand, they show growing scepticism about the adequacy of anti-communism as the ideological basis of their nationhood. Their changing attitudes toward the black-and-white logic of the South Korean government in handling communism (either pro- or anti-communism) are indicative of a more flexible and still evolving self-identity of South Korean society.

The six films examined in Chapter 4 disclose the close relationship between the class experience of the people and their cultural tradition. Perspectives on class are shaped by a variety of experiences individuals have in their labour relations. With respect to contemporary Koreans' subjective perceptions of class, however, it should be noted that they still use the old class system as a significant frame of reference in determining their standing in society. The three North Korean films attempt to promote the official doctrine of a 'classless society', yet they clearly betray the fact that people do not wholeheartedly accept it in reality. Some of the working-class characters show their dissatisfaction with the inflexible stratification system enforced upon them by the government. This tendency appears to be pertinent to the recent economic crisis and policy failures in North Korea.

Many of the South Korean films made in the 1980s and 1990s tend to tackle social problems involving those who were mobilised for the arduous economic development plans during the 1960s and 1970s but have been alienated from the economic progress of their society. They address the despair and anger of the masses over socio-economic injustice. The films' critical stance on the problematic social structure and the widespread materialism that accompanies it reinforces the role of cinema as social commentator. In this regard, the function of film is diametrically opposite in North and South Korea.

Although the cinematic rendition of the ideological antagonism between the North and South Korea is certainly worthy of investigation, this study draws equal attention to their similar use of the cultural legacy from their shared past. The representation of ideology in Korean cinema exposes the political or economic needs of the present Korean society, but its fundamental root goes back to the enduring cultural traditions that have survived among the people. Film as a cultural text thus inscribes the historicity of society. Confucian tenets on social hierarchy and family life are widely incorporated into the films from both areas. The five adaptations of *Ch'unhyangjŏn*, for example, invariably stress the time-honoured Confucian family ethic based on harmony, unity and loyalty among its members. In this sense, the cultural homogeneity of traditional Korean society can be said to constitute a common undercurrent in these films, although their surface narratives capitalise on the ideological differences between the two states. Importantly, in reinforcing traditional marriage and sexual morality, and filial piety, these films suggest that Confucian patriarchal values can serve as a viable means to resolve larger political problems of the nation. The appropriation of familialism for nationhood is one of the prominent similarities between North and South Korean war films. Also, the general respect for the educated in managerial positions is another commonality between them that stems from traditional Confucian social views.

In contemporary Korean cinema, issues that merit further study abound. Since the late 1980s, the South Korean film industry has witnessed the appearance of politically conscious young directors who challenge the ideological repression of the government. They question more provocatively and more profoundly than their predecessors did the true meanings of national prosperity for Korean people, which they have achieved during three decades of military regimes. Their approaches to the historical upheavals aim at resolving their lingering effect on the present time so that Koreans as a community can reconcile with their tragic past in both political and social spheres. Their fresh angle is not confined to subject-matter alone; they attempt to differentiate themselves from the earlier film-makers in cinematic aesthetics and techniques. Their interest in 'forbidden' subjects and formal innovations should be seen as a positive indication of the maturity of the South Korean film industry at the threshold of the twenty-first century. For the serious student of film, therefore, contemporary South Korean cinema offers a variety of issues on the relation between film, ideology and aesthetics.

Contrasted with these new developments in South Korean film, recent works from North Korea still attempt to instruct the primacy of the Kim family; especially the necessity of Kim Jong Il's succession to his father and thereby the rhetoric of patriarchal lineage in the North Korean leadership. These films confirm the isolated and closed nature of their society. We should, however, be cautious in reading this as a conclusive sign of ideological stagnation of North Korean cinema. As mentioned earlier, the extreme difficulty of obtaining the latest North Korean films makes it quite challenging to understand, let alone, to describe through a cinematic lens the full implications of the failure of the socialist-style state-planning system and the potential political disorder. This difficulty does not appear to be diminished in the near future as North Korea continues to resist the outside pressure and influence in cultural and political terms.

The future of the Korean film industry depends on a host of external parameters. In the South, the factors are mainly economic whereas in the North, they are primarily political. The output of the talented young directors from the South imparts a note of hope to those interested in the future of Korean film. Their serious messages and artistic experiments deserve continued attention. Although the unstable and fluctuating economic situation and the unpredictable political future of the country make it difficult to envision a clear direction for Korean cinema, its potential as a subject for sociological research is indeed rich precisely because of its complexity as a cultural text.

Note

1 Thompson, *Ideology and Modern Culture*, p. 20.

Filmography

Korean films during the Japanese colonial period

Ŭirijŏk Kut'u (The Righteous Revenge, 1919)

production Tansŏngsa
direction Kim Tosan
script Kim Tosan
cast Kim Tosan, Yi Kyŏnghwan, Yun Hyŏk

This was the first Korean motion picture.

Hoyŏlja (Cholera, 1920)

production The Chosŏn Colonial Government
direction Kim Sorang
cast Ch'wisŏngjwa (theatre company), Ha Chiman

Further details are not available.

Changhanmong (Long Cherished Dream, 1920)

production Chosŏn Munyedan
direction Yi Kise
script Ozaki Kōyō, Yi Kise
cast Yi Kise, Ma Hojŏng

Kukkyŏng (The National Borders, 1923)

production Songjuk Kino Drama
direction Kim Tosan
script Kim Tosan
cast Kim Tosan, Pak Sunil

Wŏlha-ŭi Maengse (Plighted Love under the Moon, 1923)

production The Chosŏn Colonial Government
direction Yun Paengnam
script Yun Paengnam
cast Yi Wŏlhwa, Kwŏn Ilch'ŏng, Mun Suil

This was the first Korean feature film.

Ch'unhyangjŏn (The Tale of Ch'unhyang, 1923)

production Tonga Culture Association
direction Hayagawa Sōtarō
script Hayagawa Sōtarō
cast Kim Kyosŏng, Han Ryong

Changhwa Hongnyŏnjŏn (The Tale of Changhwa and Hongnyŏn, 1924)

production Tansŏngsa Studios
direction Pak Chŏnghyŏn
script Kim Yŏnghwan
cast Kim Okhŭi, Kim Sŏlja

Unyŏngjŏn (The Story of Unyŏng, 1925)

production Chosŏn Kinema
direction Yun Paengnam
script Yun Paengnam
cast Kim Uyŏn, An Chonghwa

Shimch'ŏngjŏn (The Tale of Shimch'ŏngjŏn, 1925)

production Paeknam Productions
direction Yi Kyŏngson
script Yi Kyŏngson
cast Na Un'gyu, Ch'oe Tŏksŏn, Kim Uyŏn

Ssangongnu (Jade Tears, 1925)

production Koryŏ Studios
direction Yi Kuyŏng
script Yi Kuyŏng
cast Kim Chŏngryun, Kim Sojin, Cho Ch'ŏngsŏng, Kim T'aekyun

Mŏngt'ŏngguri (Fool, 1926)

production Kyerim Film Association
direction Yi P'ilu
script No Suhyŏn, Yi P'ilu
cast Yi Wŏnkyu, Kim Sojin

Changhanmong (Long Cherished Dream, 1926)

production Kyerim Film Association
direction Yi Kyŏngson
script Ozaki Kōyō, Yi Kyŏngson
cast Kim Chŏngsuk, Chu Samson, Shim Hun

Arirang (Arirang, 1926)

production Chosŏn Kinema
direction Na Un'gyu
script Na Un'gyu
cast Na Un'gyu, Shin Ilsŏn, Nam Kungun

P'unguna (A Lucky Adventurer, 1926)

production Chosŏn Kinema
direction Na Un'gyu
script Na Un'gyu
cast Na Un'gyu, Kim Chŏngsuk, Chu In'gyu

Tŭljwi (Field Mouse, 1927)

production Chosŏn Kinema
direction Na Un'gyu
script Na Un'gyu
cast Na Un'gyu, Shin Ilsŏn

Nakhwayusu (Mutual Love, 1926)

production Kŭmgang Kinema
direction Yi Kuyŏng
script Yi Kuyŏng, Kim Yŏnghwan
cast Pok Hyesuk, Yi Wŏngyong

Yurang (Wondering, 1928)

production The Chosŏn Film Art Association
direction Kim Yuyŏng
script Kim Yongp'al
cast Cho Kyŏnghui, Sŏ Kwangje, Im Hwa, Kim Changsu, Ch'a
Namgon, Kang Kyŏnghui

Sarang-ŭl Ch'ajasŏ (Searching for Love, 1928)

production Naun'gyu Productions
direction Na Un'gyu
script Na Un'gyu
cast Na Un'gyu, Yi Kŭmryong, Kim Ok, Yun Pongch'un, Yi
Kyŏngson

Hon'ga (Imbecile Street, 1929)

production Seoul Kino
direction Kim Yuyŏng
script Kim Yuyŏng
cast Im Hwa, Yi Yŏnghŭi, Pak Yŏnho, Nam Kungun

Amno (The Dark Road, 1929)

production Namhyang Kinema
direction Kang Ho (Tokko Sŏng)
script Kang Yŏnghui, Kang Ho (Tokko Sŏng)
cast Kang Ho (Tokko Sŏng), Pak Kyŏngok, Yi Changhŭi, Yi
Hongnae

K'ŭn Mudŏm (A Big Tomb, 1930)

production X Kinema
direction Yun P'ongch'un, Pak Yunsu
script Yun P'ongch'un
cast Yun P'ongch'un, Pak Yunsu

Namp'yŏn-ŭl Kyŏngbidae-ro (To Send a Husband to a Border
Garrison, 1931)

production Wŏnsan Productions
direction Simada Shō
script Simada Shō
cast Na Un'gyu, Toyama Minoru

Chihach'on (The Underground Village, 1931)

production Ch'ŏngbok Kino
direction Kang Ho

script An Sŏkyŏng
cast Kang Ch'unhŭi, Im Hwa, Yi Kyusŏl, Yi Hongnae, Yi Chŏngae, Shin Yŏng

Imjaŏmnun Narutpae (A Boat without a Boatman, 1932)

production Yushin Kinema
direction Yi Kyuhwan
script Yi Kyuhwan
cast Na Un'gyu, Mun Yebong, Kim Yŏnshil

Ch'unhyangjŏn (The Tale of Ch'unhyang, 1935)

production Kyŏngsŏng Studios
direction Yi Myŏngu
script Yi Kuyŏng
cast Mun Yebong, Han Ilsŏng, Kim Yŏnshil

This was the first Korean sound film.

Omongnyŏ (Omongnyŏ, 1937)

production Kyŏngsŏng Studios
direction Na Un'gyu
script Yi Kyuhwan
cast Yun Pongch'un, Kim Ilhae, No Jaeshin, Ch'oe Unbong, Im Unhak

Nagŭne (The Wayfarer, 1937)

production Sŏngbong Film Productions
direction Yi Kyuhwan
script Yi Kyuhwan
cast Mun Yebong, Pak Chehaeng, Wang P'yŏng

Shimch'ŏngjŏn (The Tale of Shimch'ŏng, 1937)

production Seshin Yanghaeng
direction An Sŏkyŏng
script An Sŏkyŏng
cast Sŏk Kŭmsŏng, Kim Soyŏng, Kim Shinjae

Kunyong Yŏlch'a (Troop Train, 1938)

production Sŏngbong Films, Tōhō Films
direction Sŏ Kwangje
script Yi Kyuhwan, Kikuchi Morifumi
cast Wang P'yŏng, Pak Chehaeng, Kim Yongshik, Mun Yebong

Mujŏng (The Heartless, 1938)

production Chosŏn Film Productions Ltd. Company
direction Pak Kich'ae
script Yi Kwangsu, Pak Kich'ae
cast Kim Shinjae, Yi Kŭmryong, Han Ŭnjin,

Suŏmnyo (School Fees, 1940)

production Koryŏ Film Association
direction Ch'oe In'gyu
script Yu Ch'ijin
cast Pok Hyesuk, Kim Shinjae, Mun Yebong

Chiwŏnbyŏng (The Volunteer Soldier, 1941)

production Tonga Film Productions
direction An Sŏkyŏng
script Pak Yŏnghŭi
cast Ch'oe Unbong, Mun Yebong, Yi Kŭmryong, Kim Ilhae, Yi Paeksu, Im Unhak, Kim Pokchin, Kim Yŏngok, Kim Ch'angjin

T'ayang-ŭi Aŭldŭl (Sons of the Sun, 1944)

production Chosŏn Film Productions Ltd. Company
direction Ch'oe In'gyu
script Nishigame Motosada
cast Kim Shinjae, Chu In'gyu

Sarang-gwa Maengse (Love and Pledge, 1945)

production Chosŏn Film Productions Ltd. Company
direction Ch'oe In'gyu
script Yatsumoto Ryuichi
cast Kim Shinjae, Kim Yuho, Takada Minoru

North Korean films

Nae Kohyang (My Hometown, 1949)

production Division of Film Productions of the Korean Workers' Party
direction Kang Hongshik
script Kim Sŭnggu
cast Yu Wŏnjun, Yu Kyŏngae, Mun Yebong

This was the first North Korean feature film. It was the first of a series of films to be awarded the title, People's Prize Winner.

Yonggwangro (The Blast Furnace, 1950)

production Division of Film Productions of the Korean Workers' Party
direction Min Chŏngshik
script Kim Yŏnggŭn

Further details are not available.

Kukkyŏng Subidae (The Frontier Guards, 1950)

production Film Productions Division of the Korean People's Army

Further details are not available.

Hyangt'o-rŭl Chikinŭn Saramdŭl (The People's Armed Corps Fighting in Defence of the Village, 1952)

production Film Productions Division of the Korean People's Army
direction Ch'oe Ikkyu
script Ryu Kihong
cast Song Yŏngae, Pak T'aesu, Hwang Min, Hwang Hwasuk

Tto Tashi Chŏnsŏn-ŭro (Go to the Front Line, Once Again, 1952)

production Film Productions Division of the Korean People's Army
direction Ch'ŏn Sangin
script Han Wŏnrae, Kang Ho

Further details are not available.

Chŏnt'ugi Sanyanggunjo (The Combat Unit of a Fighter Plane, 1953)

production Film Productions Division of the Korean People's Army
Further details are not available.

Chŏngch'albyŏng (Scouts, 1953)

production Film Productions Division of the Korean People's Army
direction Chŏn Tongmin
script Han Sangun
cast Pak Hak, Chŏn Unbong, Ch'oe Unbong

Shinhon Pubu (The Newly Married Couple, 1955)

production Korean Film Studios
direction Chŏn Tongmin
script Chu Tongin
Further details are not available.

Arŭmdaun Norae (The Beautiful Song, 1955)

production Korean Film Studios
direction Chŏn Tongmin
script Chu Tongin
Further details are not available.

Shimch'ŏngjŏn (The Tale of Shimch'ŏng, 1957)

production Korean Film Studios
direction Chŏn Tongmin
script Chu Tongin
Further details are not available.

Ch'unhyangjŏn (The Tale of Ch'unhyang, 1959)

production Korean Film Studios
direction Yun Ryonggyu
script Kim Sŏnggu
Further details are not available.

Pun'gyesŏn Maŭl-esŏ (The Demarcation Village, 1961)

production Korean Film Studios
direction Pak Hak
script Li Chiyong
This film was awarded the title, People's Prize Winner.
Further details are not available.

Chŏngbanggong (The Spinner, 1963)

production Korean Film Studios
direction O Pyŏngch'o
script Han Sŏng
cast Ch'oe Pushil, Song Yŏngae, Chŏng Unmo
This film was awarded the title, People's Prize Winner.

Taeji-ŭi Adŭl (The Son of the Land, 1963)

production Korean Film Studios
direction Chu Tongin
script Shin T'aeuk
cast Ŏm Kilsŏn, Sŏnu Yongsun, Kim Talyŏn

Sŏngjang-ŭi Kil-esŏ (The Path to Awakening, 1965)

production Korean Film Studios
direction Chŏn Unbong, O Pyŏngch'o, Chŏng Changhwan
script Paek Injun
cast Chŏng Kyuwan, Ŏm Kilsŏn, Ch'oe Pushil, Kim Tongshik, Hwang Yŏngil

Han Chidaejang-ŭi Iyagi I & II (The Story of a Detachment Commander I & II, 1965)

production Korean Film Studios (Wangjaesan Creative Workshop)
direction Kim Tŏkkyu
script Li Chongsun
cast Ch'oe Ch'angsu, Hong Yŏnghŭi, Sŏ Kyŏngsŏp, Hong Sunjŏng

Ch'oe Hakshin-ŭi Ilga (Ch'oe Hakshin's Family, 1966)

production Korean 2·8 Film Studios
direction O Pyŏngch'o
script Paek Injun
cast Yu Wŏnjun, Kim Sŏnyŏng, Kim Hyŏnsuk, Ch'oe Pushil, Kim Uyŏng

Ch'ŏt Kŏlŭm (The First Step, 1966)

production Korean Film Studios
direction Ryu Hosŏn
script Kim Chaeho
cast Ch'oe Pugil, Cho Kyŏngsun, Chu Sŏnghŭi

Kangmul-ŭn Hŭrŭnda (The River Flows, 1967)

production Korean 2·8 Film Studios
direction Chang Un'gang, Pak Tongyŏn
script Yu Chonghyŏk
cast Chang Kyŏnghye, Kim Yŏnghŭi, Ch'oe Taehyŏn

Yugyŏktae 5 Hyŏngje I–III (Five Guerrilla Brothers I–III, 1968–69)

production Korean 2·8 Film Studios
direction Ch'oe Ikkyu
script Pak Sŏngsu
cast Ŏm Kilsŏn, Pak T'aesu, Kim Ryongrin, Kim Sŭngo, Han Chinsŏp

This film was awarded the title, People's Prize Winner.

P'ibada (The Sea of Blood, 1969)

production Korean Film Studios
direction Ch'oe Ikkyu
script Kim Il Sung
cast Yang Hyeryŏn, Kim Sŭngo, Chŏng Taeyŏng, Li Kŭmsŏn, Chŏng Yŏnghŭi, Chŏng Unmo

This film was awarded the title, People's Prize Winner.

Sahoejuŭi Choguk-ŭl Ch'ajŭn Yŏngsu-wa Yŏngok (Yŏngsu and Yŏngok in the Social Homeland, 1969)

production Korean Film Studios
direction O Pyŏngch'o
script Li Chongsun
cast Ch'oe Ch'angsu, Cho Changrim, Yun Mansŏng

Kkotp'inun Maŭl (The Flourishing Village, 1970)

production Korean Film Studios
direction Kim Yŏngho
script Han Pokkyu
cast Kim Ryongrin, Kim Kwangnam, Pak Min, Chŏng Misuk

This film was awarded the title, People's Prize Winner.

Han Chawidanwŏn-ŭi Unmyŏng (The Fate of a Self-Defence Corps Man, 1970)

production Korean Film Studios

This film was awarded the title, People's Prize Winner.
Further details are not available.

Sagwa Ttal Ttae (When We Pick Apples, 1971)

production Korean Film Studios
direction Kim Yŏngho
script Kim Seryun
cast Chŏng Yŏnghŭi, Chŏng Misuk, Kim Seyong, Hwang Hakyun, Hwang Min

Rodong Kajŏng I & II (A Worker's Family I & II, 1971)

production Korean Film Studios
direction Ryu Hosŏn
script Pak Ponghak, Ch'oe Yongsu
cast Yi Kwangrok, Kim Ryŏngjo, Kim Ryongrin, Kim Sŭngo, Yu Wŏnjun, Kang Yŏsŏn

This film was awarded the title, People's Prize Winner.

Pulgŭn Taenggi-rŭl Ch'annŭn Sonyŏ (A Girl Looking for a Red Ribbon, 1971)

production Korean Film Studios
direction Hong Shigol
script Kim Sŏngchŏl, Kim Ryŏngsŏ
cast Chŏng Sunhŭi, Chŏn Tuyong, Kim Tŭksŏn

Kkot P'anŭn Ch'ŏnyŏ (The Flower Girl, 1972)

production Korean Film Studios
direction Pak Hak, Ch'oe Ikkyu
script Kim Il Sung
cast Hong Yŏnghŭi, Pak Hwasŏn, Kim Ryongrin, Ryu Hunam

This film was awarded the title, People's Prize Winner.

Kŭmhŭi-wa Ŭnhŭi-ŭi Unmyŏng (The Fate of Kŭmhŭi and Ŭnhŭi, 1974)

production Korean 2·8 Film Studios
direction Pak Hak, Ŏm Kilsŏn
script Paek Injun
cast Chŏng Ch'unran, Kim Sŭngo, Ch'oe Myŏnggwan, Kim Kwangmun

Pinnanŭn T'aeyang Araesŏ (Under the Bright Sun, 1976)

production Korean Film Studios
direction Yu Wŏnjun
script Kim Chumyŏng
cast Pak T'aesu, Kim Hyŏnsuk, Yu Wŏnjun, Li Rokkwang, Pak Yonghak

Nuri-e Putŭn Pŭl (Flames Spreading Over the Land, 1977)

production Korean Film Studios
direction Pak Hak, Ŏm Kilsŏn
script Paek Injun
cast Kim Junshik, Kim Ryongrin, Cho Kyŏngsun

I Sesang Kkŭt-kkaji (To the End of the Earth, 1977)

production Korean Film Studios
direction Kim Yŏngho
script Li Ch'un'gu
cast Kim Sŏnyŏng, Kim Yŏngsuk, Kang Yŏsŏn, Cho Myŏngsŏn

Poiji Annŭn Yosae (The Invisible Fortress, 1978)

production Korean Film Studios
direction Chang Un'gang
script Sŏl Juyong
cast Kim Gwangmun, Hwang Yŏngil, Chŏng Ŭigyŏm

An Chunggŭn, Idŭngbangmun-ŭl Ssoda (An Chunggŭn Shoots Itō Hirobumi, 1979)

production Korean Film Studios (Paektusan Creative Workshop
direction Ŏm Kilsŏn
cast Li Inmun, Ro Pokshil, Cho Myŏngsŏn, Hwang Yŏngil

This film was awarded the title, People's Prize Winner.
Further details are not available.

Hyŏlyuk (Flesh and Blood, 1979)

production Korean 2·8 Film Studios
direction Min Chŏngshik
script Kim Sheryun
cast Chŏn Chaeyŏn, Kang Yŏsŏn, Kim Kwangok, Kim Okhŭi, Kang Sunjŏng

Irŭmŏpnŭn Yŏngungdŭl I–IIX (Unknown Heroes I–IIX, 1979–81)

production Korean 2·8 Film Studios
direction Ryu Hosŏn, Ko Hakrim, Kim Kwangdŏk, Chang Yŏngbok
script Li Jinu
cast Kim Ryongrin, Kim Chonghwa, Chŏng Unmo, Son Taewŏn, Yun Ch'an, Pak T'aesu, Ch'oe Ch'angsu, Sŏ Kyŏngsŏp, Kim Yŏnghŭi, Sŏ Oksun, Kim Yuil, Kim Yunhong

Ch'ohaenggil (The Untrodden Path, 1980)

production Korean Film Studios
direction O Pyŏngch'o
script Han Sangun
cast Kim Chushik, Chŏn Chaeyŏn, Kwak Myŏngsŏ

Ch'unhyangjŏn (The Tale of Ch'unhyang, 1980)

production Korean Film Studios
direction Yu Wŏnjun, Yun Ryonggyu.
script Paek Injun, Kim Sŭnggu
cast Kim Yŏngsuk, Ch'oe Sŏngyu, Kim Sŏnyŏng, Yu Wŏnjun

Yŏl Nebŏn Jjae Kyŏul (The Fourteenth Winter, 1980)

production Korean Film Studios
direction Kim Yŏngho
script Li Ch'un'gu
cast Hong Yŏnghŭi, Yu Wŏnjun, Ch'oe Ch'angsu, Sŏ
Kyŏngsŏp

Paektusan (Mt. Paektu, 1980)

production Korean Film Studios
direction Ŏm Kilsŏn
script Chŏng Ikhan
cast Cho Myŏngsŏn, O P'asun, Kim Chŏngsu

Chosŏn-ŭi Pyŏl I–X (Star of Korea I–X, 1980–87)

production Korean Film Studios (Paektusan Creatve Workshop,
Poch'ŏnbo Creative Workshop)
direction Ŏm Kilsŏn
script Li Chongsun
cast Kim Wŏn, Li Chongch'ŏn, Kim Sonman, Kwak Wŏnu,
Pak Sŏng, Chŏn Chŏnghŭi

Han Tang Ilgun-ŭi Iyagi (The Story of a Party Worker, 1981)

production Korean 2·8 Film Studios
direction O Pyŏngch'o, Kim Yusam
script Sŏl Chuyong
cast Kim Ryŏngjo, Kim Tŏksŏn, Pak Pongik, Chŏng Ŭigyŏm

Wŏlmido (Wolmi Island, 1982)

production Korean 2·8 Film Studios
direction Cho Kyŏngsun
script Ch'oe Taeguk
cast Ch'oe Ch'angsu, Cho Kyŏngsun, Yun Sugyŏng, Ch'oe
Taehyŏn, Chong Ŭigyŏm

Yŏdanjang-ui Yet Sanggwan (The Brigade Commander's Former
Superior, 1983)

production Korean 2·8 Film Studios
direction Ch'ae P'unggi
script Yi Sŏngil
cast Chŏn Chaeyŏn, Li Iksŏng, Kim Ryŏnok, Kong Yongryŏl

This film was awarded the title, People's Prize Winner.

Shiryŏn-ŭl Ttulko (Get over the Trials, 1983)

production Korean Feature Film Studios
direction O Pyŏngch'o
script Han Sanghun
cast Sŏ Kyŏngsŏp, Kim Ryongrin, Chu Chongim, Kim
Kwangnam, Ra Toch'un

Manbyŏngch'o (Rhododendron, 1983)

production Korean 2·8 Film Studios
direction Pak Changsŏng
script Sŏl Juyong
cast Yang Hyeryŏn, Chŏn Ryongju, Kim Hyesŏn, Li Inmun

Tolaoji Annŭn Milsa (The Secret Messenger Who Never Returns, 1984)

    production Shin Films
     direction Ch'oe Ŭnhŭi
        script Shin Sangok
          cast Kim Chunshik, Ryang Hyesŭng, Kim Yunhong, Kim
                Chonghwa, Kim Okhŭi, Hong Sungjong, Ch'oe Ch'angsu,
                Mun Yebong

Sŏlhanryŏng-ŭi Se Ch'ŏnyŏ (Three Girls on the Sohan Ridge, 1984)

    production Korean Film Studios
     direction Ko Haknim
        script Rye Puyŏn
          cast Kim Sunhwa, Yi Kŭmsuk, Yu Kyŏngsuk

P'urŭn Sonamu I & II (The Green Pine Tree I & II, 1984)

    production Korean Film Studios (Poch'ŏnbo Creative Workshop,
                Paektusan Creative Workshop)
Further details are not available.

Pomnal-ŭi Nunsŏki I & II (Nunsok of Spring Days I & II, 1985)

    production Korean Film Studios
     direction Ko Haknim, Im Ch'angbŏm
        script Li Ch'un'gu
          cast Kim Yongmin, Kim Chunshik, Sŏ Kyŏngsŏp, Mun
                Yebong, Kim Okch'il

Sarang Sarang Nae Sarang (Love, Love, My Love, 1985)

    production Shin Films
     direction Shin Sangok (Ch'oe Ŭnhŭi)
        script Li Hyŏngsu, Han Tongho
          cast Chang Sŏnhŭi, Li Hakch'ŏl, Kim Myŏnghŭi, Son Wŭnju,
                Pang Poksun, Ch'oe Ch'angsu

Kwangju-nŭn Purŭnda (Kwangju Wants You, 1985)

    production Shin Films
     direction Chŏng Kŏnjo
        script Chu Tongin
          cast Kim Ch'ŏl, Pak Mihwa, Ch'oe Pongshik, T'ae Sanghun,
                Mun Chongbok

Sogŭm (Salt, 1985)

    production Shin Films
     direction Shin Sangok
          cast Ch'oe Ŭnhŭi
Further details are not available.

Honggildongjŏn (The Tale of Honggildong, 1986)

    production Korean 2·8 Film Studios
          cast Ch'u Sŏkpong
Further details are not available.

Ondaljŏn (The Tale of Ondal, 1986)

    production Korean 2·8 Film Studios
     direction Ha Ŭngman

script Sŏl Chuyong
cast Ch'oe Sun'gyu, Ch'oe Kŭmok, Yu Kyŏngae, Kim T'aesun, Hwang Yŏngil

Torajikkot (Bellflower, 1987)

production Korean Film Studios
direction Cho Kyŏngsun
script Yi Ch'un'gu
cast O Miran, Song Yŏnok, Kim Hyesŏn, Kim Ryŏngjo, Kim Ilhyŏn, Li Wŏnbok

Ryŏmyŏng I & II (Dawn I & II, 1987)

production Korean Film Studios (Paektusan Creative Work, Poch'ŏnbo Creative Workshop)
direction Yi Chaejun
script Paek Injun

Further details are not available.

Minjok-ŭi T'aeyang I–IV (The Sun of the Nation I–IV, 1987–90)

production Korean Film Studios (Paektusan Creative Workshop, Poch'ŏnbo Creative Workshop)
direction Ŏm Kilsŏn, Pak Ch'angsŏn
script Paek Injun, Li Ch'un'gu, Kim Hŭibong

Further details are not available.

Imkkŏkchŏngjŏn I–V (The Tale of Imkkŏkchŏng I–V, 1988–89)

production Korean Film Studios (Wangjaesan Creative Workshop)
direction Chang Yŏngbok
script Kim Seryun
cast Ch'oe Ch'angsu, Li Kyŏnghwan, Ch'u Sŏkpong, Song Man'gap, Shin Myŏnguk

Pulgŭn Tanp'ungnip I–III (Red Maple Leaves I–III, 1990)

production Korean Film Studios (Wŏlbisan Creating Group), Korean 2·8 Film Studios
direction Kim Yusam
script Li Chinu
cast Chŏng Ŭigyŏm, Chang Yusŏng, Kim Ch'unnam, Li Ch'ŏk, Kwŏn Talsu, Song Yŏnok

Choguk-kwa Unmyŏng I–VX (Nation and Destiny I–VX, 1992–99)

production Korean Film Studios, Korean 2·8 Film Studios
direction Ch'oe Sanggŭn, Pak Chŏngju, Pak Ch'uguk
script Ch'oe Sanggŭn, Shin Sangho, Li Ch'un'gu, O Chinghong
cast Ch'oe Ch'angsu, Sŏ Kyŏngsŏp, Sŏ Shinhyang, Pak Yŏngmi, Kim Sŏnnam, Pak Hyŏshin, Chŏn Chŏnghŭi, Im Sakwan, O Miran

Ŭmakka Chŏng Ryulsŏng (Chŏng Ryulsŏng, the Musician, 1992)

production Korean 2·8 Film Studios
direction Cho Kyŏngsun
script O Hyeyŏng
cast Li Wŏnbok, O Miran

South Korean Films

Chayu Manse (Hurrah! for Freedom, 1946)

production Koryŏ Productions
direction Ch'oe In'gyu
script Kim Ch'anggŭn
cast Hwang Yŏhŭi, Chŏn Ch'anggŭn, Yu Kyesŏn

Yu Kwansun (Yu Kwansun, 1948)

production Kyemŏng Productions
direction Yun Pongch'un
script Yun Pongch'un
cast Ko Ch'unhŭi, Yi Sŏn'gyŏng, Yi Ilsŏn

Yŏsŏng Ilgi (The Women's Diary, 1949)

production Chŏno Productions
direction Hong Sŏnggi
script Hong Sŏnggi
cast Chu Chŭngnyŏ, Hwang Chŏngsun

This was the first Korean film to be made in colour.

Sŏngbyŏk-ŭl Ttulko (Go through the Ramparts, 1949)

production Kimboch'ŏl Productions
direction Han Hyŏngmo
script Kim Yŏngsu
cast Yi Chipkil, Ku Chongsŏk, Kwŏn Yŏngp'al

P'ashi (Seasonal Fish Market, 1949)

production Koryŏ Productions
direction Ch'oe In'gyu
script Kim Ch'anggŭn
cast Ch'oe Chiae, Ch'oe Hyesŏng, Hwang Chŏngsun

Ch'unhyangjŏn (The Tale of Ch'unhyang, 1955)

production Tongmyŏng Productions
direction Yi Kyuhwan
script Yi Kyuhwan
cast Yi Min, Cho Miryŏng, No Kyŏnghŭi

P'iagol (P'iagol, 1955)

production Paekho Productions
direction Yi Kangch'ŏn
script Kim Chonghwan
cast Kim Chin'gyu, No Kyŏnghŭi, Yi Yech'un

Chayu Puin (Free Wife, 1956)

production Samsŏng Productions
direction Han Yŏngmo
script Chŏng Pisŏk, Kim Sŏngmin
cast Pak Am, Kim Chŏngnim, Yang Mihŭi

Tae Ch'unhyangjŏn (The Great Tale of Ch'unhyang, 1957)

production Kim Hyang
direction Kim Hyang
script Kim Hyang
cast Pak Okchin, Pak Okran

Ch'unhyangjŏn (The Tale of Ch'unhyang, 1958)

production   Seoul Colour Lab
direction   An Chonghwa
script   An Chonghwa
cast   Ch'oe Hyŏn, Ko Yumi

Kojong Hwangje-wa Ŭisa An Chunggŭn (The Emperor Kojong and the Patriot An Chunggŭn, 1959)

production   T'aebaek Productions
direction   Chŏn Ch'anggŭn
script   Yi Chŏngsŏn
cast   Kim Sŭngho, Chŏn Ch'anggŭn, Ch'oe Namhyŏn

Changmaru-ŭi Ibalsa (A Barber of Changmaru, 1959)

production   Hansŏng Productions
direction   Ch'oe Hun
script   Kim Kangyun
cast   Ch'oe Muryong, Cho Miryŏng, Kim Chimi

Pak Sŏbang (Old Pak, 1960)

production   Hwasŏng Productions
direction   Kang Taejin
script   Kim Yŏngsu
cast   Kim Sŭngho, Cho Miryŏng, Kim Chin'gyu, Chu Chŭngnyŏ,

Hanyŏ (The Housemaid, 1960)

production   Korean Art Films
direction   Kim Kiyŏng
script   Kim Kiyŏng
cast   Kim Chin'gyu, Yi Ŭnshim, Chu Chŭngnyŏ

Ah, Paekpŏm Kim Ku Sŏnsaeng (Ah, Paekpŏm Kim Ku, 1960)

production   Chungang Munhwa Films
direction   Chŏn Ch'anggŭn
script   Chŏn Ch'anggŭn
cast   Chŏn Ch'anggŭn, Cho Miryŏng

Ch'unhyangjŏn (The Tale of Ch'unhyang, 1961)

production   Hongsŏnggi Productions
direction   Hong Sŏnggi
script   Hong Sŏnggi
cast   Kim Chimi, Shin Kwishik

Sŏng Ch'unhyang (Sŏng Ch'unhyang, 1961)

production   Shin Films
direction   Shin Sangok
script   Im Hŭijae
cast   Ch'oe Ŭnhŭi, Kim Chin'gyu, Han Ŭnjin

Mabu (Horseman, 1961)

production   Hwasŏng Productions
direction   Kang Taejin
script   Im Hŭijae
cast   Kim Sŭngho, Shin Yŏnggyun, Cho Miryŏng

Obalt'an (A Stray Bullet, 1961)

production Taehan Productions
direction Yu Hyŏnmok
script Yi Bŭmsŏn, Na Soun, Yi Chonggi
cast Ch'oe Muryong, Kim Chin'gyu, Mun Chŏngsuk

Sarangbang Sonnim-gwa Ŏmŏni (My Mother and a Lodger, 1961)

production Shin Films
direction Shin Sangok
script Im Hŭijae
cast Kim Chin'gyu, Ch'oe Ŭnhŭi, Han Ŭnjin

Tolaoji Annŭn Haebyŏng (The Marine Who Never Returned, 1963)

production Taewŏn Productions
direction Yi Manhŭi
script Chang Kukchin
cast Chang Tonghwi, Ch'oe Muryong, Ku Pongsŏ

Ppalgan Mahura (Red Scarf, 1964)

production Shin Films
direction Shin Sangok
script Kim Kangyun
cast Shin Yŏnggyun, Ch'oe Ŭnhŭi, Ch'oe Muryong

Nam-gwa Puk (South and North, 1965)

production Kŭktong Enterprises
direction Kim Kidŏk
script Han Unsa
cast Shin Yŏngkyun, Ch'oe Muryong, Nam Kungwŏn

Sun'gyoja (Martyr, 1965)

production Haptong Productions
direction Yu Hyŏnmok
script Yi Chinsŏp, Kim Kangyun
cast Kim Chin'gyu, Nam Kungwŏn, Chang Tonghwi

Kaet Maul (The Sea Village, 1965)

production Taeyang Productions
direction Kim Suyong
script O Yŏngsu, Shin T'aegsŭng
cast Ko Ŭna, Shin Yŏnggyun, Hwang Chŏngsun

7 In-ŭi Yŏp'oro (Seven Women Prisoners, 1965)

production Haptong Productions
direction Yi Manhŭi
script Han Ujŏng
cast Mun Chŏngsuk, Yu Kyesŏn, Yi Minja

Pimujang Chidae (The Demilitarised Zone, 1965)

production Cheil Productions
direction Pak Sangho
script Pyŏn Hayŏng
cast Cho Miryŏng, Nam Kungwŏn, Chu Pina

Manch'u (Later Autumn, 1966)

production Taeyang Productions
direction Yi Manhŭi
script Kim Chihŏn
cast Shin Sŏngil, Mun Chŏngsuk, Kim Chŏngch'ŏl

P'aldogangsan (Sights of the Eight Provinces, 1967)

production Yŏngbang Productions
direction Pae Sŏkin
script Sŏ Kwŏnbae
cast Kim Hŭigap, Hwang Chŏngsun, Kim Chin'gyu

Tolmuji (Tolmuji, 1967)

production Taeyang Productions
direction Chŏng Ch'anghwa
script Ch'oe Kŭmdong
cast Kim Sŭngho, Nam Kungwŏn, Nam Chŏngim

Ssarigol-ŭi Shinhwa (The Legend of Ssarigol, 1967)

production Hapdong Productions
direction Yi Manhŭi
script Sŏnu Hwi, Sŏ Yunsŏng
cast Yun Chŏnghŭi, Ch'oe Namhyŏn, Kim Sŏkhun

K'ain-ŭi Huye (Scion of Cain, 1968)

production Tongyang Productions
direction Yu Hyŏnmok
script Yi Sanghyŏn
cast Kim Chin'gyu, Pak Noshik, Mun Hŭi

Miwŏdo Tashi Hanbŏn (Hate, But Once More, 1968)

production Taeyang Productions
direction Chŏng Soyŏng
script Yi Sŏngjae
cast Shin Yŏnggyun, Mun Hŭi, Chŏn Kyehyŏn

Ch'unhyangjŏn (The Tale of Ch'unhyang, 1971)

production: Yi Sŭnggu
direction Yi Sŭnggu
script Yi Sŭnggu
cast Hong Semi, Shin Sŏngil

The first Korean 70 mm film.

Hwanyŏ (The Fire Woman, 1971)

production Yujin Films
direction Kim Kiyŏng
script Kim Kiyŏng
cast Yun Yŏjŏng, Nam Kungwŏn, Chŏn Kyehyŏn

Chŭngŏn (Witness, 1973)

production Motion Picture Association of Korea
direction Im Kwŏnt'aek
script Kim Kangyun
cast Shin Ilryong, Kim Ch'angsuk, Kim Hŭira

Pyŏldŭl-ŭi Kohyang (Home of Stars, 1974)

production Hwach'ŏn Productions
direction Yi Changho
script Ch'oe Inho, Yi Hŭiu
cast An Insuk, Shin Sŏngil, Yun Ilbong

Yŏngja-ŭi Chŏnsŏng Shidae (The Best Days of Yŏngja, 1975)

production T'aech'ang Enterprises
direction Kim Hosŏn
script Cho Sŏnjak, Kim Sŭngok
cast Song Chaeho, Yŏm Poksun, Ch'oe Pulam

Samp'o Kanŭn Kil (The Route of Sampo, 1975)

production Yŏnbang Productions
direction Yi Manhŭi
script Hwang Sŏkyŏng, Yu Tonghun
cast Paek Ilsŏp, Kim Chin'gyu, Mun Suk

Pabodŭl-ŭi Haengjin (The March of the Fools, 1975)

production Hwach'ŏn Productions
direction Ha Kiljong
script Ch'oe Inho
cast Yun Munsŏp, Ha Chaeyŏng, Yi Yŏngok

Pulkkot (Flame, 1975)

production Nama Enterprises
direction Yu Hyŏnmok
script Sŏnu Hwi, Yi Ŭnsŏng, Yun Samyuk
cast Ha Myŏngjung, Kim Chin'gyu, Ko Ŭna

Kogyo Yalgae (Naughty Boys and Girls at High School, 1976)

production Yŏngbang Films
direction Sŏk Raemyŏng
script Cho Ŭnp'a, Yun Samyuk
cast Yi Sŏnghyŏn, Kim Chŏnghun, Ha Myŏngjung

Sŏng Ch'unhyangjŏn (The Tale of Sŏng Ch'unhyang, 1976)

production Kim Yŏngdŏk
direction Pak T'aewŏn
script Yi Munung
cast Chang Mihŭi, Yi Tŏkhwa, Chang Ukche, Ch'oe Mina, Shin Ku, To Kŭmbong

Kyŏul Yŏja (Winter Woman, 1977)

production Hwach'ŏn Productions
direction Kim Hosŏn
script Cho Haeil, Kim Sŭngok
cast Chang Mihŭi, Shin Sŏngil, Kim ~~Ch'uryŏn~~

Chokpo (Genealogy, 1978)

production Hwach'ŏn Productions
direction Im Kwŏnt'aek
script Kajayama Toshiyuki, Han Unsa
cast Chu Sŏnt'ae, Ha Myŏngjung, Han Hyesuk

Changma (The Rainy Spell, 1979)

    production Nama Enterprises
      direction Yu Hyŏnmok
         script Yun Hŭnggil, Yun Samyuk
            cast Yi Taegŭn, Hwang Chŏngsun, Kim Sŏkhun

Kitpal Ŏmnŭn Kisu (The Banner Bearer without a Flag, 1979)

    production Hwach'ŏn Productions
      direction Im Kwŏnt'aek
         script Sŏnu Hwi, Na Hanbong
             cast Ha Myŏngjung, Kim Yŏngae, Chu Hyŏn

Chŏnu-ga Namgin Han Madi (Words left by a Soldier, 1979)

    production Hanjin Enterprises
      direction Yi Wŏnse
         script Hwang Kilyong, Paek Kyŏl
             cast Chin Pongjin, Chang Hyŏk, Chŏn Yŏngsŏn

Param Pulŏ Choŭn Nal (A Nice Windy Day, 1980)

    production Tonga Film Expert Corporation
      direction Yi Changho
         script Ch'oe Ilnam, Sŏ Chŏngmin
             cast An Sŏnggi, Kim Sŏngch'an, Yi Yŏngho

Tchakk'o (Tchakk'o, 1980)

    production Samyŏng Films
      direction Im Kwŏnt'aek
         script Kim Ch'unghŭi, Song Kilhan
             cast Kim Hŭira, Ch'oe Yunch'ŏl, Pang Hŭi

P'imak (The Death Cottage, 1980)

    production Segyŏng Enterprises
      direction Yi Tuyong
         script Yun Samyuk
             cast Yu Chiin, Nam Kungwŏn, Kim Yun'gyŏng

Toshi-ro Kan Ch'ŏnyŏ (Maidens Who Went to the City, 1981)

    production T'aehŭng Enterprises
      direction Kim Suyong
         script Kim Sŭngok
             cast Yu Chiin, Kŭm Pora, Yi Yŏngok

Mandala (Mandala, 1981)

    production Hwach'ŏn Productions
      direction Im Kwŏnt'aek
         script Kim Sŏngdong, Yi Sanghyŏn, Song Kilhan
             cast An Sŏnggi, Chŏn Musong, Pang Hŭi

Ŏdum-ŭi Chashiktŭl (Children of Darkness, 1981)

    production Hwach'ŏn Productions
      direction Yi Changho
         script Hwang Sŏkyŏng, Yi Changho
             cast Na Yŏnghŭi, An Sŏnggi, Kim Hŭira

Sebon-ŭn Tchalkke, Sebon-ŭn Kilge (Three Times Shortly, Three Times Long, 1981)

production Tonga Film Expert Corporation
direction Kim Hosŏn
script Yi Ŏryŏng, Chi Sanghak, Hong P'a
cast Song Chaeho, Chang Mihŭi, Ch'oe Pulam

Nanjangi-ga Ssoaollin Chakŭn Kong (A Little Ball Launched by a Dwarf, 1981)

production Hanjin Enterprises
direction Yi Wŏnse
script Cho Sehŭi, Hong P'a
cast An Sŏnggi, Chon Yangja, Kim Ch'uryŏn

Kkobangdongne Saramdŭl (Slum Dwellers, 1982)

production Hyŏnjin Film Productions
direction Pae Ch'angho
script Yi Tongch'ŏl, Pae Ch'angho
cast Kim Poyŏn, An Sŏnggi, Kim Hŭira

Paekkuya Hwŏlhwŏl Nalji Mara (White Sea Gull, Don't Fly High, 1982)

production Ujin Films
direction Chŏng Chinu
script Song Kilhan
cast Ha Chaeyŏng, Na Yŏnghŭi, Chang Hyŏk

Pul-ŭi Ttal (Daughter of the Flames, 1983)

production Tonga Film Expert Corporation
direction Im Kwŏnt'aek
script Song Kilhan, Han Sŭngwŏn
cast Pak Kŭnhyŏng, Pang Hŭi, Kim Hŭira

Pabo Sŏnŏn (A Declaration of Fools, 1983)

production Hwach'ŏn Productions
direction Yi Changho
script Yi Tongch'ŏl, Yun Shimon
cast Yi Pohŭi, Kim Myŏnggon, Yi Hŭisŏng

Mulleya Mulleya (Mulleya Mulleya, 1983)

production Hallim Films
direction Yi Tuyong
script Im Ch'ung
cast Wŏn Migyŏng, Shin Ilryong, Ch'oe Sŏngho

Kwabuch'um (Widow's Dance, 1983)

production Hwach'ŏn Productions
direction Yi Changho
script Yi Tongch'ŏl, Im Chint'aek
cast Yi Pohŭi, Pak Wŏnsuk, Pak Chŏngja

Korae Sanyang (Whale Hunting, 1984)

production Samyŏng Films
direction Pae Ch'angho
script Ch'oe Inho
cast An Sŏnggi, Yi Misuk, Kim Ch'ŏlsu

Ku Hae Kyŏul-ŭn Ttattuthaenne (Warm It Was That Winter, 1984)

  production Segyŏng Enterprises
   direction Pae Ch'angho
      script Yi Munung
        cast An Sŏnggi, Yi Misuk, Yu Chiin

Kipko P'urŭn Pam (Deep Blue Night, 1984)

  production Tonga Film Expert Corporation
   direction Pae Ch'angho
      script Ch'oe Inho
        cast An Sŏnggi, Chang Mihŭi, Chin Yuyŏng

Murŭp-kwa Murŭp Sai (Between Knee and Knee, 1984)

  production T'aehŭng Enterprises
   direction Yi Changho
      script Yi Chanho
        cast Yi Pohŭi, An Sŏnggi, Im Sŏngmin

Kilsottum (Kilsottŭm, 1985)

  production Hwach'ŏn Productions
   direction Im Kwŏnt'aek
      script Song Kilhan
        cast Kim Chimi, Shin Sŏngil, Han Soryong

Ŏudong (Ŏudong, 1985)

  production T'aehŭng Enterprises
   direction Yi Changho
      script Pang Kihan, Yi Hyŏnhwa
        cast Yi Pohŭi, An Sŏnggi, Pak Wŏnsuk

Ŏmi (Mother, 1985)

  production Hwangkisŏng Films
   direction Pak Ch'ŏlsu
      script Kim Suhyŏn
        cast Yun Yŏjŏng, Chŏn Hyesŏn, Shin Sŏngil

Ticket (1986)

  production Chimi Films
   direction Im Kwŏnt'aek
      script Song Kilhan, Ku Chungmo
        cast Kim Chimi, Chŏn Seyŏng, Yi Hyeyŏng

Hwangjini (Hwangjini,1986)

  production Tonga Film Expert Corporation
   direction Pae Ch'angho
      script Ch'oe Inho
        cast Chang Mihŭi, An Sŏnggi, Chŏn Musong, Shin Ilryong

Ssibaji (Surrogate Mother, 1986)

  production Shinhan Films
   direction Im Kwŏnt'aek
      script Song Kilhan
        cast Kang Suyŏn, Yi Kusun, Yun Yangha

Seoul Hwangje (Seoul Jesus, 1986)

production Hyŏnjin Films
direction Chang Sŏnu, Sŏnu Wan
script Chang Sŏnu, Sŏnu Wan
cast Kim Myŏnggon, O Sumi, An Yongnam

Kippŭn Uri Chŏlmŭn Nal (Our Sweet Days of Youth,1987)

production T'aehŭng Enterprises
direction Pae Ch'angho
script Pae Ch'angho
cast An Sŏnggi, Hwang Shinhye, Chŏn Musong

Nagŭne-nŭn Kil-esŏdo Shwiji Annŭnda (A Wayfarer Never Rests on the Road, 1987)

production P'an Productions
direction Yi Changho
script Yi Changho
cast Kim Myŏnggon, Yi Pohŭi, Ch'u Sŏkyang

Adada (Adada, 1987)

production Hwach'ŏn Productions
direction Im Kwŏnt'aek
script Kye Yongmuk, Yun Samyuk
cast Shin Hyesu, Han Chiil, Pak Ung

Sŏng Ch'unhyang (Sŏng Ch'unhyang, 1987)

production Chŏng Hwaja
direction Han Sanghun
script Han Sanghun
cast Yi Nasŏng, Kim Sŏngsu, Yŏn Kyujin, Sa Mija, Kim Sŏngch'an, Kwak Ŭn'gyong

Hello, Imkkŏkchŏng (Hello, Imkkŏkchŏng, 1987)

production Hwangkisŏng Films
direction Pak Ch'ŏlsu
script Chi Sanghak
cast Yi Hansu, Kim Myŏnggon, Han Aegyŏng, Yi Yŏngha

Maech'un (Prostitution, 1988)

production Ch'unu Films
direction Yu Chinsŏn
script Yi Hŭiu
cast Na Yŏnghŭi, Ma Hŭngshik

America, America (1988)

production Chimi Films
direction Chang Kilsu
script Song Kilhan
cast Yi Pohŭi, Kil Yongu, Kim Chimi, Shin Sŏngil

Ch'ilsu-wa Mansu (Ch'ilsu and Mansu, 1988)

production Tonga Film Expert Corporation
direction Pak Kwangsu
script Ch'oe Insuk
cast An Sŏnggi, Pak Chunghun, Pae Chongok

Ah! Kkum-ŭi Nara (Oh, the Land of Dreams, 1988)

production Changsan'gonmae
direction Chang Tonghong

This film was banned from release by the government.
Further details are not available.

Aje Aje Para Aje (Come, Come, Come Upward, 1989)

production T'aehŭng Enterprises
direction Im Kwŏnt'aek
script Han Sŭngwŏn
cast Kang Suyŏn, Yu Inch'on, Han Chiil

Umukpaemi-ŭi Sarang (Love in Umukpaemi, 1989)

production Mogad Korea
direction Chang Sŏnu
script Pak Yŏnghan
cast Pak Chunghun, Ch'oe Myŏnggil, Yu Hyeri

Seoul Mujigae (Seoul Rainbow, 1989)

production Kŭktong Screen
direction Kim Hosŏn
script Im Yusun
cast Kim Chusŭng, Kang Rina, Chu Hosŏng

Ch'urakhanŭn Kos-ŭn Nalgae-ga Itta (Things That Have Wings Fall Down, 1989)

production Tanam Entertainment
direction Chang Kilsu
script Yi Munyŏl, Chang Kilsu
cast Kang Suyŏn, Son Ch'angmin

Talma-ga Tongtchok-ŭro Kan Kkadalg-ŭn? (Why Has Bodhi Dharma Left for the East?, 1989)

production Paeyonggyun Productions
direction Pae Yonggyun
script Pae Yonggyun
cast Yi P'anyong, Shin Wŏnsŏp

Kuro Arirang (Kuro Arirang, 1989)

production Hwach'ŏn Productions
direction Pak Chongwŏn
script Yi Hayŏng
cast Ok Sori, Yi Kyŏngyŏng, Ch'oe Minshik

P'aop Chŏnya (The Night before the Strike, 1990)

production Changsan'gonmae
direction Chang Tonghong
script Kong Such'ang

This film was banned from release by the government.
Further details are not available.

Mayumi (Mayumi, 1990)

production Kil Films
direction Shin Sangok
script Shin Pongsŭng

    cast Kim Sora, Yi Hakchae, Shin Sŏngil, Yun Ilbong, Yun Yangha, Ch'oe Chongwŏn, Yi Hosŏng

Nambugun (Southern Guerrilla Forces, 1990)

production Nam Productions
direction Chŏng Chiyŏng
script Chŏng Chiyŏng
cast An Sŏnggi, Ch'oe Minsu, Yi Hyeyŏng, Ch'oe Chinshil

Changgun-ŭi Adŭl (The Son of a General, 1990)

production T'aehŭng Enterprises
direction Im Kwŏnt'aek
script Yun Samyuk
cast Pak Sŏngmin, Yi Iljae, Shin Hyŏnjun, Kim Hyŏngil

Kudŭl-do Uri-ch'ŏrŏm (Black Republic, 1990)

production Tonga Film Export Corporation
direction Pak Kwangsu
script Yun Taesŏng, Kim Sŏngsu, Pak Kwangsu
cast Mun Sŏnggŭn, Shim Hyejin, Pak Chunghun

Ŭnma-nŭn Tolaoji Annŭnda (Silver Stallion, 1991)

production Hanjin Entertainment
direction Chang Kilsu
script Chang Kilsu, Cho Chaehong
cast Yi Hyesuk, Kim Poyŏn, Chŏn Musong, Son Ch'angmin

Kaebyŏk (Fly High Run, 1991)

production Ch'unu Films
direction Im Kwŏnt'aek
script Kim Yŏngok
cast Yi Tŏkhwa, Yi Hyeyŏng, Yi Sŏkku, Kim Myŏnggon

Kyŏngmajang Kanŭn Kil (Road to the Race Track, 1991)

production T'aehŭng Enterprises
direction Chang Sŏnu
script Ha Ilji, Chang Sŏnu
cast Kang Suyŏn, Mun Sŏnggŭn, Kim Poyŏn

Hayan Chŏnjaeng (White Badge, 1992)

production Taeil Films
direction Chŏng Chiyŏng
script Chŏng Chiyŏng, Cho Yŏngch'ŏl
cast An Sŏnggi, Yi Kyŏngyŏng, Shim Hyejin, Kim Sejun

Myŏngja, Akkiko, Sonya (Myŏngja, Akkiko, Sonya, 1992)

production Chimi Films
direction Yi Changho
script Song Kilhan
cast Kim Chimi, Kim Myŏnggon, Yi Yŏngha, Yi Hyeyŏng

Uri-ŭi Ilgŭrŏjin Yŏngung (Our Twisted Hero, 1992)

production Taedong Entertainment
direction Pak Chongwŏn
script Chang Hyŏnsu, No Hyojŏng
cast Ch'oe Minshik, Shin Ku, Ko Chŏngil, Hong Kyŏngin

T'aebaek Sanmaek (The T'aebaek Mountains, 1993)

production T'aehŭng Enterprises
direction Im Kwŏnt'aek
script Cho Chŏngnae, Song Nŭnghan
cast An Sŏnggi, Kim Myŏnggon, Kim Kapsu, Shin Hyŏnjun, O Chŏnghye, Pang Ŭnjin, Chŏng Kyŏngsun

Sŏp'yŏnje (Sŏp'ŏnje, 1993)

production T'aehŭng Enterprises
direction Im Kwŏnt'aek
script Kim Myŏnggon
cast Kim Myŏnggon, O Chŏnghye, Kim Kyuch'ŏl, An Pyŏnggyŏng, Ch'oe Tongjun, Shin Chaegŏl, Kang Sŏnsuk

Kyŏlhon Iyagi (Marriage Story, 1993)

production Ikyŏng Films
direction Kim Ŭisŏk
script Kim Ŭisok
cast Ch'oe Minsu, Shim Hyejin

Kŭ Sŏm-e Kago Shiptta (To the Starry Island, 1993)

production Pakkwangsu Films
direction Pak Kwangsu
script Im Ch'ŏlu, Yi Ch'angdong, Pak Kwangsu
cast An Sŏnggi, Mun Sŏnggŭn, Shim Hyejin, Ch'oe Hyŏngin

Hwaŏmgyŏng (Passage to Buddha, 1993)

production T'aehŭng Enterprises
direction Chang Sŏnu
script Ko Ŭn, Chang Sŏnu
cast O T'aekyŏng, Kim Hyesŏn, Wŏn Migyŏng, Yi Hyeyŏng, Chŏng Suyŏng, Yi Hojae, Shin Hyŏnjun, Tokko Yŏngjae,

Two Caps (1994)

production Kangusŏk Productions
direction Kang Usŏk
script Kim Sŏnghong
cast An Sŏnggi, Pak Chunghun, Chi Suwŏn

Nŏ-ege Na-rŭl Ponaenda (To You from Me, 1994)

production Cine 2000
direction Chang Sŏnu
script Chang Chŏngil, Chang Sŏnu, Ku Sŏngju
cast Chŏng Kyŏngsun, Chŏng Sŏnggyŏng, Yŏ Kyundong, Mun Sŏnggŭn

Tu Yŏja Iyagi (The Story of Two Women, 1994)

production Pak T'aehwan
direction Yi Chŏngguk
script Yu Sanguk, Yi Chŏngguk
cast Kim Sora, Yun Yusŏn, Chŏng Tonghwan, Kim Hŭira, Nam Sujŏng, Kim Chaesŏng, Kim Pŏkhŭi

Hollywood Kid-ŭi Saengae (Life of Hollywood Kids, 1994)

production Yŏnghwa Sesang
direction Chŏng Chiyŏng
script An Chŏnghyo
cast Ch'oe Minsu, Tokko Yŏngjae

Dr Bong (1995)

production Hwanggisŏng Films
direction Yi Kwanghun
script Yuk Chŏngwŏn
cast Han Sŏkkyu, Kim Hyesu

Muso-ŭi Ppul-ch'ŏrŏm Honjasŏ Kara (Go Alone Like a Rhino's Horn, 1995)

production Obyŏngch'ŏl Productions
direction O Pyŏngch'ŏl
script Kong Chiyŏng
cast Kang Suyŏn, Shim Hyejin, Yi Miyŏn

Terrorists (1995)

production Sŏnik Films
direction Kim Yongbin
script Kim Yongbin
cast Ch'oe Minsu, Tokko Yŏngjae

Ŭnhaengnamu Ch'imdae (Gingko Tree Bed, 1996)

production Shin Cine
direction Kang Chegye
script Kang Chegyu
cast Han Sŏkkyu, Shim Hyejin, Chin Hŭigyong

Arŭmdaun Ch'ŏngnyŏn Chŏn T'aeil (A Single Spark, 1996)

production Cine 2000
direction Pak Kwangsu
script Pak Kwangsu
cast Hong Kyŏngin, Kim Sŏnje, Mun Sŏnggŭn

Kaegatŭn Nal-ŭi Ohu (A Hot Roof, 1996)

production Sun Films
direction Yi Minyong
script Yi Minyong, Song Chaeri, Chang Chin
cast Song Oksuk, Ha Yumi, Son Suk, Hwang Misŏn, Chŏng Sŏngyŏng, Im Hŭisuk

Ch'ukche (Festival, 1996)

production T'aehŭng Enterprises
direction Im Kwŏnt'aek
script Yi Ch'ŏngjun, Yuk Sanghyo
cast An Sŏnggi, O Chŏnghye, Han Ŭnjin, Chŏng Kyŏngsun, Pak Sŭngt'ae, Yi Kŭmju, Yi Kyŏngae

Haksaeng Pugun Shinwi (Farewell My Darling, 1996)

production Yŏngsŏng Productions
direction Pak Ch'ŏlsu
script Pak Ch'ŏlsu
cast Ch'oe Sŏng, Mun Sŏngdŏk, Mun Chŏngsuk

Love Story (1996)

production STC
direction Pae Ch'angho
script Pae Ch'angho
cast Pae Ch'angho, Kim Yumi

301, 302 (1996)

production Pak Ch'ŏlsu
direction Pak Ch'ŏlsu
script Yi Sŏgun
cast Pang Ŭnjin, Hwang Shinhye

Kkonnip (A Petal, 1996)

production Yang Pyŏngju
direction Chang Sŏnu
script Ch'oe Yun
cast Yi Chŏnghyŏn, Mun Sŏnggŭn, Yi Yŏngran

Taeji-ga Umul-e Ppajin Nal (The Day a Pig Fell into the Well, 1996)

production Hong Sangsu
direction Hong Sangsu
script Ku Hyosŏ
cast Cho Ŭnsuk, Kim Ŭisŏng, Yi Ŭnggyŏng

Chidokhan Sarang (Their Last Love Affair, 1996)

production Cine 2000
direction Yi Myŏngse
script Yi Myŏngse
cast Kang Suyŏn, Kim Kapsu

Jungle Story (1996)

production Free Cinema
direction Kim Hongjun
script Kang Hun
cast Yun Tohyŏn, Kim Ch'anghwan, Cho Yŏngwŏn

Corset (1996)

production Myŏng Films
direction Chŏng Pyŏnggak
script Ch'oe Munhŭi
cast Yi Hyeŭn, Yi Kyŏngyŏng, Kim Sŭngu

Ch'orok Mulgogi (Green Fish, 1997)

production East Film
direction Yi Ch'angdong
script Yi Ch'angdong
cast Mun Sŏnggŭn, Han Sŏkkyu, Shim Hyejin

Jŏpsok (The Contact, 1997)

production Myŏng Films
direction Chang Yunhyŏn
script Kim Ŭnjŏng
cast Han Sŏkkyu, Chŏn Toyŏn

Kŏjinmal (Lies, 1998)

production Shin Cine
direction Chang Sŏnu
script Chang Chŏngil, Chang Sŏnu
cast Yi Jaeun, Kim T'aeyŏn, Chŏn Hyejin, Han Kwant'aek

Arŭmdaun Shijŏl (Spring in My Hometown, 1998)

production Paektudaegan
direction Yi Kwangmo
script Yi Kwangmo
cast Yi In, Song Oksuk, An Sŏnggi

Misulgwan Yŏp Tongmulwŏn (The Zoo Adjacent to the Art Gallery, 1999)

production Cine 2000
direction Yi Chŏnghyang
script Yi Chŏnghyang
cast Yi Ch'unhŭi, Shim Ŭnha, An Sŏnggi, Han Ch'ŏlsu

Shwiri (Shwiri, 1999)

production Kangjegyu Films
direction Kang Chegyu
script Kang Chegyu
cast Han Sŏkkyu, Ch'oe Minshik, Yu Chungwŏn, Yi Myŏnghyŏn

Injŏngsajŏng Kot Ŏptta (Nowhere to Hide, 1999)

production T'aewŏn Entertainments
direction Yi Myŏngse
script Yi Myŏngse
cast An Sŏnggi, Chang Tonggŏn

Juyuso Sŭpkyŏk Sagŏn (The Petrol Station Hijack, 1999)

production Cinema Service
direction Kim Sangjin
script Kim Sangjin
cast Yi Sŏngjae, Yu Osŏng, Yu Chit'ae, Kang Sŏngjin

Happy Ending (1999)

production Myŏng Films
direction Chŏng Chiu
script Chŏng Chiu
cast Ch'oe Minshik, Chŏn Toyŏn, Chu Chinmo

Nae Maŭm-ŭi P'unggŭm (Harmonium in My Memory, 1999)

production Art Hill
direction Yi Yŏngjae
script Hag Ŭnch'an, Yi Yŏngjae
cast Chŏn Toyŏn, Yi Pyŏnghŏn, Yi Miyŏn

Pakha Sat'ang (Peppermint Candy, 2000)

production East Film
direction Yi Ch'angdong
script Yi Ch'angdong
cast Sŏl Kyŏnggu, Mun Sori, Kim Yŏjin

Ch'unhyangdyŏn (The Tale of Ch'unhyang, 2000)

production T'aehŭng Enterprises
direction Im Kwŏnt'aek
script Cho Sanghyŏn
cast Yi Hyojŏng, Cho Sŭngu, Yi Chŏnghyŏn, Kim Sŏngnyŏ

Bibliography

The bibliography is in two parts: the first gives English-language publications, the second gives Korean publications.

English-language publications

Adorno, Theodor W., 'Scientific experiences of a European scholar in America', in Donald Feming and Bernard Bailyn (eds), *The Intellectual Migration: Europe and America, 1930–60* (Cambridge, MA, Harvard University Press, 1969), pp. 338–70.

Adorno, Theodor W., *The Cultural Industry: Selected Essays on Mass Culture*, ed. J. M. Bernstein (London, Routledge, 1991).

Adorno, Theodor W. and Max Horkheimer, *Dialectic of Enlightenment*, trans. John Cumming, new edn (London, Verso, 1979).

Agger, Ben, *Cultural Studies as Critical Theory* (London, Falmer Press, 1992).

Althusser, Louis, 'From capital to Marx's philosophy', in Althusser, Louis, and Étienne Balibar, *Reading Capital*, trans. Ben Brewster (London, NLB, 1970), pp. 11–69.

Althusser, Louis, 'The errors of classical economics', in Althusser, Louis, and Étienne Balibar, *Reading Capital*, trans. Ben Brewster (London, NLB, 1970), pp. 91–118.

Althusser, Louis, *Lenin and Philosophy and Other Essays*, trans. Ben Brewster (London, Monthly Review Press, 1977).

Althusser, Louis, 'Ideology and ideological state apparatuses', in *Lenin and Philosophy and Other Essays*, trans. Ben Brewster (London, Monthly Review Press, 1977), pp. 121–73.

Althusser, Louis, *Essays on Ideology* (London, Verso, 1984).

Althusser, Louis, *For Marx*, trans. Ben Brewster (London, Verso, 1996).

Althusser, Louis and Étienne Balibar, *Reading Capital*, trans. Ben Brewster (London, NLB, 1970).

An, Tae Sung, *North Korea in Transition: From Dictatorship to Dynasty* (Westport, Connecticut, Greenwood Press, 1983).

Anderson, Benedict, *Imagined Communities* (London, Verso, 1991).

Andrew, J. Dudley, *The Major Film Theories: An Introduction* (London, Oxford University Press, 1976).

Andrew, J. Dudley, *Concepts in Film Theory* (Oxford, Oxford University Press, 1984).

Barrett, Michèle, *The Politics of Truth: from Marx to Foucault* (Cambridge, Polity, 1991).

Barthes, Roland, *Mythologies*, trans. Annette Lavers (London, Vintage, 1993).

Baudry, Jean-Louis, 'Ideological effects of the basic cinematographic apparatus', in Bill Nichols (ed.), *Movies and Methods Volume II: An Anthology* (Berkeley, University of California Press, 1985), pp. 531–42.

Bauman, Zygmunt, *Hermeneutics and Social Science: Approach to Understanding* (London, Hutchinson & Co., 1978, repr. Gregg Revivals, 1992).

Benjamin, Walter, 'The work of art in the age of mechanical reproduction', in *Illuminations*, trans. Harcourt Brace Jovanovich (London, Cape, 1970), pp. 211–44.

Bennett, Tony *et al.* (eds), *Culture, Ideology and Social Process* (London, Batsford, 1981).

Bennett, Tony *et al.* (eds), *Popular Culture and Social Relations* (Milton Keynes, Open University Press, 1986).

Benton, Ted, *The Rise and Fall of Structural Marxism: Althusser and his Influence* (London, Macmillan Publishers, 1984).

Berger, Arthur A., *Cultural Criticism* (Thousand Oaks, Sage Publications, 1995).

Bhabha, Homi K., 'The other question: the stereotype and colonial discourse', *The Sexual Subject: A Screen Reader in Sexuality* (London, Routledge, 1992), pp. 312–31.

Bottomore, T. B., *Class in Modern Society* (London, George Allen & Unwin, 1965).

Bourdieu, Pierre, *Distinction: A Social Critique of the Judgement of Taste* (Cambridge, MA, Harvard University Press, 1984).

Cahiers du Cinéma, (editors of) 'John Ford's *Young Mr Lincoln*', in Bill Nichols (ed.), *Movies and Methods Volume I: An Anthology* (Berkeley, University of California Press, 1976), pp. 493–529.

Chin, In-sook, *A Classical Novel Ch'unhyangjon* (Seoul, Korean Centre, International PEN, 1970).

Comolli, Jean-Louis and Jean Narboni, 'Cinema/ideology/criticism', in Bill Nichols (ed.), *Movies and Methods Volume I: An Anthology* (Berkeley, University of California Press, 1976), pp. 22–30.

Crapanzano, Vincent, 'Hermes' dilemma, the masking of subversion in ethnographic description', in James Clifford and George E. Marcus (eds), *Writing Culture* (Berkeley, University of California Press, 1986), pp. 51–76.

Cumings, Bruce, *The Origin of the Korean War: Liberation and the Emergence of Separate Regimes, 1945–1947*, vol. I (Princeton, Princeton University Press, 1990).

Cumings, Bruce, *The Origin of the Korean War: The Roaring of the Cataract, 1947–1950*, vol. II (Princeton, Princeton University Press, 1990).

Cumings, Bruce, 'The corporate state in North Korea', in Hagen Koo (ed.), *State and Society in Contemporary Korea* (Ithaca, Cornell University Press, 1993), pp. 13–50.

Denzin, Norman K., *Images of Postmodern Society: Social Theory and Contemporary Cinema* (London, Sage Publications, 1991).

Dissanayake, Wimal (ed.), *Colonialism and Nationalism in Asian Cinema* (Bloomington, Indiana University Press, 1994).

Eagleton, Terry, *Criticism and Ideology: A Study in Marxist Literary Theory* (London, Routledge, 1976).

Fiske, John and John Hartley, *Reading Television* (London, Routledge, 1978).

Foucault, Michel, *The History of Sexuality I: An Introduction*, trans. Robert Hurley (London, Penguin Books, 1979).

Foucault, Michel, *Michel Foucault: Power, Truth, Strategy*, ed. Meaghan Morris and Paul Patton (Sydney, Fedal Publications, 1979).

Foucault, Michel, *Discipline and Punish: The Birth of the Prison*, trans. Alan Sheridan (London, Penguin Books, 1979).

Foucault, Michel, *Power/Knowledge: Selected Interviews and Other Writings 1972–1977*, ed. Colin Gordon, trans. Colin Gordon and others (New York, Harvester Press, 1980).

Foucault, Michel, 'Power and strategies', in Colin Gordon (ed.), *Power/Knowledge: Selected Interviews and Other Writings 1972–1977*, trans. Colin Gordon and others (New York, Harvester Press, 1980), pp. 134–45.

Foucault, Michel, *Michel Foucault: Politics, Philosophy, Culture*, ed. Lawrence D. Kritzman, trans. Alan Sheridan and others (London, Routledge, 1988).

Foucault, Michel, 'Critical theory/intellectual history', in Lawrence D. Kritzman (ed.), *Michel Foucault: Politics, Philosophy, Culture*, trans. Alan Sheridan and others (London, Routledge, 1988), pp. 17–46.

Foucault, Michel, 'Power and sex', in Lawrence D. Kritzman (ed.), *Michel Foucault: Politics, Philosophy, Culture*, trans. Alan Sheridan and others (London, Routledge, 1988), pp. 110–24.

Foucault, Michel, *The Order of Things: An Archaeology of the Human Sciences* (London, Routledge, 1989).

Gadamer, Hans-Georg, *Truth and Method*, trans. Willam Glen-Doepel (London, Seed & Ward, 1989).

Geertz, Clifford, *The Interpretation of Culture* (London, Fontana, 1993).

Geertz, Clifford, *Local Knowledge* (London, Fontana, 1993).

Giddens, Anthony, *The Class Structure of the Advanced Societies* (London, Hutchinson, 1973).

Giddens, Anthony, 'The nations as power-container', in John Hutchinson and Anthony D. Smith (eds), *Nationalism* (Oxford, Oxford University Press, 1994), pp. 34–5.

Gledhill, Christine, 'Recent developments in feminist criticism in theory', in Gerald Mast and Marshall Cohen (eds), *Film Theory and Criticism: Introductory Readings*, 3rd edn (New York, Oxford University Press, 1985), pp. 817–45.

Gramsci, Antonio, *Selections from the Prison Notebooks*, ed. and trans. Quintin Hoare and Geoffrey Nowell-Smith (London, Lawrence & Wishart, 1971).

Gramsci, Antonio, *Selections from Cultural Writings*, ed. David Forgacs and Geoffrey Nowell-Smith, trans. William Boelhower (London, Lawrence & Wishart, 1985).

Griffin, Roger, 'Nationalism', in *Contemporary Political Ideologies* (London, Pinter Publishers, 1993), pp. 147–68.

Hall, Stuart, *The Hard Road to Renewal: Thatcherism and the Crisis of the Left* (London, Verso, 1988).

Harvey, Sylvia (ed.), *May 1968 and Film Culture* (London, British Film Institute, 1978).

Heath, Stephen, 'Differences', in *The Sexual Subject: A Screen Reader in Sexuality* (London, Routledge, 1992), pp. 47–106.

Heywood, Andrew, *Political Ideologies: An Introduction* (London, Macmillan Press, 1992).

Hill, John, *Sex, Class and Realism: British Cinema 1956–1963* (London, British Film Institute, 1986).

Hirst, Paul, 'Althusser and the theory of ideology', in *On Law and Ideology* (London, Macmillan, 1979), pp. 40–74.

Hobsbawm, Eric and Terence Ranger (eds), *The Invention of Tradition* (Cambridge, Cambridge University Press, 1992).

Horkheimer, Max, 'The latest attack on metaphysics', in Stanley Aronowitz (ed.), *Critical Theory: Selected Essays*, trans. Mettew O'Connell and others (New York, Herder and Herder, 1972), pp. 132–87.

Horkheimer, Max, 'Traditional and critical theory', in Stanley Aronowitz (ed.), *Critical Theory: Selected Essays*, trans. Mettew O'Connell and others (New York, Herder and Herder, 1972), pp. 188–243.

Howard, Michael, 'War and nations', in John Hutchinson and Anthony D. Smith (eds), *Nationalism* (Oxford, Oxford University Press, 1994), pp. 254–7.

Howells, Richard, 'The interpretation of popular culture as modern myth' (unpublished doctoral thesis, University of Cambridge, 1994).

Hutchinson, John, and Anthony D. Smith (eds), *Nationalism* (Oxford, Oxford University Press, 1994).

Inglis, Fred, *Media Theory: An Introduction* (Oxford, Blackwell Publishers, 1990).

Jameson, Frederic, *Marxism and Form* (Princeton, NJ, Princeton University Press, 1972).

Jameson, Fredric, 'Class and allegory in contemporary mass culture, *Dog Day Afternoon* as a political film (1979)', in *Signatures of the Visible* (London, Routledge, 1992), pp. 35–54.

Jameson, Fredric, '*Diva* and the French socialism (1982)', in *Signatures of the Visible* (London, Routledge, 1992), pp. 55–62.

Johnston, Claire, 'Women's cinema as counter-cinema', in Bill Nichols (ed.), *Movies and Methods Volume I: An Anthology* (Berkeley, University of California Press, 1976), pp. 208–17.

Johnston, Claire, 'Towards a feminist film practice, some theses', in Bill Nichols (ed.), *Movies and Methods Volume II: An Anthology* (Berkeley, University of California Press, 1985), pp. 315–27.

Kellner, Douglas, *Media Culture: Cultural Studies, Identity and Politics between the Modern and the Postmodern* (London, Routledge, 1995).

Kim, Il Sung, 'On eliminating dogmatism and formalism and establishing *Juche* in ideological work: Speech to Party propaganda and agitation workers', 28 December 1955, in *Kim Il Sung Works 9: July 1954–December 1955* (Pyongyang, Foreign Language Publishing House, 1982). pp. 395–417.

Kim, Il Sung, 'Let us embody the revolutionary spirit of independence, self-sustenance and self-defence more thoroughly in all branches of state activities', 16 December 1967, in *Kim Il Sung Works 21* (Pyongyang, Foreign Language Publishing House, 1985), pp. 408–67.

Kim, Jong Il, *The Character and the Actor* (Pyongyang, Foreign Language Publishing House, 1987).

Kim, Jong Il, *The Cinema and Directing* (Pyongyang, Foreign Language Publishing House, 1987).

Koo, Hagen (ed.), *State and Society in Contemporary Korea* (Ithaca, Cornell University Press, 1993).

Koo, Hagen, 'Strong state and contentious society', in Hagen Koo (ed.), *State and Society in Contemporary Korea* (Ithaca, Cornell University Press, 1993), pp. 231–49.

Korean Film Export & Import Corporation, *Korean Film Art* (Pyongyang, Korean Film Export & Import Corporation, 1985).

Kuhn, Annette, *Women's Picture: Feminism and Cinema*, 2nd edn (London, Verso, 1994).

Leak, Andrew, *Barthes: Mythologies* (London, Grant & Cutler, 1994).

Lee, Young-il and Young-chol Choe, *The History of Korean Cinema*, ed. Motion Picture Promotion Corporation, trans. Richard Lynn Greever (Seoul, Jimoondang, 1988).

Marx, Karl, *Karl Marx: Selected Writings*, ed. David McLellan (Oxford, Oxford University Press, 1977).

Marx, Karl, 'Preface to *A Contribution to the Critique of Political Economy*', in David McLellan (ed.), *Karl Marx: Selected Writings* (Oxford, Oxford University Press, 1977), pp. 388–92.

Marx, Karl and Frederick Engels, *The German Ideology I & III*, ed. and trans. R. Pascal (New York, International Publishers, 1963).

Marx Karl and Frederick Engels, 'The communist manifesto', in David McLellan (ed.), *Karl Marx: Selected Writings* (Oxford, Oxford University Press, 1977).

Marx, Karl and Frederick Engels, *On Literature and Art* (Moscow, Progress Publishers, 1978).

Mast, Gerald and Marshall Cohen (eds), *Film Theory and Criticism: Introductory Readings*, 3rd edn (New York, Oxford University Press, 1985).

Mast, Gerald and Marshall Cohen, 'Film, psychology, society and ideology', in Gerald Mast and Marshall Cohen (eds), *Film Theory and Criticism: Introductory Readings*, 3rd edn (New York, Oxford University Press, 1985), pp. 669–74.

McLellan, David, *Ideology*, 2nd edn (Buckingham, Open University Press, 1995).

Mulvey, Laura, 'Visual pleasure and narrative cinema', *Screen*, 16:3 (1975), 6–18.

Nichols, Bill (ed.), *Movies and Methods Volume I: An Anthology* (Berkeley, University of California Press, 1976).

Nichols, Bill, *Ideology and the Image: Social Representation in the Cinema and Other Media* (Bloomington, Indiana University Press, 1981).

Nichols, Bill (ed.), *Movies and Methods Volume II: An Anthology* (Berkeley, University of California Press, 1985).

Palmer, Richard E., *Hermeneutics: Interpretation Theory in Schleirmarcher, Dilthey, Heidegger and Gadamer* (Evanston, IL, Northwestern University Press, 1969).

Parkin, Frank, *Class Inequality and Political Order: Social Stratification in Capitalist and Communist Societies* (Frogmore, Granada Publication, 1972).

Parkin, Frank, *Marxism and Class Theory: A Bourgeois Critique* (London, Tavistock, 1979).

Polan, Dana B., 'Powers of vision, visions of power', *Camera Obscura: A Journal of Feminism and Film Theory*, 18 (1988), 106–19.

Poulantzas, *Class in Contemporary Capitalism*, trans. David Ferbach (London, NLB, 1975).

Pollack, Griselda, 'What's wrong with "image of women"?', in *The Sexual Subject: A Screen Reader in Sexuality* (London, Routledge, 1992), pp. 135–45.

Pribram, E. Deidre (ed.), *Female Spectators: Looking At Film and Television* (London, Verso, 1988).

Rosenstone, Robert A., *Visions of the Past: The Challenge of Film to Our Idea of History* (Cambridge, MA, Harvard University Press, 1995).

Rayns, Tony, 'Korea's new wavers', *Sight and Sound*, 4:11 (1994), 22–5.

Said, Edward W., *Orientalism: Western Conceptions of the Orient* (London, Penguin Books, 1985).

Saudners, Peter, *Social Class and Stratification* (London, Routledge, 1990).

Scase, Richard, *Class* (Buckingham, Open University Press, 1992).

Screen Reader 1: Cinema/Ideology/Politics (London, Society for Education in Film and Television, 1977).

Short, K. R. M. (ed.), *Feature Films as History* (London, Croom Helm, 1981).

Silverman, Kaja, *The Subject of Semiotics* (Oxford, Oxford University Press, 1983).

Smith, Anthony D., *Theories of Nationalism* (London, Gerald Duckworth & Company, 1971).

Sorlin, Pierre, *The Film in History: Restaging the Past* (Oxford, Basil Blackwell Publisher, 1980).

Spellerberg, James, 'Technology and ideology in the cinema', in Gerald Mast and Marshall Cohen (eds), *Film Theory and Criticism: Introductory Readings*, 3rd edn (New York, Oxford University Press, 1985), pp. 761–75.

Stam, Robert and Louise Spence, 'Colonialism, racism, and representation, an introduction', in Bill Nichols (ed.), *Movies and Methods Volume II: An Anthology* (Berkeley, University of California Press, 1985), pp. 632–49.

Standish, Isolde, 'Korean cinema and the new realism, text and context', in Wimal Dissanyake (ed.), *Colonialism and Nationalism in Asian Cinema* (Bloomington, Indiana University Press, 1994), pp. 65–89.

Storey, John, *An Introductory Guide to Cultural Theory and Popular Culture* (Hertfordshire, Harvester Wheatsheaf, 1993).

Suh, Dae-Sook, *Kim Il Sung: The North Korean Leader* (New York, Columbia University Press, 1988).

Suh, Jae-Jean, 'Theoretical revision of *Juche* thought and nationalism in North Korea', *The Korean Journal of National Unification*, 2 (1993), 7–29.

Telotte, J. P., *Voices in the Dark: The Narrative Patterns of Film Noir* (Urbana, University of Illinois Press, 1989).

Thompson, E. P., *The Making of the English Working Class* (London, Victor Gollancz, 1980).

Thompson, John B., *Studies in the Theory of Ideology* (Cambridge, Polity Press, 1984).

Thompson, John B., *Ideology and Modern Culture: Critical Social Theory in the Era of Mass Communication* (Cambridge, Polity Press, 1990).

Turner, Graeme, *British Cultural Studies: An Introduction*, 2nd edn (London, Routledge, 1996).

Vincent, Andrew, *Modern Political Ideology*, 2nd edn (Oxford, Blackwell Publisher, 1995).

Weber, Max, 'The nation', in John Hutchinson and Anthony D. Smith (eds), *Nationalism* (Oxford, Oxford University Press, 1994), pp. 21–5.

Williams, Linda (ed.), *The Sexual Subject: A Screen Reader in Sexuality* (London, Routledge, 1992).

Williams, Linda (ed.), *Viewing Positions: Ways of Seeing Film* (New Brunswick, Rutgers University Press, 1994).

Williams, Raymond, *Marxism and Literature* (Oxford, Oxford University Press, 1977).

Wilson, Rob, 'Melodramas of Korean national identity, from *Mandala* to *Black Republic*', in Wimal Dissanyake (ed.), *Colonialism and Nationalism in Asian Cinema* (Bloomington, Indiana University Press, 1994), pp. 90–104.

Zavarzadeh, Ma'sud, *Seeing Films Politically* (Albany, State University of New York Press, 1991).

Korean publications

An, Chonghwa, *Han'guk Yŏnghwa Ch'ŭngmyŏn Pisa* (Undisclosed Korean Film History) (Seoul, Ch'unch'ugak, 1962).

Board of National Unification, *Pukhan-ŭi Yŏn'gŭk Yŏnghwa* (North Korean Theatre Drama and Film) (Seoul, Board of National Unification, 1979).

Board of National Unification, *Nambukhan Yŏnghwa mit Mudae Yesul Pigyo* (A Comparison of North–South Korean Films and Theatre Arts) (Seoul, Board of National Unification, 1986).

Board of National Unification, *Pukhan, T'ongil Yŏngu Nonmunjip* (Collection of Essays on North Korea and Korean Unification) (Seoul, Board of National Unification, 1990).

Cho, Hŭimun, 'Han'guk yŏnghwa kitchŏm-e kwanhan yŏn'gu' (A study of the beginnng of Korean film), in Chŏngok Kim (ed.), *Han'guk Yŏnghwa-ŭi Saeroun Palgyŏn* (A New Discovery of Korean Film) (Seoul, Korean Film Academy, 1993), pp. 7–42.

Cho, Hŭimun, 'Han'guk yŏnghwa-ŭi saengsŏng' (The development of Korean film), *Korean Film Critiques*, 5 (1993), 28–80.

Cho, Hŭimun, '"Han'guk yŏnghwa"-ŭi kaenyŏmjŏk chŏngŭi-wa kijŏm-e kwanhan yŏn'gu' (A study of the major concepts in Korean film and its beginning), *Yŏnghwa Yŏn'gu* (Film Study), 11 (1995), 7–29.

Cho, Yunje, *Ch'unhyangjŏn* (The Tale of Ch'unhyang) (Seoul, Ŭlyumunhwasa, 1983).

Ch'oe, Chinyong, and others (eds), *Han'guk Yŏnghwa Chŏngch'aek-ŭi Hŭrŭm-gwa Saeroun Chŏnmang* (The Trends and the New Perspective of Korean Film Policy) (Seoul, Chimmundang, 1994).

Ch'oe, Ch'ŏkho, *Pukhan Yesul Yŏnghwa* (North Korean Art Film) (Seoul, Sinwŏn Munhwasa, 1989).

Ch'oe, Ch'ŏl, and Sŏnggyŏng Sŏl (eds), *Sŏlhwa, Sosŏl-ŭi Yŏn'gu* (A Study of the Myth and the Novel) (Seoul, Chŏngŭmsa, 1984).

Ch'oe, Chunghwi, and Hoyun Li (eds), *Chosŏn Yŏnghwa Yŏn'gam* (Korean Film Yearbook) (P'yŏngyang, Munye Publishing House, 1987).

Ch'oe, Changjip, 'Minjujuŭiro-ŭi ihaeng-gwa nodong undong' (Transition to democracy and labour movement), in Chang, Ŭlbyŏng, and others, *Nambukhan Chŏngch'i-ŭi Kujo-wa Chŏngmang* (The Structures and Prospects of North and South Korean Politics) (Seoul, Hanul Academy, 1994), pp. 136–70.

Ch'oe, Ŭnhŭi, and Sangok Shin, *Kim Jong Il Wangguk 1 & 2* (The Kingdom of Kim Jong Il 1) (Seoul, Dong-A Ilbo, 1988).

Ch'oe, Yŏngch'ŏl, 'Ilje shingmin ch'iha-ŭi yŏnghwa chŏngch'aek' (Film policies under the Japanese colonial rule), in Yi, Chunggŏ, and others, *Han'guk Yŏnghwa-ŭi Ihae*: Arirang-*esŏbut'ŏ* Ŭnma-nŭn Tolaoji Annŭnda-*kkaji* (Understanding Korean Films: From *Arirang* to *Silver Stallion*) (Seoul, Yeni, 1992), pp. 217–42.

Chŏn, Kwangyŏng, *Shin Sosŏl Yŏn'gu* (A Study of the New Novel) (Seoul, Saemunsa, 1986).

Chŏn, Yangjun, and Hyoin Yi, and Chŏngha Yi (eds), *Redigo 2 Chip: Saeroun Han'guk Yŏnghwa-rŭl Wihayŏ* (Ready Go 2: For the New Korean Film) (Seoul, Iron-gwa Shilch'ŏn, 1988).

Chŏn, Yangjun, and Kich'ŏl Chang (eds), *Tatchin Hyŏnshil, Yŏllin Yŏnghwa: Yu Hyŏnmok Kamdok Chakp'umjip* (Closed Reality, Open Film, The Works of Yu Hyŏnmok, the Director) (Seoul, Che 3 Munhaksa, 1992).

Chŏng, Sŏngmu, *Shidae-wa Munhak Yesul-ŭi Hyŏngt'ae* (An Era and the Form of Literature and Art) (P'yŏngyang, Social Science Publishing House, 1987).

Chosŏn Chungang (ed.), *Chosŏn Chungang Yŏn'gam 1988* (Chosŏn Chungang Year Book 1988) (P'yŏngyang, Chosŏn Chungang T'ongshinsa, 1988).

Cultural Development Research Institute, *Munhwa Yesul T'onggye Charyojip* (Collection of Culture and Art Static Data) (Seoul, Korean Culture and Arts Foundation, 1989).

Cultural Development Research Institute, *Han'guk-ŭi Munhwa Yesul Hyangsu Shilt'ae-wa Chŏngch'aek Taeŭng Pangan* (The Actual Conditions of Enjoyment of Korean Culture and Art and the Corresponding Policy) (Seoul, Korean Culture and Art Foundation, 1989).

Cultural Planning Committee, *Che 7 ch'a 5 Kaenyŏn Kyehoek: Munhwa Pumun Kyehoekan* (The Seventh Five-year Program, The Cultural Plan) (Seoul, Ministry of Culture, 1991).

Han, Chŭngmo, and Sŏngmu Chŏng, *Juche-ŭi Munye Iron Yŏn'gu* (A Study on the *Juche* Theory of Literature and Art) (P'yŏngyang, Social Science Publishing House, 1983).

Hŏ, Ch'ang, 'Yŏnghwa sŏngjang karomangnŭn kŏmyŏl chedo' (The censorship that hinders the growth of film), *Korean Film Critiques*, 8 (1996), 209–18.

Hwang, Hyŏnt'ak, *Han'guk Yŏngsang Sanŏmnon* (A Study of the Korean Visual Media Industry) (Seoul, Nanam, 1995).

Kang, Hyŏndu, *Pukhan Mass Mediaron* (A Study of North Korean Mass Media) (Seoul, Nanam, 1997).

Kim Chaeyong, *Pukhan Munhak-ŭi Ihae* (Understanding of North Korean Literature) (Seoul, Munhak-kwa Chisŏngsa, 1994).

Kim, Chisŏk, and others, *Han'guk Yŏnghwa Ilkki-ŭi Chŭlgŏum* (The Pleasure of Reading Korean Film) (Seoul, Ch'aek-kwa Mŏngsang, 1995).

Kim, Chŏngok (ed.), *Han'guk Yŏnghwa-ŭi Saeroun Palgyŏn* (A New Discovery of Korean Film) (Seoul, Korean Film Academy, 1993).

Kim, Chongwŏn, 'Ch'och'anggi Han'guk yŏnghwasa kisul-ŭi munjejŏm-gwa saeroun kijŏm-ŭi cheshi' (The problems of describing the early Korean film history and a redefinition of the beginning of Korean film), *Korean Film Critiques*, 5 (1993), 11–28.

Kim, Ch'unt'aek, *Urinara Kojŏn Sosŏlsa* (A History of Korean Classical Narratives) (Seoul, Han'gilsa, 1993).

Kim, Dong-Uk, *Ch'unhyangjŏn Yŏn'gu* (A Study of *Ch'unhyangjŏn*) (Seoul, Yonsei University Press, 1985).

Kim, Il Sung, *Kim Il Sung Chŏjak Sŏnjip 1* (Selected Works of Kim Il Sung 1) (P'yŏngyang, Korean Workers' Party Publishing House, 1967).

Kim, Il Sung, *Kim Il Sung Chŏjak Sŏnjip 2* (Selected Works of Kim Il Sung 2) (P'yŏngyang, Korean Workers' Party Publishing House, 1968).

Kim, Il Sung, *Kim Il Sung Chŏjak Sŏnjip 4* (Selected Works of Kim Il Sung 4) (P'yŏngyang, Korean Workers' Party Publishing House, 1968).

Kim, Il Sung, *Kim Il Sung Chŏjak Sŏnjip 5* (Selected Works of Kim Il Sung 5) (P'yŏngyang, Korean Workers' Party Publishing House, 1972).

Kim, Il Sung, *Kim Il Sung Chŏjak Sŏnjip 6* (Selected Works of Kim Il Sung 6) (P'yŏngyang, Korean Workers' Party Publishing House, 1974).

Kim, Il Sung, *Kim Il Sung Chŏjak Sŏnjip 3* (Selected Works of Kim Il Sung 3) (P'yŏngyang, Korean Workers' Party Publishing House, 1975).

Kim, Il Sung, 'Yŏngha-nŭn hososŏng-i nopaya hamyŏ hyŏnshil-boda apsŏ nagaya handa' (Film should strongly appeal to the masses and advance them more than reality) (17 January 1958), in *Kim Il Sung Chŏjak Sŏnjip 12* (P'yŏngyang: Korean Workers' Party Publishing House, 1981), pp. 5–13.

Kim, Il Sung, 'Hyŏngmyŏngjŏk munhak yesul-ŭl ch'angjakhalde daehayŏ' (Concerning the creation of revolutionary literary art) (7 November 1964), in *Kim Il Sung Chŏjak Sŏnjip 18* (P'yŏngyang, Korean Workers' Party Publishing House, 1982), pp. 436–8.

Kim, Il Sung, 'Hyŏngmyŏng chuje chakp'um-esŏŭi myŏt kaji sasang mihakchŏk munje' (Some ideological and aesthetic problems in revolutionary works) (10 January 1967), in *Kim Il Sung Chŏjak Sŏnjip 21* (P'yŏngyang, Korean Workers' Party Publishing House, 1983), pp. 13–28.

Kim, Il Sung, *Kim Il Sung Chŏjak Sŏnjip 9* (Selected Works of Kim Il Sung 9) (P'yŏngyang, Korean Workers' Party Publishing House, 1987).

Kim, Jong Il, *Yŏnghwa Yesulron* (The Theory of Cinematic Art) (P'yŏngyang, Korean Workers' Party Publishing House, 1973).

Kim, Jong Il, *Juche Hyŏngmyŏng-ŭi Uiŏp-ŭl Wansŏng-ŭl Wihayo 2 (1972–1973)* (For Accomplishing the Great Achievement of *Juche* Revolution 2) (P'yŏngyang, Korean Workers' Party Publishing House, 1987).

Kim, Jong Il, *Kim Jong Il Chŏjaksŏn* (Selected Works of Kim Jong Il), ed. Kyŏngnam University Far-East Research Institute (Seoul, Kyŏngnam University Far-East Research Institute, 1991).

Kim, Jong Il, 'Sahoejuŭi kŏnsŏl-esŏ kun-ŭi wich'i-wa yŏkhal' (The army's position and role in the socialist reconstruction), in Kyŏngnam University Far-East Research Institute (ed.), *Kim Jong Il Chŏjaksŏn* (Selected Works of Kim Jong Il) (Seoul, Kyŏngnam University Far-East Research Institute, 1991), pp. 1–34.

Kim, Jong Il, 'Marx–Leninjuŭi-wa *Juche* sasang-ŭi kich'i-rŭl nop'i tŭlgo naagaja' (Let us move forward with Marxism–Leninism and *Juche* Idea) in Kyŏngnam University Far-East Research Institute (ed.), *Kim Jong Il Chŏjaksŏn* (Selected Works of Kim Jong Il) (Seoul, Kyŏngnam University Far-East Research Institute, 1991), pp. 163–86.

Kim Jong Il, *Kim Jong Il Chŏjak Sŏnjip 1* (P'yŏngyang, Korean Workers' Party Publishing House, 1992).

Kim Jong Il, 'Saeroun hyŏngmyŏng munhak-ŭl kŏnsŏlhalde daehayŏ' (Concerning the creation of the new revolutionary literary art) (7 February 1966), in *Kim Jong Il Chŏjak Sŏnjip 1* (P'yŏngyang, Korean Workers' Party Publishing House, 1992), pp. 113–14.

Kim Jong Il, 'Pandang panghyŏngmyŏng punjadŭl-ŭi sasang yŏdok-ŭl ppurippaego tang-ŭi *Yuil* sasang ch'egye-rŭl seulde daehayŏ' (Concerning the eradication of the poisonous thoughts of the anti-party, anti-revolutionary elements and the establishment of *Yuil* thought) (25 June 1967), in *Kim Jong Il Chŏjak Sŏnjip 1* (P'yŏngyang, Korean Workers' Party Publishing House, 1992), pp. 230–1.

Kim Jong Il, 'Tabujak yesul yŏnghwa *Minjok-kwa Unmyŏng*-ŭi ch'angjak sŏnggwa-e t'odaehayŏ munhak yesul kŏnsŏl-esŏ saeroun chŏnhwan-ŭl ilŭk'ija' (Let's reach a new turning point in the construction of literature and art, based on the creative result of the multi-volume art film *The Nation and Destiny*) (23 May 1992) in *Chosŏn Chungang Nyŏn'gam 1993* (Chosŏn Year Book 1993) (P'yŏngyang, Chosŏn Changang T'ongshinsa, 1993), p. 50.

Kim, Sunam, *Han'guk Yŏnghwa Chakka Yŏn'gu* (A Study of Korean Film Directors) (Seoul, Yeni, 1995).

Kim, Sunam, 'Yun Paengnam-ŭi yŏnghwa insaeng yŏn'gu' (A study of Yun Paeknam's film and life), in *Han'guk Yŏnghwa Chakka Yŏn'gu* (A Study of Korean Film Directors) (Seoul, Yeni, 1995), pp. 37–62.

Kim, Sunam, 'Na Un'gyu-ŭi minjok yŏnghwa chaego' (Reconsideration of the nationalistic film of Na Un'gyu), in *Han'guk Yŏnghwa Chakka Yŏn'gu* (A Study of Korean Film Directors) (Seoul, Yeni, 1995), pp. 63–90.

Kim, Sunam, '*Mise-en-scène* yŏnghwa-ŭi taega Shin Sangok' (Shin Sangok, the master of *Mise-en-scène*), in *Han'guk Yŏnghwa Chakka Yŏn'gu* (A Study of Korean Film Directors) (Seoul, Yeni, 1995), pp. 191–227.

Kim, Sunam, 'Han'guk yŏnghwa-ŭi chaengjŏm-gwa kŭ pansŏng' (A reflection of the issues of Korean film), *Korean Film Critiques*, 8 (1996), 219–28.

Korean Cinema Critics League, *Yŏnghwa P'yŏngron 2* (Korea Cinema Critic 2) (Seoul, Wŏnbanggak, 1990).

Korean Association of Professors of Film Studies (ed.), *Yŏnghwa-ran Muŏsh-in'ga* (What is Cinema?) (Seoul, Chishik Sanŏpsa, 1994).

Korean Motion Pictures Promotion Corp. (ed.), *Han'guk Yŏnghwa 70 Nyŏn Taep'yojak 200 Sŏn* (Seventy Years of Korean Filmdom) (Seoul, Tongmyŏng Print, 1989).

Korean Motion Pictures Promotion Corp. (ed.), *Han'guk Yŏnghwa Yŏn'gam* (Korean Film Year Book) (Seoul, Tongmyŏng Print, 1990).

Kwŏn, Yŏngmin, and others, *Pukhan Munhwa Yesul Yŏn'gu-ŭi Panghyang* (A Direction of Study on North Korean Culture and Art) (Seoul, The Korean Culture Art Foundation, 1990).

Kyŏngnam University Far-East Research Institute (ed.), *Pundan Pansegi Nambukhan-ŭi Sahoe-wa Munhwa* (Half a Century of North and South Korean Societies and Cultures) (Seoul, Kyŏngnam University Far-East Research Institute, 1996).

Linguistics Research Institute of Social Science Board (ed.), *Munhak Yesul Sajŏn* (Literature and Art Dictionary) (P'yŏngyang, Social Science Publishing House, 1972).

Literature Research Institute of Social Science Board (ed.), *Juche Sasang-*

e Kich'ohan Munye Iron (The Juche-Oriented Theory on Literature and Art) (P'yŏngyang, Social Science Publishing House, 1975).

Min, Pyŏngnok, 'Saeroun Han'guk yŏnghwa sanŏp-e taehan koch'al' (An examination of the new Korean film industry), in Chŏngok Kim (ed.), Han'guk Yŏnghwa-ŭi Saeroun Palgyŏn (A New Discovery of Korean Film) (Seoul, Korean Film Academy, 1993), pp. 191–224.

Ministry of Culture and Information, Haengjŏng Paeksŏ (An Administrative White Paper) (Seoul, Ministry of Culture and Information, 1976).

Ministry of Culture and Information, Haengjŏng Paeksŏ (An Administrative White Paper) (Seoul, Ministry of Culture and Information, 1986).

National Film Research Institute (ed.), Minjok Yŏnghwa 1 (National Film 1) (Seoul, Ch'in'gu, 1989).

National Film Research Institute (ed.), Minjok Yŏnghwa 2 (National Film 2) (Seoul, Ch'in'gu, 1990).

National Film Research Institute, 'P'aŏp Chŏnya-ŭi sŏnggong-gwa kŭ p'yŏngga' (The fruits of The Night before the Strike and an evaluation) in National Film Research Institute (ed.), Minjok Yŏnghwa 2 (National Film 2) (Seoul, Ch'in'gu, 1990), pp. 173–205.

North Korea Research Institute (ed.), Pukhan Ch'ongnam (A Survey of North Korea) (Seoul, North Korea Research Institute, 1980).

Paek, Chihan (ed.), Pukhan Yŏnghwa-ŭi Ihae (Understanding North Korean Film) (Pusan, Ch'in'gu, 1989).

Pak, Hyŏnch'ae, and Ch'angryŏl Chŏng (eds), Han'guk Minjokchuŭiron 3 (Korean Nationalism 3) (Seoul, Ch'angjak-kwa Pip'yŏngsa, 1985).

Pak, Myŏngjin, 'Pukhan yŏnghwa-ŭi t'ŭksŏng-gwa kŭ shilt'ae (The characteristics and reality of North Korean film), in Cultural Development Institute (ed.), Pukhan Munhwa Yesul Yŏn'gu-ŭi Panghyang (The Direction of North Korean Culture and Art) (Seoul, Korean Culture and Art Foundation, 1990), pp. 357–412.

Pyŏn, Inshik, 'Inbonjuŭi-ranŭn kitpal innŭn kisu Im Kwŏnt'aek' (Im Kwŏnt'aek, the banner bearer with the flag called humanism), Korean Film Critiques, 6 (1994), 73–88.

Pyŏn, Chaeran, '1930 nyŏndae chŏnhu KAPF yŏnghwa hwaldong yŏn'gu' (A study of the KAPF film movement in the late 1920s and the early 1930s) in National Film Research Institute (ed.), Minjok Yŏnghwa 2 (National Film 2) (Seoul, Ch'in'gu, 1990), pp. 219–40.

Seoul Film Group, Saeroun Yŏnghwa-rŭl Wihayŏ (For the New Korean Film) (Seoul, Hangminsa, 1983).

Shim, Chiyŏn, Haebang Chŏngguk Nonjaengsa 1 (The History of Debates on the Post-Liberation 1) (Seoul, Hanul, 1986).

So, Yŏnho, and Kangryŏl Yi, Pukhan-ŭi Kongyŏn Yesul 1 (North Korean Performance Art 1) (Seoul, Koryŏwŏn, 1990).

Social Science Publishing House (ed.), Munhwa Yesul Chakp'um-ŭi Chongja-e Kwanhan Iron (A Theory on the Seed of Literature and Art Works) (P'yŏngyang, Social Science Publishing House, 1977).

Social Science Publishing House (ed.), 'Kyoyuk-kwa Munhak Yesul-ŭn Saramdŭl-ŭi Hyŏngmyŏngjŏk Segyegwan-ŭl Seunŭn te Ibajihayŏya Handa'-e Taehayŏ (About 'Education and Literature-Art Should Serve to Teach People the Revolutionary World of View') (P'yŏngyang, Social Science Publishing House, 1974).

Social Science Publishing House (ed.), Uri Tang-ŭi Munye Chŏngch'aek (Our Party's Policy of Literature and Art) (P'yŏngyang, Social Science Publishing House, 1973).

Sŏl, Sŏnggyŏng, *Ch'unhyangjŏn Hyŏngsŏng-gwa Kyet'ong* (The Development and Classification of *Ch'unhyangjŏn*) (Seoul, Chŏngŭmsa, 1986).

Son, Hoch'ŏl, and others, *Han'guk Chŏnjaeng-gwa Nambukhan Sahoe-ŭi Kujojŏk Pyŏnhwa* (The Korean War and the Structural Changes of South and North Korean Society) (Seoul, Kyŏngnam University Far-East Research Institute, 1991).

Sŏ Chaejin, *Pukhan Sahoe-ŭi Kyegupkaldŭng Yŏn'gu* (A Study of Class Conflict in North Korea) (Seoul, National Unification Institute, 1996).

Three Years After Liberation Research Group of History Problem Research Institute, *Haebang 3 Nyŏnsa Yŏn'gu Immun* (An Introduction to Study Three Years After Liberation) (Seoul, Kkach'i, 1989).

Unification Problem Research Institute (ed.), *Pukhan Kyŏngje Charyojip: Pukhan Sahoejuŭi Shilch'e-wa Iron* (A Collection of North Korean Economic Data: The Facts and Theory of North Korean Socialist Economy) (Seoul, Minjok T'ongil, 1989).

Yi, Chŏngha, 'Pak Kwangsu interview', in Hyoin Yi (ed.), *Han'guk-ŭi Yonghwa Kamdok 13 In* (Thirteen Korean Film Directors) (Seoul, Yŏllin Ch'aektŭl, 1994), pp. 239–50.

Yi, Chunggŏ, 'Han'guk yŏnghwasa' (Korean film history), in the Korean Association of Professors of Film Studies (ed.), *Yŏnghwa-ran Muŏsh-in'ga* (What is Cinema?) (Seoul, Chishik Sanŏpsa, 1986), pp. 183–210.

Yi, Chunggŏ, 'Han'guk yŏnghwasa yŏn'gu' (A study of Korean film history), in Yi, Chunggŏ *et al.*, *Han'guk Yŏnghwa-ŭi Ihae*: Arirang-*esŏbut'ŏ* Ŭnmanŭn Tolaoji Annŏnda-*kkaji* (Understanding Korean Films: From *Arirang* to *Silver Stallion*) (Seoul, Yeni, 1992), pp. 13–70.

Yi, Chunggŏ, 'Ilje shidae uri yŏnghwa' (Our film in the Japanese colonial period), in Yi, Chunggŏ *et al.*, *Han'guk Yŏnghwa-ŭi Ihae*: Arirang-*esŏbut'ŏ* Ŭnmanŭn Tolaoji Annŭnda-*kkaji* (Understanding Korean Films: From *Arirang* to *Silver Stallion*) (Seoul, Yeni, 1992), pp. 139–54.

Yi, Hyoin, *Han'guk Yŏnghwa Yŏksa Kangŭi 1* (Lecture on Korean Film History 1) (Seoul, Iron-gwa shilch'ŏn, 1992).

Yi, Hyoin, 'Haebang chikhu Han'guk yŏnghwagye-ŭi yŏnghwa undong' (The film movement in post-Liberation period), *Korean Film Critiques*, 5 (1993), 81–96.

Yi, Hyoin, *Han'guk-ŭi Yŏnghwa Kamdok 13 In* (Thirteen Korean Film Directors) (Seoul, Yollin Ch'aektŭl, 1994).

Yi, Onjuk, *Pukhansahoe Yŏn'gu: Sahoehakchŏk Chŏpkŭn* (A Study on North Korea, Sociological Approach) (Seoul, Seoul University Press, 1989).

Yi Sŏngdŏk, 'Rodong kyegŭp-ŭi saenghwal ch'ŏlhak-ŭl kuhyŏnhan segyejŏkin kŏljak (1)' (The world's great work materialising the philosophy of life of the working class), *Chosŏn Yŏngha* (Chosŏn Film), 267 (September 1995), p. 40.

Yi, Uyŏng, *Nambukhan Munhwa Chŏngch'aek Pigyo Yŏn'gu* (A Comparative Study of North and South Korean Culture Policies) (Seoul, the Research Institute for National Unification, 1994).

Yi, Uyŏng, *Kim Jong Il Munye Chŏngch'aek-ŭi Chisok-kwa Pyŏnhwa* (The Continuity and Changes of Kim Jong Il's Literature and Art Policy) (Seoul, the Research Institute for National Unification, 1997).

Yi, Uyŏng, 'Pukhan yŏnghwa-e pich'in Kim Jong Il ch'osang' (A portrait of Kim Jong Il as reflected in North Korean film), *Shin Dong-A*, September 1994, 252–65.

Yu, Ch'ijin, 'Ch'unhyangjŏn kaksaek-e kwanhayŏ' (About adaptation of *Ch'unhyangjŏn*), in Ch'ŏl Ch'oe and Sŏnggyŏng Sol (eds), *Sŏlhwa, Sosŏl-ŭi Yŏn'gu* (A Study of Myth and Novel) (Seoul, Chŏngŭmsa, 1984), pp. 205–7.

Yu, Hyŏnmok, *Han'guk Yŏnghwa Paldalsa* (Korean Film History) (Seoul, Hanjin, 1980).

Yun, Tŏkhŭi, and Kim Tot'ae, *Nambukhan Sahoe Munhwa Kongdongch'e Hyŏngsŏng Pangan* (Towards Formation of the North and South Korean Social, Cultural Community) (Seoul, the Research Institute for National Unification, 1992).

Index